SMOKEY, ROSIE AND YOU!

THE HISTORY AND PRACTICE OF MARKETING PUBLIC PROGRAMS

SMOKEY, ROSIE AND YOU!

THE HISTORY AND PRACTICE OF MARKETING PUBLIC PROGRAMS

David A. Ehrlich
Alan R. Minton
with Dr. Diane Stoy
The Track Center for Marketing Public Programs
www.marketingpublicprograms.org

Published by The Track Center for Marketing Public Programs
A division of The Track Group, Inc. – Alexandria VA
www.trackg.com

ISBN 978-1-934248-33-1
ISBN 1-934248-33-9
LCN 2007929588

FRONT COVER IMAGES:
Smokey Bear
See Page 64 to learn about Smokey Bear
The name and character of *Smokey Bear* are the property of the United States, as provided by 16 U.S.C. 580p-1 and 18 U.S.C. 711, and are used with the permission of the Forest Service, U.S. Department of Agriculture. Reprinted with permission as an official licensee.

Rosie the Riveter
We Can Do It!
See Page 60 to learn about Rosie the Riveter
Created by J. Howard Miller. Produced by Westinghouse for the War Production Coordinating Committee.
National Archives (NARA) Still Picture Branch (NWDNS-179-WP-1563)

Cover concept and design by The Track Group, Inc.

BACK COVER IMAGES:
The posters on the back cover and selected others reprinted in this book are from the collection *By the People, For the People: Posters from the WPA, 1936-1943.* Library of Congress.

Dedication

This book is dedicated to those professionals working in government who share their passions with the public everyday through creative and innovative outreach and communication efforts.

According to the Ad Council, Smokey Bear is the fictional star of the longest running public service campaign in US history. Since 1944, Smokey has been busy raising public awareness about the need to protect America's forests. So far, Smokey's forest fire prevention campaign has reduced the number of acres lost each year from 22 to 4 million.

My earliest personal experience with a public campaign designed to change the behavior of the American public is Smokey Bear. As a child, I lived a few minutes from The Department of Environmental Conservation in New Paltz, NY. In the early 1970s, I had no idea about the mission of this Department. All I knew then was that I could walk to an office behind my house to obtain very large, very colorful cardboard posters with Smokey Bear and other fun images. I looked forward to the new posters and accumulated a nice collection over the years. I think the people working in the office enjoyed seeing us visit in search of the newest posters - each with a message about preventing forest fires.

It's probably no coincidence that now, some thirty years later, my work involves creating multimedia, interactive educational outreach programs for children and adults, including EPA's mascot "Thirstin" shown below. My personal experience with Smokey is similar to the experience of many other Americans who began thinking differently about the role of women in the workforce after seeing Rosie the Riveter during World War II, or EPA's Thirstin and the many new other icons being created in the 21st century.

EPA's Thirstin mascot representing Safe Drinking Water

Icons like these are the friendly faces of a world in which outreach efforts by hundreds of government agencies are focused on thousands of important issues that affect our lives and our country every day.

David Ehrlich, President
The Track Group

Contents

Evolution of Betty Crocker's official portrait.
Original from 1936 and 1996 update. Source: General Mills Corporation.

Preface

The likeness of Betty Crocker, one of the most well-known brand icons, has changed seven times since first being introduced in 1936. People have started paying money to buy bottled water even though in many places safe water is available and almost free. The comfort of a familiar place has drawn people to purchase higher-priced coffee. These three marketing-related changes in the private sector occurred this past century. Why the changes? We at the Track Center for Marketing Public Programs pose this question to our students in our "Marketing Public Programs" course, a course attended primarily by federal employees involved in communication and outreach efforts.

A lively discussion takes place as we explore the changes in society that have caused these and other marketing-related events to occur. We hear that people have changed, with their expectations evolving as new products have been introduced. We hear that we live in a different world than our parents, with new demands being created on people's time and lifestyles. We hear that marketing has become more sophisticated and that it has been effective at persuading many to purchase products previously thought of as unnecessary.

I Want You For The U.S. Army. 1941.
Source: Library of Congress

After a vigorous discussion concludes, we show students an image of Uncle Sam and ask the same question, "Why the changes?" Some students chuckle and say, "Nothing has changed, Uncle Sam looks exactly the same as he did in 1918." Like Betty Crocker at first, Uncle Sam was a reflection of the times when he was first created. Yet, unlike Betty Crocker, Uncle Sam has not changed with the changing times. He still bears the same strong resemblance to the early presidents as he did when he was first introduced.

Today, he lives on as a familiar, albeit odd-looking, uncle. A new discussion revolves around this contrast and the notion that most, if not all, successful corporations continually update their marketing efforts and offerings, while the common perception of the government is that government is not in the business of marketing and is not widely adopting leading-edge marketing techniques.

Because many in the government speak about the "general public" frequently when discussing outreach efforts, we at the Track Center for Marketing Public Programs conduct video interviews of tourists walking in the mall in Washington, DC to help our students better understand the mindset of their largest identified target audience. We show people the same image of Uncle Sam, and we ask them to comment on whom he resembles and what he means to them. We frequently hear that he looks like President Lincoln and that he is a trusted uncle looking over their shoulder. People readily acknowledge that, while not reflective of our nation's diversity, Uncle Sam is a symbol that remains a familiar face to the government. We wonder how Uncle Sam might have evolved if he had taken a path similar to Betty Crocker, who is actually a reflection of seventy-five real-life women of diverse backgrounds and ages thought by the company to represent the true Betty Crocker.

We contrast the motivation that drives corporations to remain not only relevant, but also one step ahead of the culture—the threat of extinction—with the motivation of the federal government, which has little such threat. The threat of extinction pushes businesses to get inspiration from many sources to stay in tune with and act on trends unfolding in the marketplace, actively scanning what other businesses and organizations are doing that might be important to pursue. The federal government may literally require an act of Congress for it to change the way it conducts its affairs and in most cases will not perish if it fails to evolve. It will largely just be less effective than it could be.

This being said, some areas within the federal government are highly motivated to actively market their programs because there are potentially dire consequences for the nation. The military requires new recruits constantly in order to meet the mission of defending the nation with an all-volunteer force. The Centers for Disease Control and Prevention (CDC) is highly motivated to proactively address new threats such as a potential bird flu pandemic. Accordingly, we often look to the military and public health as prime examples of leading-edge marketers within the public sector.

Another line of questions that we bring up during our person-on-the-street video interviews is behavior change. We ask people if they have any bad habits, and if so, what would it take to get them to change their behavior. One young woman stated that she couldn't think of any bad behaviors that she might engage in. We rephrased the question a second time and asked if she could think of any behaviors she might want to change. At this point, she casually mentioned smoking. The fact that she might not even consider smoking a bad behavior that needs changing is revealing.

When asked to identify the risks of smoking, respondents were usually able to easily rattle off a handful of well-known risks, including lung disease. This shows us that promoting behavior change is not simply about the target audience knowing the facts. Rather, it is a very complex effort that requires an understanding of how the target market perceives an issue, what obstacles to action exist for the target market, and what will resonate with, motivate, and enable specific target segments to undertake real behavior change.

This is not unlike the goal of corporations, who must ultimately promote a change in behavior in their target market in order to stay relevant. Corporate America understands that marketing is the key to unlocking the desired changes in their target market, and they know that effective marketing is much more involved than simple outreach efforts. The "sale" that the military is trying to make would be among the most challenging compared to the typical goal of a company. Compare asking someone to sign up for a potentially lethal assignment relative to a purchase of a new car. The fact that the military is successful as an all-volunteer force shows that the government is leveraging marketing even when tasked with promoting a very tough behavior.

For many within the government, the word "marketing" is associated with selling and symbolizes something that might be difficult to get funding for. At a minimum, many might suggest that it is inappropriate for federal agencies to conduct a marketing campaign in the same way that a commercial organization would. A chief marketing officer is a common role within any company, while the government tends to have public affairs and outreach staff who are more likely to be responsive to media inquiries or provide well-vetted, base-level communications, versus a proactive, full-blown strategic marketing campaign that is constantly evolving with the changing environment and needs of the marketplace and is strategically planned based on research and insights into identified target segments.

Whether you call it marketing, outreach, communications, or public affairs, the fact is that the government must conduct marketing to some degree to remain relevant to a majority of the public and fully achieve the objectives of the various agencies. There is an obligation to the nation to educate, inform, and help shape the public dialog toward the greater good of individuals and the society at large. This marketing is directed at many audiences (often referred to as stakeholders), including the "general public," internal management, Congress, business, tribes, states and counties, non-profits, and international audiences. All of the audiences need information and can obtain value from much of what the government has to share.

Smoking Stacks Attract Attacks. Phil von Phul.
[1940 or 1941] Source: Library of Congress
Prints and Photographs Division

This book looks at the long history of government marketing going back to the early part of the last century and helps create an awareness of the vast opportunities to market public programs in the twenty-first century. Today, if you don't take the lead and shape the message proactively concerning issues related to the mission of your agency, others, including news organizations and the bloggers, will fill the void. Many of us received a negative impression of the Federal Emergency Management Agency (FEMA) after hurricane Katrina. It is likely, however, that the FEMA organization has done many positive things in recent years. Perhaps expectations were misguided about the role of FEMA and exactly what they could and could not do in a given situation. Every agency has the opportunity to be proactive in communicating the good they do, as well as helping people make real changes in their lives that will benefit us all.

While the government typically does not take on marketing to "promote the agency" at the same time as undertaking communication campaigns to reach the public, it often becomes clear through a public campaign what value and relevance an agency has. For example, while the U.S. Department of Agriculture (USDA) is promoting eating right and the food pyramid or the Environmental Protection Agency (EPA) is promoting conservation through use of Energy Star appliances, both organizations indirectly receive positive impressions about how they are actively contributing to the public good and society overall.

As the movement toward a more non-regulatory environment continues, the emphasis on marketing becomes even more critical, since voluntary action starts with the "What's in it for me?" mindset of the audience. The Energy Star program started and remains a program that is all about voluntary membership and actions taken by partner organizations as well as the general public. The EPA and Department of Energy (DOE) relied on a very strategic plan in the beginning, and mastered the art of leverage and tipping points to make great voluntary progress toward their goals, while participants were rewarded in multiple ways and became more entrenched in the program.

During our person-on-the-street video, we ask people to speak about how the federal government benefits their life on a day-to-day basis. We show this part of the video in class to show that while some people may know many details about their specific programs and the overall role of the government, in fact, the vast majority of the public has much more limited knowledge about this topic. Many of the individuals in the video strain to think of a single impact on their daily life, yet we know that the daily freedoms that allow us all to flourish and be who we want to be is a product of the many actions taken by the government.

Most of our students realize that we are a safer and more educated society because of actions taken by the federal government. Whether we step on an airplane, drink tap water, drive on a national highway in a car with airbags, or purchase a piece of fruit or a prescription drug, we benefit by the actions of government. It is a real shame that the government is not getting credit for much of the positive. An emphasis on what is not working is usually featured on the news and this often forms people's perception of government.

The Track Center for Marketing Public Programs wrote this book, and developed our Marketing Public Programs training course and website, to address this disconnect between what the government can and does accomplish every day to benefit the citizens of this country and the entire world and what people often perceive. We aim to help level the playing field between private enterprises that are actively involved in marketing and government agencies that have varying experience and marketing plans in place, but for whom marketing is just one among many priorities. Government can also learn a lot not only from what the commercial and non-profit marketers do, but also from what highly motivated agencies such as military and public health do in the government.

The real limit is less about financial resources, and instead more about awareness of what can be done and thinking outside the box when it comes to messaging and methods used to resonate with our target markets to promote real action. Sol Salinas, a founder of the EPA Energy Star program, makes the point that when the predecessor to Energy Star was started, it did not have large budgets in terms of staff or financial resources. Rather, a few key tipping points occurred that turned an idea into a hugely successful national program. We include Energy Star among several of our case studies in this book to give you insight into what is possible and the opportunities that you have to make a difference in society and to have a measurable impact on the lives of many individuals.

Every time we see Smokey Bear or Rosie the Riveter, we are inspired and are reminded that you, too, can create the next Smokey or Rosie. When we created Thirstin, a mascot representing clean water for the EPA, we knew he could be as influential as Smokey or Rosie within its targeted audience. The opportunity to create a positive change in society is very exciting. Imagine being responsible for changing the lives of people by simply having a vision and executing a strategic plan focused on change. The opportunity is yours and due to the power of the web, you can promote change with much less funding than ever before. Thirstin is being distributed as a mascot in children's interactive web-based games and booklets at a minimal cost, and over the years, thousands of school-age children will learn about safer drinking water and things they can do to help protect the environment.

We envision this book as a helpful guidebook for those who are charged with developing public programs. Many of our students and clients' careers within the government have evolved into a communications role. Many were not formally trained in marketing, yet they face challenges that require an in-depth knowledge of marketing public programs. This book aims to address several key areas, including:

THE ROOTS OF MARKETING PUBLIC PROGRAMS.
In Part 1, you will find that you are not alone. Rather, as perhaps an "accidental" marketing professional who is serving the public good in the twenty-first century, you are part of a community of professionals with roots that date back to the days of the Revolutionary War. In this section, you will learn many fascinating details about how marketing was used in

both war and peace—how the marketing techniques evolved with emerging technologies like the radio and television—and how marketing professionals worked to demonstrate the positive impact of their efforts on the greater society. After reading Part 1, you may feel some camaraderie with marketing geniuses like the Sons of Liberty, John Paul Jones, Teddy Roosevelt, and even FDR. At the very least, you will develop a new appreciation for the long, historical traditions created by those Americans who have marketed public programs over the last two centuries. Throughout this book, we have included many images of classic campaigns conducted by the Works Progress Administration (WPA) in the early twentieth century as inspiration and as a reminder that marketing within the government is not something new.

THE TRENDS OF TODAY AND TOMORROW.

In Part 2, we switch gears and shift our focus to ten of the top trends in the United States today. Why talk about trends in a book about marketing? Because today's marketing professionals need to be in the know about the complicated society in which we live. Rather than running a slow second behind the corporate world, today's marketing professionals who serve the public want and need to be on top of the latest trends so that their programs can be leaders in the field of marketing—just as their predecessors have been in years past. You'll find Part 2 a lively read with interesting analysis on such diverse topics as blogging, bariatric surgery, and bowling alone.

LEARN FROM THE BEST.

In Part 3, we share four case studies of high-visibility campaigns complete with some history and interesting interviews with thought leaders in the four different fields of women and heart disease, seat belts, military recruiting, and energy conservation. If you have any preconceived notions about the need to use an exact "formula" for the campaign you are developing, you will change your mind after reading this section. Each campaign—successful in its own right—had its own unique features. Each had individuals who experienced "ah-ha" moments, which were the seeds that grew powerful public programs that really did change our lives for the better. Each had twists and turns along the way, and each one has a great story to tell. After reading this section, you will think differently each time you buckle up your seat belt or buy a light bulb.

PLANNING YOUR CAMPAIGN.

In Part 4, we have provided you with the links to our TRACK worksheets which will serve as practical guideposts for you as you start getting on track with planning your program or campaign. In this section, we have also explained each worksheet so that you understand how and when to use it in your planning process.

After reading this book, you will have taken a journey back into the annals of public marketing history, gazing into America's crystal ball, hearing from some of the most successful government marketers and gearing up for some exciting marketing work.

Writing this book has been a journey for us as well, and we would like to thank our clients and students within the federal government who are involved in marketing public programs on a daily basis. In researching the case studies, we appreciate the time and information provided by Terry Long, NHLBI Communications Director; Dr. James Nichols, former Director of the Federal Office of Research and Traffic Records, NHTSA; Sol Salinas, formerly with EPA and an early champion of the Energy Star program; Maria Vargas of EPA; and Don Nail, public affairs representative for the North Carolina Governor's Highway Safety Program. We'd also like to thank the following individuals who assisted in editing the manuscript: Shereen Kandil, Matthieu Pierre, and Robert Spencer.

We invite you to become involved in the dialog and consider participating by sharing your successes and challenges. Visit (www.marketingpublicprograms.org) to learn about how you can become involved and view hundreds of campaigns as well as videos of your peers discussing the challenges and opportunities of marketing public programs.

Now, let's start our journey by looking at how it all got started, the history of marketing public programs.

Part One:
The Roots of Marketing Public Programs

George Washington Crossing the Delaware. Emanuel Gottlieb Leutze, 1851.
Source: Metropolitan Museum of Art, New York, NY

THE ROOTS OF PUBLIC MARKETING—RESISTANCE, REVOLUTION, AND REFORM

The roots of marketing are deeply embedded in the history of man. Communication channels and tools may have been different in years past, but as today, using information to arouse emotions, influence viewpoints, confront morality, and change behavior is very much a part of the human story. For example, Virgil used his Georgics as a vehicle for encouraging food production for the growing population. The walls of Pompeii were inscribed with appeals that encouraged participation in elections. And the precursor to today's farm bulletins were found in Iraq as early as 1800 BC—with instructions for farmers on seeding, harvesting, and controlling rodents [4].

Yet those who market public programs in the twenty-first century owe a debt of gratitude to a small band of crusaders whose moxie and daring techniques laid the foundation for American public marketing—Samuel Adams and his fellow revolutionaries. In their highly organized campaigns to influence public opinion during the revolt of the American colonies against England, Adams and his compatriots "understood the importance of public support and knew intuitively how to arouse it and channel it"[4]. Working from the "shadows," the revolutionaries are believed to have been masters at using every conceivable avenue of communication available to them during colonial times—"pens, pulpits, platforms, staged events, symbols, leaking, and political organization" to get their message across about the American Revolution. Consider the following examples that demonstrate the revolutionaries' intuitive grasp of the basic principles of public marketing.

Adams et al knew that organization was key to sparking public action and in 1766, the "Sons of Liberty" was established. Their savvy sense about the value of symbols and slogans for public campaigns was evident in their creation of the Liberty Tree and the enduring slogan, which is repeated in American History classes today—"Taxation without representation is tyranny." They knew the power of staging media events—such as the Boston Tea Party—which would garner public attention, arouse public sentiment, and recruit others to work for the cause. They established the original American gold standard for relentlessly staying on message through the use of a saturated, sustained campaign to increase awareness and arouse public support for the Revolution [4, 5, 6].

26TH President Theodore "Teddy" Roosevelt (1901-1909).
Source: Library of Congress

TEDDY ROOSEVELT AND THE GREENING OF THE OVAL OFFICE

The colorful, larger-than-life Theodore "Teddy" Roosevelt was an activist, politician, big game hunter, cattleman, police commissioner, negotiator, winner of the Nobel Peace prize and the Congressional Medal of Honor, conservationist, naturalist, explorer, and advocate for the "strenuous life." Roosevelt became the youngest U.S. President at age 42. He had a long history of public service and activism before the assassination of President William McKinley. Roosevelt's lifetime activism on behalf of natural resources, his conservation policies, and his pure genius in sponsoring the federal government's first large-scale publicity program have been credited with "saving much of America's resources from gross exploitation"[7].

In 1887, Roosevelt founded the Boone and Crockett Club, an organization devoted to responsible hunting practices and the conservation of natural resources. During his six-year tenure as the organization's president, Roosevelt became a powerful advocate for fair hunting standards and the creation of conservation laws. He lobbied Congress to encourage the protection of the forests of Yellowstone, which had been declared a national park in 1872. Roosevelt's influence on Congress led to Congressional action which increased the power of the American presidency to protect natural resources, a power he would later put to good use during his presidency. Roosevelt was also instrumental in creating the first national zoo in 1889 [5].

In 1897, Roosevelt became Assistant Secretary of the U.S. Navy—a reward for his tireless campaigning for President William McKinley. After war was declared with Spain, Roosevelt resigned as Navy Secretary and volunteered to fight at the front with the "Rough Riders," an eclectic, all-volunteer cavalry of Western cowboys, frontiersmen, miners, Eastern athletes, and sons of prominent citizens [6].

Roosevelt's notoriety as head of the Rough Riders propelled him full force into the world of politics, and in 1898, he was elected as the new Governor of New York. His two-year term of office evolved into a platform for what would become his life-long, relentless advocacy on behalf of natural resources. Roosevelt became the first New York governor to advocate publicly for the protection of wild birds, animals, and flowers. He promoted wise use of forest resources and forest management based on scientific principles and ended corruption within the Fisheries, Forest and Game Commission. Eventually Roosevelt's advocacy led to greater protection of the State's forests, and better public understanding of conservation and the importance of the preservation of species [4].

PUSHING FOR CHANGE WITH PRESIDENTIAL POWER

Historical sources [5] suggest that by the time Roosevelt became President in 1901, there was low public awareness of the impact of unlimited use of natural resources. In the wake of continuing westward expansion and industrialization, half of the country's timber had already been lost. There was rampant waste of topsoil and nonrenewable minerals and excessive hunting which left some animal species (such as passenger pigeons and bison) extinct or near extinction. In his travels, Roosevelt had personally witnessed the environmental effects of uncontrolled industrial growth, the destruction of grasslands from overgrazing, the thinning of the buffalo herds, and the loss of some big game species.

Shortly after taking the presidential oath of office, he began using his presidential power and the platform of the White House to continue his lifelong crusade to raise public awareness about the need for conservation and to preserve the natural environment. In his first presidential address, Roosevelt announced a national blitz of activities that focused on conservation of resources, protection of forests and wildlife, and governmental oversight of management practices used with natural resources. He quickly established fifty-one bird reserves, four game preserves and one hundred fifty national forests.

In addition to his tenacious commitment to public education about conservation, his savvy use of multiple media channels, and his enduring ability to stay on message, Roosevelt worked tirelessly to push through a litany of legislative acts that would leave a permanent mark on the country's landscape and on his legacy. These included the Reclamation Act which allowed for the conversion of non-arable land and the settlement of the Western United States; the creation of Pelican Island Federal Bird Reservation, the country's first federal wildlife refuge; consolidation of the

General Land Office, U.S. Geological Survey, and Bureau of Forestry into the U.S. Forestry Service; passage of the Antiquities Act, which gave the President the power to establish national monuments; creation of the Inland Waterways Commission, which focused on developing waterways and preserving clean water; and the establishment of the National Conservation Commission, which later produced the first national report on the country's dwindling natural resources [5].

In 1908, Roosevelt used presidential proclamation to protect the eight hundred thousand acres of the Grand Canyon National Monument in Arizona from destruction by developers. In the same year, Roosevelt organized a historic three-day conference on conservation for the nation's governors [7]. From the Oval Office at the White House, Roosevelt sent promotional letters to the governors and the country's most influential leaders that said, "It seems time for the country to take account of its natural resources and to enquire how long they are likely to last" [8]. Roosevelt delivered the conference's opening address, which he entitled "Conservation as a National Duty." The success of the conference led to the creation of the National Conservation Commission, which from 1908 to 1923, assumed the national leadership for monitoring natural resources and guiding conservation efforts.

LEAVING A LASTING LEGACY

President Teddy Roosevelt left a lasting legacy in American history. What began in 1903 as a single act of presidential protection of the three-acre Pelican Island Bird Reservation in Florida is now the National Wildlife Refuge System. According to the U.S. Fish and Wildlife Service [9], this national system has now grown to 94 million acres, with 520 refuges and more than three thousand waterfowl production areas.

According to Gifford Pinchot, Roosevelt's fellow conservationist and the first head of the U.S. Forest Service, "The greatest work that Theodore Roosevelt did for the United States, the great fact which will give his influence vitality and power long after we shall all have gone to our reward, is ... that he changed the attitude of the American people toward conserving the natural resources" [5]. In short, Roosevelt achieved his goal of helping the American public realize a simple but inevitable truth—that the natural resources of the country were not infinite.

But a deeper look at Roosevelt's strategy reveals the real genius of his sophisticated marketing sense. Roosevelt was extraordinarily skilled at crafting the public message of conservation and casting it as a social, democratic movement. He viewed land as an "economic resource" which must be conserved and managed to protect the long-term economic and political strength of the country. Loss of any wilderness or wildlife, Roosevelt believed, would weaken the national history of the United States and its national identity. Conservation could achieve the economic goal of providing the greatest good for the greatest number over the greatest period of time [10].

During his Presidency, Roosevelt was incredibly successful at leveraging the strong emotional connection between conservation and the strength of American democracy. Roosevelt relentlessly promoted that good citizenship was synonymous with conservation and that it was simply undemocratic and unpatriotic for any citizen to exploit and waste precious natural resources. Public lands and natural resources belonged to the public, Roosevelt said, and they did not exist for the unrestricted use of private industry. His legislative activism was driven by his practical belief that lofty, democratic, and sometimes romantic ideals could easily fall by the wayside if they were not linked to "wise laws" and resolute law enforcement.

Roosevelt also holds another distinction in the history of public marketing. He is believed to be the first public figure to promote the seminal idea that current generations have a responsibility to preserve resources for future generations. In a 1907 Arbor Day address, Roosevelt summarized his view of the link between the present generation and the future:

> We of an older generation can get along with what we have, though with growing hardship; but in your full manhood and womanhood you will want what nature once so bountifully supplied and man so thoughtlessly destroyed; and because of that want you will reproach us, not for what we have used, but for what we have wasted... So any nation which in its youth lives only for the day, reaps without sowing, and consumes without husbanding, must expect the penalty of the prodigal whose labor could with difficulty find him the bare means of life [11].

Thus, the long reach and the legacy of Teddy Roosevelt—the green President—live on.

MARKETING WAR—THE CHARGE OF THE CREEL COMMITTEE

In 1918, nine years after leaving office, former President Teddy Roosevelt spoke in Baltimore on behalf of another patriotic cause—Liberty Loans and the U.S. war effort. Film records [12] show Roosevelt wearing a mourning armband for his dead war hero son, Quentin, walking across the field of Oriole Baseball Park with Liberty Loan officials, and delivering a rousing speech with a wide swath of American flags as the backdrop. Roosevelt was lending his persona to what had become a huge public marketing endeavor—the raising of patriotic fervor and funds to support America's involvement in World War I (WWI). In the lead-up to the U.S. declaration of war in April 1917, President Woodrow Wilson created the Committee on Public Information. He appointed Missouri newspaperman and former editor of the Rocky Mountain News, George Creel, as chairman of what would later be known as the Creel Committee. The Committee would become one of the most organized, massive, creative, and controversial public marketing campaigns in American history. The sweeping mandate for the Creel Committee's work reflected Wilson's sobering view of the gravity of the circumstances, the implications of the war, and the need to enroll the American public in the war effort. In his "war address" to the Congress on April 2, 1917, Wilson soberly said:

> It is a fearful thing to lead this great peaceful people into war, into the most terrible and disastrous of all wars, civilization itself seeming to be in the balance. But the right is more precious than peace, and we shall fight for the things which we have always carried nearest our hearts—for democracy, for the right of those who submit to authority to have a voice in their own governments, for the rights and liberties of small nations, for a universal dominion of right by such a concert of free peoples as shall bring peace and safety to all nations and make the world itself at last free [13].

In this pro-democracy, pro-war context, Creel and his cronies became public relations agents for the U.S. war effort at home and abroad. Their propaganda machine stirred up plenty of controversy and left an astonishing legacy that opened a wide window on the worldly power of mass communication.

CHANNELING MULTIPLE CHANNELS

The members of the Creel Committee were masters of their craft who used a dazzling array of sources and channels to promote the war effort. In an era without television or the Internet, the Committee created many channels and saw to it that all were running at top speed during the two frenetic years of the campaign [14]. In addition to thousands of news releases, slides, and publications of every size, sort, and style, the Creel Committee created and marketed the war through varied channels, such as:

1. A speaker's bureau of notable Americans (like former President Teddy Roosevelt and silent film star Charlie Chaplin) and regular citizens who would visit public events and movie houses. With a background of blaring patriotic tunes, these "Four-Minute Men" would make emotional appeals to their fellow citizens to either buy Liberty Bonds, donate to the Red Cross, or join the armed forces. In total, there were seventy-five thousand speakers who gave 755,190 speeches in support of the Great War. Many of these represent Creel's attempt at segment marketing where he matched the speakers and the speeches with the target audiences [16].

2. The recruitment of America's filmmakers who agreed to produce pro-war silent films such as "Pershing's Crusaders," "America's Answer," and "Under Four Flags," which would be shown in theaters with a musical backdrop of patriotic tunes.

3. The production and wide distribution of "Red, White and Blue Books" with war promotions of the Allied cause by prominent academic scholars.

4. The creation of a treasure chest of artistic talent who would put their pens to work creating war posters, pro-war cartoons, window cards, newspaper advertisements, seals, and buttons which extolled the virtues of civic support and engagement during war time. Some work by the Committee's Division of Pictorial Publicity lives on in infamy (such as posters which showed the German enemy as a bloodthirsty savage "the Hun"), while others such as James Montgomery Flagg's portrait of "Uncle Sam" have achieved iconic status. Originally published as the cover for the July 6, 1916, issue of Leslie's Weekly, Flagg's portrait of "Uncle Sam" is considered to be "the most famous poster in the world" with over four million copies printed between 1917 and 1918, when the United States began sending troops into war zones [17].

5. Successful enlistment of the country's newspapers as conduits for war advertisements. Said the New York Times, "Liberty Loans had to be advertised throughout the country. Publicity did just that. Five times, at short intervals, the newspapers of the nation stepped into line and 'put across' to the man at the breakfast table, and in his office, in the factory, in the mines—in every phase of commerce and industry, in fact, the need for digging down deep into his pocket and 'coming across.' It worked. Beautifully and efficiently" [18].

6. Creation of civic channels through which pro-war information could be quickly disseminated. These include networks of schools, churches, fraternal groups, teachers, and chambers of commerce. Even Boy Scouts lent their foot power as they delivered

copies of President Wilson's addresses to American homes.

7. The use of wireless radio to spread military messages to other lands. In a 1922 article, Creel summarized the impact of the radio in the campaign: "In the fight for 'the verdict of mankind'—propaganda, to use the hackneyed word—America put her chief dependence on radio, finally reaching a peak of operation that used the air lanes of the whole world, reaching every country on the globe with the American message. Germany's collapse was moral as well as physical, and in this disintegration of enemy morale, radio was the principal and the determining factor" [19].

As Creel concluded, "There was no part of the great war machinery that we did not touch, no medium of appeal that we did not employ. The printed word, the spoken word, the motion picture, the telegraph, the cable, the wireless, the poster, the sign-board—all these were used in our campaign to make our own people and all other peoples understand the causes that compelled America to take arms" [15].

Liberty Bonds became an important way of funding the war, and part of the first truly integrated marketing campaigns.
C.R. Macauley. 1917. Source: Library of Congress

CREATING A HUNDRED-YEAR LEGACY

During WWI, public relations experts known as the Creel Committee created a two-year blitz of "breathtaking scope of activities" [20], which have left a lasting legacy in the world of public marketing. Their work demonstrated the power of mass communication [21], by creating new professionals called "public relations agents," whose job was to manipulate the "symbols of public opinion" to promote civic causes [20]. This committee laid the foundation for using publicity and advertising to make "nationalism an American religion" [22]. George Creel's 1920 memoir [15] summarized the $4 million marketing effort:

> It was the fight for the minds of men, for the 'conquest of their convictions,' and the battle-line ran through every home in every country. It was in this recognition of Public Opinion as a major force that the Great War differed most essentially from all previous conflicts. The trial of strength was not only between massed bodies of armed men, but between opposed ideals, and moral verdicts took on all the value of military decisions. ... In all things, from first to last, without halt or change, it was a plain publicity proposition, a vast enterprise in salesmanship, the world's greatest adventure in advertising.

United States Army. Social Hygiene Division. "Will You Be a Free Man or Chained." 1918. Poster. Source: Library of Congress

MEDICINE VERSUS MORALITY—THE FIGHT AGAINST VENEREAL DISEASE IN WORLD WAR I

As George Creel and his Committee for Public Information spread volumes of pro-war propaganda around the country and the world, the U.S. government and society-at-large grew increasingly concerned about the dreaded spread of venereal disease (VD). It was well known that VD had devastating effects on "individuals, families and communities" [23] and that at the turn of the century, a thriving prostitution industry had become an outgrowth of industrialization and a threatening source of syphilis and gonorrhea.

The spread of VD among U.S. servicemen, however, presented a danger, not only to the personal health and well being of soldiers, their wives, and children, but also to the essential military might of the American forces in Europe. The threat was so great that the U.S. Public Health Service created a Division of Venereal Disease in 1918 to help control the spread of VD among servicemen and essential war workers [24].

TACKLING THE TABOOS

Although Teddy Roosevelt had successfully connected conservation with good citizenship and the Creel Committee had linked America's involvement in WWI with pure patriotism, decision makers faced a dilemma of a different kind with a sensitive issue like VD. The very nature of sexually transmitted diseases was different because any educational campaign that focused on preventing VD required "breaking powerful taboos against even mentioning the subject in polite society" [23]. It was difficult to argue with two basic premises—that campaigns to reduce the incidence of VD must focus on military readiness and the need for servicemen to be "100 percent efficient to win the war," and that military personnel should be encouraged to practice abstinence [25]. But beyond these quite simplistic ideas, there was little agreement about the marketing strategy for VD prevention and control in the military.

Military officials, educators, and social reformers of the time wrestled with a major dilemma—should VD prevention efforts take a purely objective medical stance and or should the social reform movement of the era capitalize on spread of VD as an attractive soapbox for ardent preaching about social, cultural, and moral values? In his retrospective on VD [26], historian Allan Brandt summarized the dilemma this

way: "Should there be a disease prevention effort that recognized that many young American men would succumb to
the charms of French prostitutes, or should there be a more
punitive approach to discourage sexual contact?" Brandt
suggested that the heart of the dilemma rested on a widely
held view of VD as "both a punishment for sexual miscon-
duct and an index of social decay" and that, ultimately, the
tension between medicine and Victorian morality impeded
national efforts to control the spread of VD [26].

LEVERAGING LOOSE WOMEN AND THE GRIM REAPER

Although marketing campaigns used a variety of media
such as films, lectures, pamphlets, and demonstrations to
represent either purist positions or blended viewpoints on
this medicine vs. morality issue, patriotic posters became
the "heaviest artillery" in this propaganda war within the
war [27]. Many of these reflected the attitudes of social hygiene
reformers, the moral crusaders of the early twentieth century who worked to close down red-light districts in American cities and educate soldiers about the dangers of "illicit
sexual behavior" [27]. More progressive thinkers advocated
using both the objective medical approach (research and
medical treatment) and the moral viewpoint that focused
on fighting prostitution, vice, and moral decay. The progressive voices believed that "solutions required enlightenment"
and that "scientific research and publicity would conquer
any hindrance to human advancement" [23]. Progressive organizations worked to provide "wholesome" recreation for
"the boys" while they labeled VD as "the Invisible Enemy .
. . the epitome of all that is unclean, malignant and menac-
ing." Contrasting views of the VD issue were captured in
a film "Fit to Fight" which showed some servicemen who
fell to "temptation and languished in hospitals" while others

kept "clean" for the girls back home and went on to "manly" triumphs [23].

Documents available in the historical collection at the National Library of Medicine [28] provide visual evidence of the powerful, dark, fearful messages of VD prevention efforts. The words syphilis and gonorrhea were taboo, but there were two recurring themes—women and death. Women were painted as seductresses and the root of all evil. All women—even those who seemed wholesome and pure—were portrayed as potential sources of disease. The serious health effects of VD were clearly captured by the heavy, overarching theme of death as depicted by skull-and-crossbones, black capes, and tombstones. The moralistic messages of the era are exemplified in the classic 1918 ball-and-chain poster that links venereal disease and "enslaving habits" (such as sexual indiscretion and interaction with prostitutes) with a loss of personal and political freedom. The message asked soldiers to choose between being free or being "chained" by the results of their sexual indiscretion. This strategy was seen as part of a larger campaign to "define a male sex role that was at once powerful and virile yet pure and virginal by combining a high sense of moralism with a confident masculinity"[27].

OPENING THE CLOSET

For historians, marketing professionals, military strategists, and public health officials, the archives of WWI offer a fascinating look into the social milieu of the era and the way that public marketers used powerful, value-laden messages to address the interplay between medicine and morality. However, the success of the U.S. military in leveraging those messages to prevent VD among American troops in WWI is a matter of debate. Brandt [26] concluded that the United States would have been more successful if it had taken a more direct approach like New Zealand, which simply skirted the morality issue and provided soldiers with condoms. Although the American military encouraged soldiers to practice abstinence, its primary VD prevention strategy was, according to Brandt, an "after-the-fact, and largely ineffective, chemical prophylaxis" [26], which was combined with the threat of court martial if a soldier contracted a venereal disease.

According to Family Health International [25], statistics on the success of military efforts to reduce VD were not published, although there are reports that several million men received emergency VD treatment after unprotected sexual activity. There are other estimates that suggest that more than three hundred eighty-three thousand soldiers were diagnosed with VD between April 1917 and December 1919 with the loss of seven million days of active duty. Only an epidemic of influenza was a more common illness among servicemen than VD [26]. Nevertheless, the collective public marketing efforts raised awareness about the dangers of VD in WWI, challenged the status quo, and brought the subject "out of the closet" [23] where they laid the groundwork for future public health marketing campaigns in the years to come.

*Stamp out venereal diseases. E. Fuhr: The H.C. Miner Litho. Co.,
[between 1918 and 1920]. Source: Library of Congress*

INTERMEZZO: BATTLES OF A DIFFERENT SORT

With a background of patriotism, industrialization, and
immigration, the intermezzo between the two world wars
unfolded as an American battlefield of a different sort. This
was a time in which battles with foreign forces were replaced
with homegrown conflicts about morality, power, social justice, rights, and reform—conflicts that became catalysts for

bold activism, historic legislation, social reform, and continued evolution of the marketing craft.

WAGING A BATTLE AGAINST BOOZE

The success (and later demise) of the Anti-Saloon League of America is a case in point. The League, which was established in Ohio in 1893 as the Ohio Anti-Saloon League, was an outgrowth of the temperance movement, an organized reform effort designed to discourage or totally prohibit the consumption of intoxicating liquors. Concerns about temperance date far back in history, although temperance associations established in New York in 1808 and in Massachusetts in 1813 [29] were the immediate predecessors of the Anti-Saloon League. Pro-temperance efforts by the American clergy sparked the formation of more than six thousand local temperance groups by the 1830s. The movement moved through periods of inactivity and frenetic activism until waves of immigration after the turn of the century re-kindled the fervor surrounding temperance. Historical sources [29] suggest, "the influx of immigrants into the U.S. made alcohol consumption a battleground between "drys," who were often native-born, and "wets," who were often immigrants—with the typical "wet" being a German brewer or saloon owner.

The American tempest swirling around temperance was similar to the strategic conflicts involved in the WWI marketing campaigns focused on VD prevention. Central to the conflict was the intricate interplay among the different concerns about excessive drinking. Woven into the arguments were the deleterious health effects of alcohol consumption, the social and financial effects of drinking on the family, workforce, and society, the overarching concern about drunkenness and crime, and the declining morals associated with industrialization.

The work of the Anti-Saloon League tells a story about the group's belief in the power of the printed word to influence public opinion. The League developed its own publishing house, the American Issue Publishing Company, and used its landmark publication, the American Issue, to blanket the public with pro-temperance propaganda. It was reported [31] that at the peak of its promotional work, the League issued more than forty tons of anti-liquor publications every month. Buoyed by its early success, the League developed a national campaign to legalize Prohibition which would make possession and intake of alcohol illegal. Pro-Prohibition parades and petitions to Congress would soon follow, along with hefty promises that Prohibition would lower crime and improve the quality of American life.

The League was similar to the Creel Committee in its clever use of anti-German sentiment to leverage support for the national cause of Prohibition. Since many U.S. brewers were of German ancestry, the League built on the success of war advertisements such as "The Hun" to create themes of pro-Prohibition patriotism and morality. These efforts successfully led to the 1917 passage of the Eighteenth Amendment to the U.S. Constitution and its ratification in 1919.

The resulting battle about booze in American life found pro- and anti-Prohibition voices activating every conceivable channel to send their messages about the cause. As the temperance pendulum swung back and forth, anti-temperance supporters fought Prohibition full force as they gained momentum during the "roaring twenties" and the "jazz age"—a time in American history characterized by economic expansion, post-war consumerism, growing rights for women, literary achievement, musical creativity, the invention of the automobile and the radio, growing interest in sports, dancing, and defying the social norms of the past [32].

In tandem, Americans' continued interest in finding, selling, and drinking illegal alcohol, which led to the dark side of Prohibition—speakeasies (so named by the bartenders direction to customers to "speak easy" to avoid detection), the smuggling of alcohol, and organized crime. Within this environment, gangster Al Capone controlled "speakeasies, bookie joints, gambling houses, brothels, horse and race tracks, nightclubs, distilleries and breweries at a reported income of $100,000,000 a year" [33]. By the end of the decade, the tide in America had turned. After the stock market crash in 1929 and the beginning of the Great Depression, the end of Prohibition was in sight. Al Capone, who had earned a reputation as "the single greatest symbol of the collapse of law and order in the U.S. during the 1920s Prohibition era," was in jail [33]. In 1933, the Twenty-First Amendment to the Constitution was introduced, and in 1934, the ratification of the Amendment ended Prohibition, the Anti-Saloon League and other temperance groups, and one of the most colorful eras in American history [30].

Head of suffrage parade, Washington, D.C., 1913.
Source: George Grantham Bain Collection (Library of Congress)

WINNING THE VOTE FOR WOMEN

No discussion of publicity programs in the intermezzo between the world wars would be complete without a look at the women's suffrage movement, which culminated in the passage of the Nineteenth Amendment to the Constitution in 1920. Also called the Susan B. Anthony Amendment, this law finally guaranteed the most basic civil right, voting, for America's women [34]. The slow and painstaking victory came after more than seventy years of activism by a huge, colorful cast of characters who "lectured, wrote, marched, lobbied, and practiced civil disobedience to achieve what many Americans considered a radical change of the Constitution" [35].

Leading the way in the twentieth century was Alice Paul, who is credited with bringing the attention-getting tactics of British suffragists to the American movement [36]. In 1916 it was Paul and her militant colleagues who formed the National Woman's Party and pressured President Wilson to back congressional passage of a constitutional amendment by picketing the White House and actually chaining themselves to the White House fence. In 1918, the President announced that women's suffrage was urgently needed as a "war measure" and in 1919, the woman suffrage constitutional amendment passed by a narrow margin.

Decisions about strategy within the movement involved controversial and often contentious conversations about advocacy vs. agitation. While some groups, such as the National American Woman Suffrage Association, argued for a state-by-state strategy and others like Alice Paul advocated for a federal amendment, all the women (and men) involved in the women's suffrage movement used marketing tactics, which triggered intense public reaction, civil disobedience, hunger strikes, and for some, jail sentences. Beyond their crowning achievement of giving women the vote, the suffragettes left behind a legacy that today might qualify as some of the best practices in public marketing. Consider the following.

LINKING THE CAUSE TO LIBERTY

The movement officially began back in 1848, when Elizabeth Cady Stanton, Lucretia Mott, and three other women's rights reformers organized the first women's rights convention in Seneca Falls, NY. Although this convention is notable because it was the first of its kind, what distinguishes the event in the annals of marketing history is Stanton's "Declaration of Sentiments" address [36] in which she set forth the injustices experienced by American women. In the tradition of Teddy Roosevelt and George Creel, Stanton used her pen to successfully link women's suffrage with the American pursuit of liberty and the U.S. Constitution.

Modeled after the Declaration of Independence, Stanton's crafted her "Declaration of Sentiments" as a litany that carefully and forcefully enumerated broad injustice against women. In addition to being excluded from voting, Stanton pointed out that, among many injustices, women were "legally dead in the eyes of the law, not allowed to enter professions such as medicine or law, forced to pay property taxes although they had no representation in the levying of these taxes, given no means to gain an education since no college or university would accept women students, robbed of their self-confidence and self-respect, and made totally dependent on men" [36]. At the end of her address, Stanton concluded:

Now, in view of this entire disenfranchisement of one-half the people of this country, their social and religious degradation—in view of the unjust laws above mentioned, and because women do feel themselves aggrieved, oppressed, and fraudulently deprived of their most sacred rights, we insist that they have immediate admission to all the rights and

privileges which belong to them as citizens of these
United States [36].

Stanton's powerful connection of suffrage to liberty was
seen as a true stroke of genius, a real act of militancy, and a
hopeful sign of better times ahead for American women.

SAYING IT WITH SYMBOLS

One of the real accomplishments of the suffrage movement was the astonishing success in which, in the pre-tele-
vision age, the leaders created and used symbols as tools of
political advocacy. This was no small task given the widely
divergent voices of the movement and the prevailing views
of women as subservient dependents of men whose role was
limited to childbearing and domestic chores. It has been
said that imagery is a window into the relationship between
ideology and politics. For the suffragettes, symbols provided
the path for unifying the divided voices of the movement,
broadcasting a clear, central message about suffrage to a
much wider audience, securing a place for suffrage in the
American public consciousness, and succeeding at the ultimate goal—assuring voting rights for women [37].

As they worked to create the political imagery of suffrage,
leaders of the movement drew upon the extensive repertoire
of symbols from the past. There were those created by men
in America's political parties of the 19th century—examples
in which "potent images of the soldier-statesman, the log
cabin common man, the rough-and-ready frontiersman, and
the political sage" were used as tools to achieve popular political support. There were those borrowed and adapted to
American usage from the British suffrage movement, such
as the "Herald/Angel," a female figure shown sometimes
with wings or blowing a trumpet. This allegorical symbol
was based on an angelic figure created by Sylvia Pankhurst
for the British movement. Herald figures, suggest histori-

ans, follow in the "long tradition of idealized Goddesses of Liberty and Justice, and the figures America and Columbia"—the "classical figures of women representing America, Democracy, Liberty, and Justice, which had been in American political use since the time of the Revolution" to represent abstract civic virtues, and the personification of countries and political parties [37].

Suffragettes used these examples as a foundation for crafting distinctive symbols which represented the new female political culture. According to the National Women's History Project:

> Themes of women as moral arbiters of society, keepers of cultural tradition and agents of cultural transmission, nurturers of children, philanthropists to the less fortunate, and mothers of the race were extensively emphasized. These themes fit perfectly with the prevailing cultural concepts, held by both men and women, about the role of women in society. Stressing these themes opened up the arsenal of suffrage arguments to a wide range of new strategies and persuasive tactics [37].

Historical analysis of the symbols [37] shows that light is a major theme in which the sun or torch moves from west to east – a symbolic choice that represents the early success of the movement first in western states and then spreading from west to east. The symbol of "enlightenment" was believed to be a good fit with the American concept of woman's traditional, esteemed role of preserver and transmitter of culture. In addition, Suffrage materials displayed excellent, imaginative graphics; yet, they are idealized, "contained," and restrained, like the mainstream suffragists themselves.

The images, like the movement, never seriously questioned, challenged, or attacked woman's role in society or the capitalistic economic order. Mainstream suffragists correctly perceived that if the suffrage drive were to succeed it must be couched in terms making the vote a necessary tool to competently maintain woman's proper sphere. Woman's purpose was to redeem the nation through social ministry and bring it to greater righteousness through reform and uplifted politics, by protecting home, children, and society. Much of the imagery demonstrates that suffrage had become, ultimately, a mainstream political movement [37].

CAMPAIGNING WITH COLOR

The savvy marketers of the suffrage movement are great role models as campaign planners who left no campaign detail to chance. In addition to the astute creation and use of symbols, they chose the colors of their campaign selectively and symbolically. Historical analysis has shown that two primary color palettes were used—the indigenous American tradition of gold or yellow coupled with a variety of subordinate colors, and the borrowed use of the British suffrage colors—purple, white, and green, and its American variant purple, white, and gold [37].

The choice of the yellow/gold palette had originated with the work of Elizabeth Cady Stanton and Susan B. Anthony's in Kansas in 1867. Sources suggest that:

> The pro-suffrage forces adopted the Kansas state symbol, the sunflower as their own. Thereafter, the flower and the color gold or yellow were associated with the suffrage cause. Suffrage supporters used gold pins, ribbons, sashes, and yellow roses to denote their cause. During the nation's centennial celebrations in 1876, suffrage supporters sang "The Yellow Ribbon" song that associated the color with "God's own primal color; born of purity and light" and with the "flame of freedom's fires" [37].

As the "distinguishing badge" of the woman suffragette, the sunflower was viewed as an appropriate symbol of righteousness because it "faced the light and followed the course of the sun." The color gold also appeared as the backdrop of sunburst or rays of sun behind the Herald/Angel figures or in the figure's torch. This was believed to represent "the dawn of a new day" which would occur when women could vote [37]. The color gold, combined with the simple slogan of "Votes for Women," also appeared on millions of buttons, pins, pennants, and parade materials.

It has been estimated [38] that the campaign for women's suffrage included "57 years of campaigning, 56 referenda to male voters, 480 efforts to get state legislatures to submit suffrage amendments, 277 campaigns to get state party conventions to include women's suffrage planks, 47 campaigns to get state constitutional conventions to write women's suffrage into state constitutions, 30 campaigns to get presidential party conventions to adopt women's suffrage planks into party platforms, and 19 successive campaigns with 19 successive Congresses." Add to that a literal army of ordinary and extraordinary activists—marketing savvy with symbols, slogans, and colors, outrageous tactics, limited resources, drama, prejudice, incredible obstacles, and pure grit. Symbolized by the sunflower, the suffrage movement ended with a victory for the sun as American women won the most basic American civil right—the vote.

NEW DEAL, NEW WAR

When Democrat Franklin Delano Roosevelt was sworn in as the Thirty-second President of the United States in 1933, he told the American people, "We have nothing to fear but fear itself." In the midst of the Great Depression, Roosevelt saw his role as the great soother and reformer who would calm the fear in the country, restore American confidence, and build programs that would lift the United States out of the Depression and on the road to a full economic recovery. Roosevelt, fifth cousin to President Teddy Roosevelt, wasted no time in creating the New Deal, a term given to the plethora of federal programs designed to take care of the needy, promote economic recovery, and reform the financial institutions of the country.

During the first hundred days of the Roosevelt's first of four terms, the Congress passed a blitz of fifteen major pieces of legislation that established New Deal agencies and programs. Taken from a reference in a campaign speech in which Roosevelt had promised a "new deal for the American people" [39], these New Deal programs became known by recognizable acronyms referred to as "alphabet soup" by Roosevelt's critics at the time, and etched in history since then.

History [40, 41] has recorded the wide swath of social and economic activity sparked by New Deal initiatives in such areas as banking and finance, unemployment, agriculture, industry, and labor. These included:

RECONSTRUCTION FINANCE CORPORATION, (A HOOVER AGENCY) expanded under Jesse Holman Jones to make large loans to big business. Ended in 1954;

FEDERAL EMERGENCY RELIEF ADMINISTRATION (FERA), a Hoover program to create unskilled jobs for relief; replaced by WPA in 1935;

UNITED STATES BANK HOLIDAY, 1933: closed all banks until they became certified by federal reviewers;

CIVILIAN CONSERVATION CORPS (CCC), 1933: employed young men to perform unskilled work in rural areas; under Army supervision; separate program for Native Americans;

Tennessee Valley Authority (TVA), 1933: effort to modernize very poor region (most of Tennessee), centered on dams that generated electricity on the Tennessee River; still exists;

Agricultural Adjustment Act (AAA), 1933: raised farm prices by cutting total farm output of major crops (and hogs);

National Recovery Act (NRA), 1933: industries set up codes to reduce unfair competition, raise wages and prices;

Public Works Administration (PWA), 1933: built large public works projects; used private contractors (did not directly hire unemployed);

Federal Deposit Insurance Corporation (FDIC) / Glass-Steagall Act: insured deposits in banks in order to restore public confidence in banks; still exists;

Securities Act of 1933, created the SEC, 1933: codified standards for sale and purchase of stock, required risk of investments to be accurately disclosed; still exists;

Civil Works Administration (CWA), 1933–34: provided temporary jobs to millions of unemployed;

Indian Reorganization Act, 1934: moved away from assimilation;

Social Security Act (SSA), 1935: provided financial assistance to the elderly and handicapped, paid for by employee and employer payroll contributions; re-

quired years of contributions, so first payouts were
1942; still exists;

WORKS PROGRESS ADMINISTRATION (WPA), 1935: a
national labor program for 2+ million unemployed;
created useful construction work for unskilled men;
also sewing projects for women and arts projects for
unemployed artists, musicians, and writers;

NATIONAL LABOR RELATIONS ACT (NLRA) / Wagner Act,
1935: set up National Labor Relations Board to
supervise labor-management relations; in 1930s
it strongly favored labor unions. Modified by Taft-
Hartley (1947); still exists;

JUDICIAL REORGANIZATION BILL, 1937: gave President
power to appoint a new Supreme Court judge for every judge seventy years or older; failed to pass Congress;

FAIR LABOR STANDARDS ACT (FLSA), 1938: established
a maximum normal work week of forty hours, and a
minimum pay of forty cents/hour; still exists.

It's not surprising that the chemistry between such intense, speedy creation of so many New Deal agencies, acts,
and activities during the 1930s and the unsettling uncertainty of the times led to extraordinary social debate. In private and public spaces, there was ongoing controversy about
the real meaning of the New Deal. It was reported [41] that
Americans wanted the government to take greater responsibility for the welfare of its people. But, with Roosevelt's New
Deal poised to create the basis for the modern U.S. welfare
state, there was a smoldering unease about the rise of big
government.

While there was general agreement that the federal government should balance the federal budget and defend the nation, there was plenty of disagreement about the best way to end the Depression. Points of view included [42] "trust-busters," who advocated for vigorous enforcement of anti-trust laws as a means of breaking up concentrated business power; "associationalists" who wanted to encourage cooperation between business, labor, and government by establishing associations and codes supported by the three parties; and "economic planners," who sought to create a system of centralized national planning. Roosevelt is reported to have said, "take a method and try it. If it fails, admit it frankly, and try another. But above all, try something" [42].

In this milieu of competing perspectives and compelling American needs, a battle emerged for ideas in the public space and an unprecedented wealth of new, challenging marketing opportunities. There were concepts to be explained, programs to be sold, people to be convinced, reforms to be enacted, and legislative battles to be won. The new, expanded need for marketing and public relations had entered a new era—one in which interest in government, the use of the radio and cartooning as political tools, a blue American eagle, and a woman named Rosie would come into their own.

Work Pays America. Artist: Vera Block. Federal Art Project, New York, between 1936-1941 Source: Library of Congress

MARKETING THE NEW DEAL

The marketing madness that surrounded the short life of the National Recovery Administration (NRA) is a good example of patriotic New Deal marketing. Led by former General Hugh S. Johnson, the NRA was based on a fairly simplistic concept: The country's business, labor, and government leaders would establish codes of fair practices for industry specific prices, production levels, minimum wages, and maximum hours. All American businesses would be asked to accept a stopgap "blanket code"—a minimum wage of between twenty and forty cents an hour, a maximum workweek of thirty-five to forty hours, and to end child labor. Ultimately, the goal of the NRA was "ending ruinous competition, overproduction, labor conflicts, and deflating prices, and stabilizing the economy" [43].

Save Your Eyes - Use Your Goggles. Federal Art Project [1936 or 1937].
Source: Work Projects Administration Poster Collection (Library of Congress)

To mobilize political support for the NRA, Johnson launched an intense marketing effort with the NRA "Blue Eagle" as its icon. Following in the tradition of Teddy Roosevelt and George Creel, Johnson cleverly linked the NRA with fervent patriotism. Participating businesses were asked to publicize their support by displaying an NRA "Blue Eagle" poster in the window, and putting the symbol on products. The patriotic tone and the pressure to comply is evidenced by an official NRA letter sent to businesses: "You were asked to display the Blue Eagle as evidence of your promise to do your part and as a symbol of your faith in the ability of American trade and industry to defeat depression by united effort" [43].

With the NRA blue eagle leading the way, Johnson and his NRA publicity machine organized massive public rallies and "spectacular torchlight parades" in which thousands of citizens rallied around the cause. Hollywood was asked to lend a helping hand in producing public service pieces such as the one in which comedian Jimmy Durante promoted the NRA in an "official featurette patriotically contributed by the motion picture industry" [44]. The meaning of the NRA's messages was clear—participation was patriotic, and unwillingness to go along was selfish and downright unpatriotic.

It is generally believed [43] that the NRA was a success and failure. Amidst the ongoing conflict between public and private interests, the NRA's codes abolished child labor and established the precedent of federal regulation of minimum wages and maximum hours. Large numbers of unskilled workers joined unions. However, the wages were often below what labor demanded, and large occupational groups, such as farm workers, fell outside the codes' coverage. Title I of the NRA was overturned by the U.S. Supreme Court on May 27, 1935, in the A.L.A. Schechter Poultry Corp. vs. United States case, in which the Schechter Corporation allegedly disobeyed the requirements of a "Code of Fair Competition for the Live Poultry Industry of the Metropolitan Area in and about the City of New York" [43]. By that time, more than seven hundred industries had been codified, four million unemployed people had been absorbed into industrial jobs, and nearly 23 million workers were under codes.

The Works Project Administration (WPA), which was the second part of the NRA, was allowed by the court to stand. As one of the largest public works projects in history, the WPA went on to spend billions on reforestation, flood control, rural electrification, water works, sewage plants, school buildings, slum clearance, student scholarships, and other projects. Although economists and labor historians continue to debate the impact of the NRA, it is safe to say that the New Deal gave marketers a rich patriotic platform for practicing their craft.

President Franklin D. Roosevelt, during "Fireside chat", 1937. Source: History Department at the University of San Diego

REACHING OUT WITH RADIO

If there were a perfect match between a medium and a messenger, it would be FDR and his famous "fireside chats."

Although George Creel put the wireless to shrewd use in WWI, it is FDR who is best known for leveraging radio technology as a tool of leadership and influence during one of the most difficult times in U.S. history—the Great Depression and World War II.

It's been said that no American leader, then or since, used the radio so effectively [45]. Radio represented the "most direct means of access to the American people," and during the 1930s there was a radio in almost every home. This was a time when families typically spent several hours a day gathered together, listening to their favorite radio programs [46]. As unemployment hovered around 33 percent, banks were closed, and despair commonplace, Roosevelt began broadcasting his chats on national networks. Beginning on March 12, 1933, with the first chat on his administration's plan to repair the nation's banking crisis, FDR discussed critical issues with the nation thirty-one times. With his calm, reassuring voice, Roosevelt shared his hopes and plans for the troubled nation. The masses gathered around radios and listened intently to FDR.

After he invited "people from all walks of life" to "tell me your troubles" by writing to him directly, millions of letters flooded the White House. It has been reported that these letters detailed the emotions experienced by the citizens during these radio addresses, and that they felt that FDR "entered their homes and spoke to each of them." One man said, "I never saw him but I knew him. Can you have forgotten how, with his voice, he came into our house, the President of the United States, calling us friends" [46].

In today's crowded, competitive media markets, marketers can learn much from Roosevelt's strategic genius in reaching out through the radio. To achieve maximum saturation, Roosevelt broadcast his thirty-one chats at 10:00 p.m. Eastern time, a time "early enough that Easterners were still awake but late enough that even people on the West Coast would be home from their day's activities" [46].

Special care was taken to make his addresses "accessible and understandable to ordinary Americans." Sources [46] suggest that FDR's speechwriters "always used basic language when preparing the Fireside Chats—eighty percent of the words FDR chose were among the 1,000 most commonly used words in the English vocabulary."

The chats occurred at pivotal times and covered specific topics of great national importance. In addition, FDR and his speechwriters were masters of storytelling, with anecdotes and analogies that explained the complex issues facing the United States at the time. For example, FDR used a baseball analogy to describe the first two months of the New Deal: "I have no expectations of making a hit every time I come to bat. What I seek is the highest possible batting average, not only for myself, but for the team" [46].

Although the President exuded confidence in his leadership and his many programs, he used the fireside chats to tell the public that the fate of the nation rested in their hands. By referring to his audience in terms of "you" and "we," FDR reinforced a sense of national identity, encouraged individual participation in the nation's activities, and forged an intimate relationship between the president and the public [46]. Referred to as "one of the greatest uses of mass media in history" [47], the fireside chats became a successful channel in which the American public believed that they were in conversation with their president in the midst of a national crossroads.

Construction of a Dam. William Gropper, 1939. Oil on canvas.
Source: Department of the Interior Museum

DRAWING FOR THE CAUSE

No discussion of marketing during the New Deal would be complete without mention of the army of artists who put their pens to work influencing public opinion of FDR's massive social reform agenda. The political, social, and emotional issues swirling around FDR sparked a tsunami of cartoons that depicted every conceivable view of the change, contempt, and courage of the times. The thousands of New Deal cartoons that appeared in the popular press have been thoroughly analyzed and are preserved in the annals of history. Archivists [48, 49] suggest that the massive collections of New Deal cartoons published during FDR's presidency open a window not just on American history but also into the growing sophistication of political cartooning as an artistic craft.

Analysis of cartooning strategy demonstrates the thoughtful technique used in this medium. It has been shown [48], for example, that cartoons are typically drawn at four different levels. The first is a straightforward depiction of an event or issue, which does not express the artist's opinion. In the second type, the artist uses a metaphor that captures the essence of the point. The artist expresses a clear opinion in the third type, while at the most complex level, the artist skillfully combines metaphors and opinion.

The 1930s also gave birth to "Federal One," which used government funds to support the work of unemployed artists, musicians, actors, and writers through the Federal Art Project (FAP), the Federal Music Project, the Federal Theatre Project, and the Federal Writers' Project. This massive endeavor is symbolic of the values-laden New Deal as an era of both reform and survival. Although the FAP was designed as an employment vehicle for unemployed artists, it was also viewed as a vehicle for reinforcing the goals of the New Deal, bringing art to the masses and enriching their lives with culture. Artists from the specialties of easel painting, sculpture, photography, mural painting, and graphic arts were hired to work, teach others about artistic techniques, and inspire others to appreciate the value of art in American life.

In stark contrast to the sardonic satire of the black and white, pen and paper newspaper cartoons of the New Deal, the mural art of the Works Progress Administration (WPA)— emblazoned by a palette of oil colors and mythic imagery— lives on today as a legacy of one of the first government-sponsored art projects in our nation's history. According to the Library of Congress [50], which houses one of the largest collections of WPA posters, the "silkscreen, lithograph, and woodcut posters were designed to publicize health and safety programs; cultural programs including art exhibitions, theatrical, and musical performances; travel and tourism; educational programs; and community activities in seventeen states and the District of Columbia." The posters were primarily printed on poster board, although they were also produced as one-sheet and multi-sheet designs which were sometimes signed by the artist.

The WPA murals add another dimension to the study of media in marketing public programs. In contrast with the stinging satire used in political cartoons, the large, vividly colored murals of the WPA capitalized on mythology, imagery, and symbols for transmitting direct and subliminal messages to the viewing public. These were similar to the figures used in the women's suffrage movement. In some of the federal collections [50], the WPA workers are seen in heroic poses reminiscent of military heroes. The artists are careful to show the workers laboring in unison to complete a great public works project. Beneath the colors lie a powerful message about the need for unity during troubled times and the power of collective action.

Overall, the FAP is reported [50] to have employed more than five thousand artists and produced over two million posters from thirty-five thousand designs. Today, the two thousand surviving posters bear witness to FDR's marketing genius in providing the American public with jobs, hope, and culture.

Waging War with Words and Women

The genius of FDR and his leadership on the global stage would soon be put to the grand test when the United States entered World War II (WWII). For those Americans who worked in marketing, advertising, and public relations, this time of international trial and tribulation would usher in an era of unprecedented professional opportunity. On June 13, 1942, FDR issued "Executive Order 9182," which established the Office of War Information "in recognition of the right of the American people and of all other peoples opposing the Axis aggressors to be truthfully informed about the common war effort" [51]. Placed within the Office for Emergency Management in the Executive Office of the President, the Office of War Information (OWI) would absorb the Office of Facts and Figures, the Division of Information of the Office for Emergency Management, the Office of Government Reports, and the Foreign Information Service in the Office of Coordinator of Information.

The OWI was given an enormous mission. According to its first Director—newsman and radio commentator Elmer Davis—it was "a war agency, which owes its existence solely to the war, and was established to serve as one of the instruments by which the war will be won" [52].

In short, "the OWI was charged with selling the war" [53]. The immense, complex work facing OWI and its legions of professionals was made easier by the fact that the American public had seen the great power of organized information firsthand—through the work of the Creel Committee in WWI and more recently, with the plentiful marketing programs of FDR's New Deal. Yet, OWI's task was great, for the government needed to energize and mobilize an isolationist public to support a war on two fronts—in the Pacific and in Europe. And in practical terms, "war production had to be bolstered, war bonds to be sold, materials and manpower had to be conserved, rationing had to be accepted by the public, and the morale of those at the front and those at home had to be bolstered during the long hard sacrifice of wartime" [54]. What followed was a period of unprecedented intensity in which the OWI would utilize a variety of media—posters, movies, radio programs and newsreels—to shape and deliver positive, consistent messaging which would influence, persuade, warn, encourage, and ultimately, enroll the public in support of the massive war effort.

I Want You For The U.S. Army. 1941. Source: Library of Congress

PENNING PERSUASION WITH POSTERS

With pen and paintbrush in hand, the advertisers and artists of WWII put the tools of their trade to work on behalf of the war effort. All the artists were Americans and many were specifically hired by OWI. Although these artists used multiple media channels, posters emerged as an ideal medium for using color, graphics, snappy sayings, and sometimes stark imagery to spread pro-war messages about freedom and democracy. It has been suggested that the popularity of posters as tools of war propaganda was significantly enhanced by innovations in printing technology and distribution strategies. One U.S. Office of War Information official is reported to have said: "We want to see posters on fences, on the walls of buildings, on village greens, on boards in front of City Hall and the Post Office, in hotel lobbies, and in the windows of vacant stores...shouting at people from unexpected places with all the urgency which this war demands" [55].

Careless Talk Costs Lives. Artist: Al Doria. WPA War Services of LA, 1941-1943.
Source: Work Projects Administration Poster Collection (Library of Congress)

Initially OWI had planned to centrally design and distribute all war materials, but other government agencies, branches of the military, businesses (such as General Electric, the House of Seagram, and the Stetson Hat Company), Madison Avenue advertisers, and commercial illustrators were asked to lend their pens after the task overpowered OWI resources. Museum directors and curators lent their expertise with the selection of designs, while community-based volunteer defense councils helped to develop local distribution systems.

Historical collections of WWII posters [55] show that the war artists created a wide repertoire of posters with the recurring themes of American patriotism and independence, a unified labor force with both men and women, the conservation and rationing of food and materials, security, the notion that behavior on the home front affected success on the battlefront, and the need for citizens to support fundraising for the war effort. Many of the catchy sayings such as "loose lips might sink ships" (the House of Seagram), "keep mum—the world has ears" (OWI), "teamwork wins—You build 'em, we'll sail 'em" (United States Maritime Commission), and "The sound that kills: don't murder men with idle words" (OWI), found their way into daily street chat.

Build For Our Navy! R. Muchley. Between 1941 and 1943.
Source: Work Projects Administration Poster Collection (Library of Congress)

It has been said [56] that beneath the sayings and the slogans of WWII posters, another classic story emerged from a clash of artistic perspective and taste. On one side, there were artists who favored traditional "war art," which used a sophisticated style of contemporary art, highly stylized images, and symbolism to promote the war effort. On the other side, there were the "ad men" from the world of advertising who wanted posters to be more like ad campaigns. Criticism of each perspective was common. Posters created by the ad men were seen as superficial and sometimes inappropriately cheerful for wartime. The ad men commissioned focus

groups of factory workers to show that the point of more
stylized art posters was simply not understood by the masses. Art historians [56] suggest that the advertising specialists
in OWI "finally gained the upper hand in 1943—and from
that time, government posters looked more like magazine
illustrations, and the idea of 'war art' was abandoned."

WOMEN WORKING FOR THE WAR

Among the many memorable WWII posters, there
emerged one iconic image that would etch a unique, permanent place in U.S. history and in American life—Rosie the
Riveter, who symbolized the millions of American women
who helped the war effort by taking "men's jobs" during
WWII. During the long years of the Depression, women who
sought work had been criticized for taking scarce jobs away
from men. But the times and need for workers changed dramatically in the booming wartime. Between 1942 and 1944,
there was an "intense courtship of women by employers and
government" [57]. As part of the government sponsored "Wom-
en at Work Cover Promotion," magazines were encouraged
to create feature articles that highlighted women's desire
for glamour, good pay, and ways to show their patriotism:
"Women, you could hasten victory by working and save your
man" [57]. Many kinds of employment, not just defense and
factory work, were referred to as "war jobs" and "necessary
civilian jobs" such as grocery clerks, elevator operators, telephone operators, farmers, and ticket agents. Women were
told that if they didn't do the jobs, "our civilian life would
break down" [57].

We Can Do it. J. Howard Miller.
Source: National Archives and Records Administration

Women responded by turning out in record numbers to work in all kind of jobs, including new, challenging manufacturing jobs that had traditionally been held by men. This female work force included growing numbers of married and older women, and large numbers of African-American women who moved from low-paying domestic jobs to better-paying jobs in factories. The number of employed women grew by 6.5 million. The proportion of women in the work force rose from 25 percent at the beginning of the war to 36 percent at war's end; an increase greater than the previous four decades combined [58, 59].

A look into Rosie's history provides an interesting, inside glimpse into her development as the ultimate symbol for American women who worked during WWII. Many erroneously believe that Rosie was initially created by famous artist Norman Rockwell for the Memorial Day cover of the Saturday Evening Post on May 29, 1943. Historians suggest that Rosie really began a year earlier when the term "Rosie the riveter" first entered the public airways via a song written in 1942 by songwriters Redd Evans and John Jacob Loeb [57]:

All the day long,
Whether rain or shine,
She's a part of the assembly line.
She's making history,
Working for victory,
Rosie the Riveter.
Keeps a sharp lookout for sabotage,
Sitting up there on the fuselage.
That little girl will do more than a male will do.

Rockwell supposedly heard this song [57] since he wrote the name "Rosie" on the lunch box in his drawing.

After newspapers and magazines featured stories about the strong, powerful women who were doing men's work, the U.S. War Production Commission funded the creation of a recruitment poster with a determined female worker—complete with her hair wrapped in a bandanna, her muscular arm upraised, and a caption which read "We Can Do It!" Although the slogan "We Can Do It!" had actually been used in industry prior to the Rosie poster [57], it was Westinghouse artist J. Howard Miller who is credited with creating the signature Rosie poster.

The Rockwell version of Rosie—dirty, oversized, brawny, and wearing overalls, goggles and various pins for blood donation, victory, and her security badge—was widely disseminated during the war but historians suggest [57] that copyright restrictions limited its long-term use. The other Rosie—produced early in 1943 with federal funds by J. Howard Miller, was free of such constraints. As a result, women named Rose gained a small measure of stardom during the war. One such woman, Rose Monroe, a riveter in Michigan, made a film about selling war bonds and a commercial movie called Rosie the Riveter [57].

Historians continue to debate the effects of women working during the war. As the nation shifted its production to a peacetime economy, female industrial workers were laid off from their jobs at nearly double the rates of men [58]. By 1947, the percentage of women in the work force had declined to 27 percent, and women quickly saw that jobs in heavy industry were no longer available to them after men returned from the war [58]. Although the number of working women never again fell to pre-war levels [57], this was a sign that a new post-war era was beginning in the country—one in which there would be a renewed interest in motherhood and traditional family life.

What would remain constant across the eras would be the enduring image of Rosie the Riveter. Today, many years after she was called into action to motivate America's women to join the workforce, Rosie's image continues to have a ubiquitous presence in American life. There are Rosie mugs, magnets, t-shirts, stationery, and mouse pads sold in shops all over the United States. Also, there is a website devoted exclusively to Rosie (www.rosietheriveter.org), numerous books, a national park in California with a memorial dedicated to her memory (www.nps.gov/rori), and an ongoing living history project (www.loc.gov/vets) sponsored by the Library of Congress.

RISING FROM THE ASHES

Although Rosie the Riveter certainly achieved wide name recognition and fame during and after WWII, she has shared the limelight with a furry, four-legged, unlikely peer—Smokey Bear. Like Rosie, Smokey has an interesting story and a persona that has had a popular public presence for more than sixty years. Unlike Rosie, whose distinctive image and wartime message of "We can do it" have remained essentially unchanged after the war years, Smokey underwent a makeover as he matured—his handlers sensed the need for him to carry a more modern message about fire prevention.

Smokey Bear poster. 1953. Source: Smokeybear.com

Many believe that Smokey began when a burned bear cub rescued from a 1950 forest fire became the living Smokey at the National Zoo in Washington, DC. But Smokey's story actually began during WWII after the Japanese bombed a California oil field near Santa Barbara, very close to the Los Padres National Forest. Although the bombing was not viewed as a major war event, it put stress on the local firefighters and sparked great concern in the United States that the country's timber resources might be in peril.

According to a Fire Service brochure [60], timber was "a primary commodity for battleships, gunstocks, and packing crates for military transports." During war time, any threat to the country's timber was dangerous to the war effort. Soon after the bombing, the U.S. Forest Service sought help from the War Advertising Council, a volunteer group of advertisers, in developing a marketing campaign centered on a new idea—enlisting the help of citizens in winning the war by preventing accidental fires.

What followed was a number of trial-and-error marketing efforts that included frightening Japanese figures with slanty eyes and big teeth and a stern "Ranger Jim." In 1944, the Walt Disney Company loaned Bambi to the fire prevention campaign for a year and his softer image was an immediate, albeit short-term, success. The search for the campaign's ultimate icon led to a bear drawn by eminent animal illustrator Albert Staehle [60]. "Smokey Bear" would be the image and the voice of the Cooperative Forest Fire Prevention Campaign (CFFPC) [61]. The bear was named Smokey after "Smokey" Joe Martin, the Assistant Chief of the New York City Fire Department from 1919 to 1930. It has been reported [60] that the campaign's radio ads were made by an announcer who "put his head in a bucket for ursine gravitas to intone, 'Only YOU can prevent forest fires'" [60].

The Forest Service soon turned to artist Rudy Wendelin, who had worked with the Forest Service in the past, to design the entire portfolio of campaign promotional materials and licensing products for Smokey and the CFFPC. It was Wendelin who oversaw "all things Smokey" until he retired in 1973. According to historical sources [60], with Wendelin's pen, Smokey's sharp claws disappeared and he was given fingers to hold the shovel and water buckets. Smokey's image was softened, and he slowly became more human, even wearing jeans to avoid appearing naked.

Smokey's well-known message, "Only YOU can prevent forest fires!" has also been modified slightly over the years to reflect concerns about wildfires and modern trends in forestry. In the 1980s, it was recognized [62] that carefully planned and executed application of fire helps to actually clear the land and return it to a natural state of health. Thus, "prescribed" fire became recognized as an effective tool for removing debris in the forest and preventing the outbreak and spread of wild fires. Experts suggested [62] that because Smokey was against any kind of fire—natural or human—he may have inadvertently ended up being "anti-nature" because suppressing all kinds of fire increases the likelihood of catastrophic fires. Reconciling Smokey's "no-fire" message with the newer, selective use of "good fires" and the reality about "wildfires" has changed fire prevention messages. These updated messages now broaden the concept of fires to any uncontrolled fire in the outdoors, directly address the issue of good fires as "nature's housekeepers," and place more emphasis on forest ecology.

But subtle changes in the country's approach to fire prevention have not eroded the immense public appeal of Smokey as one of the most enduring public service icons in the history of public marketing. He received so much mail from school children that he was awarded his own zip code—20252. His image has been honored on a postage stamp, commemorative license plates, and a host of toys. Every year, American students study fire prevention with Smokey Bear educational materials, and every day, Smokey can be found taking his message out to schools and com-

munity fire awareness events. In Capitan, New Mexico, the
Smokey Bear Museum and Park pays tribute to the coura-
geous little bear who became a living symbol for fighting
and preventing forest fires, and who is buried there.

In 2002, Smokey joined the Internet age with his own
website (www.smokeybear.com) co-sponsored by the Ad
Council, the U.S. Forest Service, and the National Association of Foresters, organizations which use royalties from
the licensing of Smokey products to fund their fire prevention activities. Smokey's website includes, "Smokey's vault,"
which contains a review of Smokey's history and a nostalgic
multimedia collection of Smokey memorabilia over the decades. At age sixty-two, the Smokey Bear campaign is the
longest running public service campaign in history and is
credited with reducing the number of acres lost annually to
fire in the United States from 22 million to 4 million.

Beyond this astounding record of endurance and impact,
Smokey's life is an example of evolutionary marketing filled
with good, practical lessons for contemporary campaigns.
Smokey's recognizable image emerged after the campaign
considered a number of unsuccessful prototypes and used
Disney's Bambi for the first year. Smokey's persona was refined over the years as he and the campaign matured. In
2000, Smokey was repositioned for a more adult audience.
After fifty years with the same message, Smokey's message
was modified in 2001 by the Ad Council (www.adcouncil.
org). This new message, "Only YOU can prevent wildfires,"
refers to any uncontrolled, outdoor fire, while Smokey's website now discusses contemporary perspectives on the use of
"good" fire. Smokey's example shows us how creative marketing can take an important safety message that began in
wartime and keep it relevant across the decades and the
generations.

When WWII ended in 1945, the country had a new president. After only eighty-two days as FDR's Vice-President,
Harry Truman became president of a nation mourning a

beloved leader and engaged in a world war. After Truman took the oath of office on April 13, 1945, he told reporters: "Boys, if you ever pray, pray for me now. I don't know if you fellas ever had a load of hay fall on you, but when they told me what happened yesterday, I felt like the moon, the stars, and all the planets had fallen on me" [63]. During his two terms of office, Truman led the nation through a tumultuous period in which he ordered the dropping of the atomic bomb on Hiroshima and Nagasaki and oversaw the nation's emergence from WWII into the transitional times that began in the second half of the twentieth century.

The end of WWII sent many women back to more traditional roles as homemakers as their soldier husbands resumed civilian jobs and headed for school, courtesy of the GI Bill, which had been signed into law by FDR on June 22, 1944. Officially known as the Servicemen's Readjustment Act of 1944, the Bill provided federal aid to help veterans adjust to civilian life in the areas of hospitalization, purchase of homes and businesses, and education [64]. Seven years after the end of WWII, approximately eight million veterans had received educational benefits, at a total cost of approximately $14 billion [64].

Aerial view of Levittown, Pennsylvania. ed Latcham, ca. 1959.
Source: National Archives and Records Administration

Returning war veterans were also responsible for other post-war phenomena—an unprecedented number of births which began the baby boom generation in 1946 and the demand for housing which led to a new concept in American life—the suburbs. Exemplified by the rows of mass-produced, two-bedroom homes in Levittown, PA, the suburbs represented a new beginning, an escape route out of the inner cities and a real slice of the American dream: "They came to own their own home—cook with their own appliances—mow their own lawn. They had GI loans in hand, babies on the way, and a '50s brand of pioneering spirit'" [65].

That pioneering spirit and optimism of the immediate post WWII period existed in parallel with emerging concerns of Americans during the Presidency of General Dwight Eisenhower, the former Supreme Allied Commander in Europe, from 1952–1961. There was racial injustice, anti-Communist paranoia, the dread of nuclear war, the emergence of the Cold War, and the end of the Korean War [66]. This was the era of relative calm, contrasts, and conflicts of a different sort—of hula hoops, Elvis, television, bomb shelters, the interstate highway system, desegregation, and the early civil rights movement.

Eisenhower's successor in the White House, John F. Kennedy, was the first Roman Catholic president. As the new, youthful, handsome president, Kennedy ushered in an era of enthusiasm that would bring back the idea of public service and bring the United States into the space age. Kennedy set the stage for his brief presidency at his inaugural address in 1961 when he called on citizens to serve with his oft-quoted injunction: "Ask not what your country can do for you—ask what you can do for your country." In his "We choose to go to the moon" speech in September, 1962, Kennedy said: "Those who came before us made certain that this country rode the first waves of the industrial revolution, the first waves of modern invention, and the first wave of nuclear power, and this generation does not intend to founder in the backwash of the coming age of space. We mean to be a part of it—we mean to lead it. For the eyes of the world now look into space, to the moon and to the planets beyond, and we have vowed that we shall not see it governed by a hostile flag of conquest, but by a banner of freedom and peace. We have vowed that we shall not see space filled with weapons of mass destruction, but with instruments of knowledge and understanding" [67]. On July 21,1969, almost seven years after Kennedy's speech and six years after his assassination in Dallas, American Neil Armstrong becomes the first man to walk on the moon.

While Kennedy's funeral in Washington DC marked a tragic time for the nation, the event became a first in the history of broadcasting. It was the 1963 Kennedy funeral that marks the first time television networks preempted their regular schedules and all commercial advertising as they switched to twenty-four-hour news coverage of the "wrenching marathon" that would conclude with the president's burial at Arlington National Cemetery on Monday, November 25, 1963 [68]. The Museum of Broadcast Communication reported that "in 1963, before the days of high-tech, globally linked, and sleekly mobile newsgathering units, the technical limitations of broadcast journalism militated against the coverage of live and fast-breaking events in multiple locations. The challenges of juggling live broadcasts from across the nation with overseas audio transmissions, of compiling instant documentaries and special reports, and of acquiring and putting out raw film footage over the air was an off-the-cuff experiment in what NBC correspondent Bill Ryan called 'controlled panic'" [68].

Family watching television. Evert F. Baumgardner, ca. 1958.
Source: National Archives and Records Administration

As the entire country and the entire world watched live broadcasts of the slain president's state funeral procession and the murder of assassin Lee Harvey Oswald, the power of television in the world was changed forever. As the Museum of Broadcast Communication concluded [68], television, which had been criticized in its early days, "immediately, almost automatically, was transformed into a participating organ of American life whose value, whose indispensability, no Nielsen audiometers could measure or statistics reveal." The unforeseen national tragedy had transformed television into a "national lifeline" for the country.

By 1963, marketing professionals were working with a toolbox filled with almost two hundred years of American marketing experience which had created campaigns that literally changed the nation. From the revolutionary days of the Sons of Liberty to the sad days of JFK's funeral, advances in technology extended the reach of marketers with new media channels such as radio, which was used so artfully by FDR, and television, which came into its own at one of the most tragic times in the country's history. A colorful cast of brilliant, eclectic marketing strategists—such as John Adams, Teddy Roosevelt, George Creel, Elizabeth Cady Stanton, Alice Paul, and FDR—had shown how massive public marketing campaigns could successfully shift public opinion and behavior by linking social issues to patriotism and democratic ideals. Aided by new printing technology, the artists and cartoonists of WWI, the New Deal, and WWII demonstrated the power of pens, paintbrushes, posters, and personalities like Uncle Sam, Rosie the Riveter, and Smokey Bear to carry marketing messages to the masses.

The country had moved from a farm-based economy to industrialization and post-industrialization and was moving swiftly toward the information age. Along the way, the United States had experienced firsthand the real power of professional communications, marketing, advertising, and public relations to harness the forces of politics, activism, and social reform into effective action. Putting a man on the moon ushered in a new American era, one in which the country would begin to experience unprecedented social and technological change. This type of change, described as "whitewater" [69], would be filled with surprises and novel situations which would take us far out of our comfort zone. In this environment, marketing professionals would be called upon to use all the tools of their trade in the ever-changing context of American life in the last half of the twentieth century and the beginning of the next. Thus, learning to work as a relentless observer of American culture became a must for all who create modern marketing campaigns. To that end, Part Two takes you on a journey through some trends in the contemporary American landscape and how modern campaigns found a way to leverage them for marketing success.

Used with the permission of the Forest Service, U.S. Department of Agriculture

By the People, For the People: Posters from the WPA, 1936-1943

The posters in this section and selected others reprinted in this book are from the collection "By the People, For the People: Posters from the WPA, 1936-1943" Library of Congress. These Work Projects Administration (WPA) posters were produced as part of the New Deal, which was introduced by President Franklin D. Roosevelt. The posters were designed to promote a variety of public marketing initiatives including community involvement and activities, support for the war effort, adoption of positive health and safety behavior, and the appreciation of the arts.

More than nine hundred of the original WPA posters are in the custody of the Library of Congress's Prints and Photographs Division.

The posters in this book are just a small collection of the creative marketing campaigns produced from 1936 to 1943. You can find more of the original silkscreen, lithograph, and woodcut posters at the Library of Congress by visiting www.loc.gov/index.html.

MILK FOR SUMMER THIRST

CREATED/PUBLISHED
Ohio: Federal Art Project, 1940

SUMMARY
Poster for Cleveland Division of Health promoting
milk, showing a young man holding a glass of milk
with the sun shining in the background.

NOTES
Date stamped on verso: Oct 14 1940

BETTER HOUSING: THE SOLUTION TO INFANT
MORTALITY IN THE SLUMS

CREATED/PUBLISHED
New York: Federal Art Project, 1936

SUMMARY
Poster promoting better housing as a solution for high
rates of infant mortality in the slums, showing a blueprint of new housing next to existing tenement buildings over which stands the figure of Death.

NOTES
Date stamped on verso: Dec 18 1936 Benj. Sheer, artist
New York City Housing Authority - Fiorello H. La Guar-
dia, Mayor - Langdon W. Post, Comm.

HELP YOUR NEIGHBORHOOD BY
KEEPING YOUR PREMISES CLEAN

CREATED/PUBLISHED
Tenement House Dept. of the City of New York: F.H.
La Guardia, Mayor: Langdon W. Post, Commission-
er. New York: Federal Art Project, 1936 or 1937

SUMMARY
Poster promoting better living conditions by keeping
tenement neighborhoods clean.

NOTES
Date stamped on verso: Apr 16 1937

YOUR WARTIME DUTY! DON'T WASTE WATER:
DO NOT LET WATER RUN A LONG TIME TO GET A DRINK: DO
KEEP WATER IN ICEBOX INSTEAD

CREATED/PUBLISHED
New York: NYC WPA War Services, between 1941
and 1943

SUMMARY
Poster for The New York City Department of Water
Supply, Gas & Electricity for a campaign to conserve
water, showing a man drinking water.

NOTES
F.H. La Guardia, Mayor
Department of Water Supply, Gas & Electricity
Patrick Quilty, Commissioner

ARE YOU HELPING WITH SALVAGE?

CREATED/PUBLISHED
So. Calif.: Work Projects Administration,
between 1941 and 1943

SUMMARY
Poster encouraging citizen participation in salvage
for the war effort, showing seaplanes and a man
welding.

OUTWITTED BY COMMUNITY SANITATION;
COMMUNITY SANITATION PLANNING KEEPS FLIES AWAY FROM
DEADLY DISEASE GERMS

CREATED/PUBLISHED
Illinois: Federal Art Project. 1940

SUMMARY
Poster promoting sanitary facilities showing a giant
fly above an outhouse.

AIR RAID PRECAUTIONS: KEEP COOL, DON'T SCREAM, DON'T
RUN, PREVENT DISORDER, OBEY ALL INSTRUCTIONS
ANGUS, CHARLOTTE, ARTIST

CREATED/PUBLISHED
Pennsylvania: Penna Art WPA, between 1941 and 1943

SUMMARY
Poster offering instructions for proper procedures
during air raids.

NOTES
Date stamped on recto: Jan 21, 1943

STAMP 'EM OUT: BUY U.S. STAMPS AND BONDS
T.A. BYRNE, ARTIST

CREATED/PUBLISHED
La.: WPA War Services of La.,
between 1941 and 1943

SUMMARY
Poster encouraging purchase of war stamps and
bonds to support the war effort, showing faces of
Hitler, Mussolini, and Hirohito.

NOTES
Date stamped on recto: Jan 21, 1943

Sew for victory

CREATED/PUBLISHED
New York: N.Y.C. W.P.A. War Services,
between 1941 and 1943

SUMMARY
Poster promoting sewing as contribution to the war
effort, showing outline of sewing machine with war
images.

NOTES
Poster design by Pistchal

IN MARCH READ THE BOOKS YOU'VE
ALWAYS MEANT TO READ

CREATED/PUBLISHED
Chicago: Ill. Art Proj., between 1936 and 1941

SUMMARY
Poster for statewide Library Project showing a wind-
blown woman and books by authors such as Scott,
Dumas, Thackeray, Dickens, Austen, and others.

NOTES
Date stamped on verso: Mar 25 1941

Used with the permission of the Forest Service, U.S. Department of Agriculture

Part Two:
Trends of Today, Pathways
for a Better Tomorrow

It was futurist John Naisbitt who said, "the most reliable way to understand the future is by understanding the present" [1]. Each and every day, statisticians, business analysts, marketers, publicists, demographers, entrepreneurs, academicians, students of popular culture, and the simply curious step right into the human battleground in which the pull of the old and allure of the new move our society forward. With their diving gear and analytic tools in place, these trend-seekers dive head first into the swirling, turbulent streams of change with the hope of seeing the light in murky waters. Like the characters in The DaVinci Code, they're searching for a holy grail—only this one is the next big trend gathering momentum as if it were a hurricane gathering speed in warm water. Searching for the next big trend is fueled by adrenaline and the anticipation of the next big business.

In this digital age, it's easy to focus our analysis of trends on giants like computer technology and biotechnology and the revolutionary changes they have brought to our world. And yet, man does not live by science and technology alone. Social, cultural, environmental, and political forces influence our lives just as much as the giants do and like a hurricane, any or all of these forces can make landfall and leave an indelible mark on our country and our individual lives. In this chapter, we look at ten trends which we think make a real difference in marketing public programs today. Looking at these trends is like looking at a freeze frame of a fast-moving film. Capturing a slice of life in this way allows us to stop, look, analyze, and reflect on patterns that shape the life and times of the public we serve. Keeping our hands on the pulse of the nation is just as critical for those who market public programs as it is for those in the world of business, although our bottom line is a grail of a different type. The marketplace of business is powered by competitive DNA—it's organic, facile, and quick to seize the next business opportunity. In contrast, the bottom line for public marketing programs is driven by public service DNA—serving the public good by stimulating positive change in attitudes and actions. To do that well, public marketers must place their cause not only in the context of the times, but also on the edge of the next emerging trend.

Welcome to the Wild Wired World:
A NEW CYBER WORLD OF DIGITAL NATIVES

Pack your surfboard, mouse, facebook, iPod, smart phone, and your spam filters. Keep you ear tuned to the digital buzz, your eye focused on the portal, and your dictionary of digital speak close at hand. Wear waders tall enough to help you navigate the never-ending streams of podcasts. Carry a good map of the blogosphere. Keep you eyes open for the walls of the past falling down before your eyes. Your mission...should you decide to accept it...is to enter the wild wired world of the new media...

In this wild new world of the twenty-first century, the old media are gasping for breath as the new media emerge in an interconnected world where the old rules simply don't apply. If media guru Marshall McLuhan (1911–1980) were alive today, he might be tempted to say that the Internet is THE medium—the most powerful force of modern times. McLuhan, the leading prophet of the electronic age, is best known for coining some familiar cyber terms (global village and surfing) and for the now famous phrase "the medium is the message" [2]. In his most popular work, (underline and italics Understanding Media: The Extensions of Man) Understanding Media: The Extensions of Man (1964), McLuhan suggested that what really mattered with the media was not the specific content transmitted but the characteristics of the medium itself. McLuhan's old wisdom is like new genius today because after taking a good hard look at the impact of the Internet, it's easy to see why we live in a whole new world.

In his bestselling book Megatrends, futurist John Naisbitt [1] hit the bullseye with his prediction that communication technology would collapse the information float in our world. Shortening the amount of time information spends in the communication channel would speed up life and business, Naisbitt said. Technology caused the death of distance and propelled us into the world of instantaneous communications. Nasibitt reminded us [2] that when President Lincoln was shot, the news reached London five days later. Today we live in the world of 24/7 cable coverage where we watch real world events unfolding in real time. *In The Lexus and the Olive Tree* [3], NY Times correspondent Thomas Friedman offered another perspective on life in the interconnected new world. "In 1990 most people hadn't heard of the Internet and very few had e-mail addresses. In less than a decade, the Internet, cell phones and e-mail have become essential tools that many people, and not only in developed countries, cannot live without," said Friedman. The Internet allows us to communicate with almost anyone, anywhere, at any time and it gives us, suggests Friedman, "a sort of universal language outside the bounds of any particular culture and a universal model of communication that allows us to connect with all sorts of people with whom we have never shared an olive grove" [3].

In his aborted project, Paul Baran composed a detailed, twelve-volume series in which he documented the vulnerability of the U.S. communication structure and proposed a new system—the "Internet" with a network of routers that could communicate with each other [5]. Rejected by the military and industry as well, Baran's concepts would later be independently replicated by researchers at the Advanced Research Projects Agency (ARPA), Massachusetts Institute of Technology, and other research facilities which were searching for a path that would lead to "a globally interconnected set of computers through which everyone could quickly access data and programs from any site" [5]. The concept of e-mail was discovered later when a computer expert working in a small Massachusetts consulting firm discovered how to modify the file transfer protocols that carry messages [5]. The discovery was kept secret for a long time before it leaked out and moved quickly to achieve widespread use and fame.

The Census Bureau [4] has looked carefully at that use and concluded that the Internet had exerted its impact in three different ways, all of which are relevant to marketing public programs today. First, the Internet has become a major media outlet for the dissemination of news. In a mere six years, the proportion of adults who used the Internet to find information on "news, weather, or sports" increased from 7 percent in 1997 to 40 percent in 2003, and the proportion using the Internet to find information on government or health services increased from 12 percent to 33 percent [3]. Second, the Census Bureau confirmed [4] what most of us already know—e-mail is replacing the telephone and print media as our primary communication mode. More than half (55 percent) of all adults used e-mail or instant messaging in 2003, as compared with 12 percent of adults in 1997. Third, as Tom Friedman had reported in his 1999 book [3], the Internet has become an integral part of the economy. Census Bureau figures show that eighteen percent of American adults conducted banking online in 2003; twelve percent of adults used the Internet to search for a job; almost half of adults (47 percent) used the Internet to find information on products or services; and about one-third of adults (32 percent) actually purchased a product or service online, compared with 2.1 percent of adults who used the Internet for "shopping" in 1997.

These realities leave no doubt that marketing public programs today means establishing a visible presence in cyber space. The Internet has truly taken on a life of its own—so much so that experts [6] call it a "success disaster"—the design of a new function that escapes into the real world and multiplies at an unseen rate before the design is fully in place.

And this is where living and working in our wild wired world has become a story much bigger and more complex than a story of information merely moving about in new and different ways. It's the story of a new generation of cyber savvy citizens who speak a brand new language—a generation that thinks in new and different ways—and one that will change the world forever. And it is a story of technology tearing down the traditional walls of the power of the past and returning us to a new version of the wild west in which cyber-cowboys rule the virtual new frontier.

GOING NATIVE

When today's marketers analyze their target audiences, they may or may not be aware that in the cyber age, there is an entire generation of Americans who are speaking a brand-new language—the digital language of computers, video games, and Internet. In his seminal work on digital game-based learning [7], Marc Prensky calls these Americans "digital natives"—those young people who were born after 1975 and who grew up clicking a mouse and playing video games. Through their constant use of computers, this "games generation" says Prensky, has developed different brain pathways and different ways of learning and interacting with information. Prensky has detailed ten characteristics of digital natives that set them apart from "digital immigrants"—those older generations who were born before 1975 and who came to learn computers at a much later age.

Prensky [7] suggests that digital natives are likely to exhibit the following characteristics—all of which have implications for educators and marketers:

1. Operating at "twitch" speed vs. conventional speed. Lots of keyboard time has increased the speed at which natives process information, and this need for speed has become an expectation of natives. They expect a fast pace of development in the classroom, at work, and in life and are unhappy if they don't have it.

2. Parallel processing vs. linear processing. Because gamers grew up multi-tasking—doing homework, listening to music and watching television at the same time—they expect to be operating on multiple tracks at one time. This is evidenced by the number of windows a native will have open on the computer at any one time.

3. Random access vs. step-by-step. Natives have grown up clicking around with a mouse and accessing information in random patterns in a highly interactive way. They may begin a story at the end or in the middle, and they avoid the traditional step-by-step, linear instructions preferred by immigrants.

4. Icons vs. text. Natives have grown up recognizing icons first and then using text to understand the icon. This increased visual acuity has implications for speed of learning and for formatting of educational materials, entertainment programs, and marketing materials.

5. Connected vs. stand-alone. Natives have grown up in a connected world with e-mail, cell phones, text and broadcast messages, and instant messaging—and they expect to always be connected to others through these tools—wherever and whenever. This connectivity may be synchronous (occurring at the same time) or at different times. As opposed to immigrants, natives are content with virtual relationships, and unlike the immigrants, do not require face-to-face contact in all relationships.

6. Active vs. passive. There are no operating manuals for the natives, who traditionally jump right into a task by clicking away. Prensky tells us [7] that hands-on exploration is second nature for natives, who thrive on active exploration and who are intolerant to passive experiences in which they cannot be fully engaged in a hands-on way. This feature also has implications for educators and marketers.

7. Play vs. work. Natives and immigrants are very different in their view of play. Natives view work through the lens of games and play, which is full of computers. On the other hand, immigrants view work as serious. To them, play is optional.

8. Payoff vs. patience. The fast feedback that comes from working with computers has made many natives intolerant of a slow payoff from any activity.

Thus, the natives expect rewards now versus later. Prensky cites the example [6] of young Bill Gates who was unwilling to stay at Harvard because he was so eager to start a computer company, now the colossal corporate giant—Microsoft.

9. Fantasy vs. reality. Natives love the fantasy in Star Wars and video games, and they expect to use some degree of fantasy and imagination in the grown-up world as well. Prensky [6] cites Yahoo's "Chief Yahoo Yahoo" or Gateway's "chief imagination officer" as examples of this phenomenon.

10. Technology as friend vs. foe. This last dimension seems obvious but natives see computers as their friends not as their enemy to be feared. Prensky [6] gives us a look through the natives' lens at their computers—it's a place to rest, to play, to talk, and to have fun.

Natives are "cognitively different" from earlier generations. They are not stimulated by interactions that do not fit with their approach to processing information. Marc Prensky concluded that these new cognitive differences cry out for new approaches to learning. And as we now know from open-source software, these digital natives expect to be actively engaged in today's new media—not a passive recipients, but as active, hands-on creators and designers. For those who create public marketing programs, this means that there may be a prerequisite to working with new media—taking a crash course in going native, learning digispeak, and developing a better understanding of how to capture the hearts, minds, and attitudes of digital natives.

OPENING THE GOLDEN CYBERGATE

A new cyber-democracy has emerged along with the Internet—a new age democracy that is rapidly toppling the traditional legions of power, changing the rules, and opening up the golden gate of opportunities for consumers to make their voices heard in the virtual world. Although this trend could be viewed—and even debated—through the lens of post-modernism, it is easy to show that the power shift that has occurred in the new media is real.

In days past, an American family took pride their collection of the Encyclopedia Britannica or the World Book Encyclopedia as the ultimate family resource for learning. A family's encyclopedia was one of its treasured heirlooms, created by "experts" who determined the "correct" subject matter and crafted an "objective" description, and then marketed door-to-door by a respected sales force. Fast forward to the present day. Need to learn about something quickly? Simple enough—you're just a click away from Wikipedia. Created by Jimmy Wales [8], Wikipedia is user-friendly, user-edited, and on the edge in terms of timeliness and accuracy. In its review of the fifty people who really matter in business today, cnn.com cited Wales' brainchild as an example of the power shift today from "institution to reader as the editorial filter." The bottom line, said CNN, is that millions of users equal a collaborative intelligence that outstrips what any one editor could ever hope to be.

There is evidence that the collaborative, interconnected network of consumers makes itself heard anywhere there is an opportunity by "creating and filtering new forms of content, anointing the useful, the relevant, and the amusing, and rejecting the rest.[8]" The clear lines that separated the consumer and business have become blurred as the huge, interactive, self-organizing user audience has taken on new roles—content developer, graphic designer, customer service representative, editor, censor, and as suggested by CNN.com, the "caretaker" of open-source technology. Whether choosing the winner on American Idol, the best sellers on Amazon, the best news stories to cover on CNN, or the latest slogans for Delta Airlines or T-Mobile—cyber consumers have a big voice of choice in the world of the new media. They also have a big play pen for meeting, greeting, and playing—in MySpace and other social networking cyber spaces.

MySpace—the online social networking mega-site with its 95 million members—has been called "the most disruptive force to hit pop culture since MTV—a nonstop global block party of music, video, and hookups"—a force which may be "the most powerful mass-media launching pad ever invented" [9]. The $580 million purchase of MySpace by News Corp's chief Rupert Murdoch has left no doubt about the perceived power that lies in transforming free space into what Murdoch and his media empire envision as a "colossal marketing machine" [9]. According to USA Today [10], the dominance of the MySpace giant is being challenged by a host of other communities in which users can "share videos with their micro-communities" (vMix.com), write on each others "walls" (Facebook.com), meet others with similar interests in "BlogRings" (Xanga.com), and learn as "citizens" who are interested in such topics as rocket science, art history, and cars (Whyville.net).

The Whyville site is especially noteworthy for marketing professionals who work with nutrition programs. Sponsored by the University of Texas and the School Nutrition Association, a citizen visits Whyville and can eat three meals a day there as he or she tracks the caloric and nutritional content of his or her diet and learns more about the link between good nutrition and health. Another example is (www. nasa.gov/audience/forkids) where kids can play games that are interactive and educational. For those with an interest in do-it-yourself game design, Microsoft has now provided a new golden opportunity for gamers with the release of free game-development tools called XNA Game Studio Express [11]. Available at www.microsoft.com/xna, the software helps gamers develop their own games for PCs. Gamers will then be invited to purchase memberships in Microsoft's "Creators Club," which will allow them to test their games on Xbox 360 systems. The fact that Microsoft has plans to allow solo game producers to demo and sell their games on their Xbox Live online service is another sign of the new cyber-democracy.

Shifting Power

The world of new media is smashing its own version of the Berlin wall—the pre-Internet power base of the traditional movers and shakers, decision makers, powerbrokers, and gatekeepers. The weapon they use? The blogosphere. Short for weblogs, a blog is a section of a website in which users can post (in reverse chronological order) an "e-journal entry of their thoughts—on an open forum communication tool that, depending on the Web site, is either very individualistic or performs a crucial function for a company"[12]. A blog can combine text, images, and links to other blogs, web pages, and other media related to its topic.

According to www.blogrankings.com, there are thousands of blogs that cover every conceivable topic such as art and culture, automobiles, books and literature, business, entertainment, relationships, health, nutrition, politics, travel, shoes, and sports. Some examples of what government agencies blog about are podcasts, developing strategic partnerships, training, different ways federal agencies should communicate with their customers and why, marketing for the federal government, and much more. The big blog tracker Technorati, available at www.technorati.com, is currently tracking 52.6 million blogs.

Similar to the borderless cyber-connections envisioned as "vibrant villages" [6], which are drawn together by shared ideas, interests, habitats, hobbies, causes, religions, and virtually any feature of human existence, blogs began about a decade ago as online opinions and chatter. But they haven't stopped there. They have added a new verb to our vocabulary and a new job to the workforce. And most importantly, blogs have become a powerful force in the world of public opinion, in commerce, in politics, and everywhere else.

Case in point—the world of art which has been steeped in tradition, control, and power dynamics of the rich and famous. Recent media reports [13] suggest that blogs have created a new world of cyber galleries with new rules, new players, and new average citizens as patrons. In these spaces, artists work in dual roles—as artists, as bloggers who post their postcard-size oil paintings on their daily blogs and sell them at affordable prices, and as art educators who are taking art to the masses in cyber space. This process is doing more than selling art and keeping the careers of aspiring artists alive. It is smashing the walls of exclusivity in which art dealers and galleries, who command high commissions, are losing their grip on "defining who is emerging and who is successful" in the art world.

In his overview of blogs in Wired Magazine [14], columnist and master blogger Andrew Sullivan believes that today's blogging phenomenon is a real and an especially potent force in the publishing world. He sees the blogosphere as "democratic journalism at its purest" and "a publishing revolution more profound than anything since the printing press." Sullivan believes that "blogging is changing the media world" and could "foment a revolution in how journalism functions in our culture." Sullivan suggests that blogs have power because they are personal, and they bypass the ancient ritual of writers working through the sometimes heavy gate of publishers and editors. Blogs also can earn a large following, great exposure, and large profits as well—Sullivan's blog, for example, reached a quarter million readers a month and began making a profit after only two years.

The sheer reach of blogs has power in the media market-place. Perhaps that's why the Harvard Business Review recognized blogs as one of the business breakthroughs in 2005 [15]—providing a big-time endorsement for business blogging and putting the world of business and media on notice that "the blogosphere will soon take its rightful place as a full-fledged media branch."

The frenetic activity in the product blogosphere can be seen as a definite move away from relying on old media such as news releases and print ads. It's a step toward building new partnerships between commercial ventures and hobby bloggers [16]. The exponential growth of blogs has stimulated concerns about rampant plagiarism [17] that is occurring in parallel with swiftly moving ideas. And, from a professional perspective, the blogoshere has created a new role in public relations—blogger relations specialist [16]—whose ultimate goal is to place "niche specific content in front of those who care the most."

This new cyber world of digital natives, MySpace devotees, and bloggers is the world of the new media, one that evolved from its roots as a military strategy to a new way of living and interacting in the everyday cyber world of the twentieth century. As Bob Dylan, now sixty-five, told us years ago with his famous song—"Times, the times are changin'."

Public Relations in the Digital Age:
SHAPING OPINIONS AND RELATIONSHIPS IN THE SHIFTING SAND

With the rise of the new media and the aging of the old, public relations (PR) is facing many challenges as its practices, tools, and mindsets morph to keep pace with the times and keep relevant in the digital age. In his 2006 overview of the industry [18], PR guru Richard Edelman viewed these challenges as a mixed blessing. "Our traditional channels are under siege, yet there are more media options," Edelman said as he urged the industry to retrain the workforce, recognize the influence of blogs, and experiment with new formats and new partnerships which tap into the essence of the PR business—conversation with multiple stakeholders.

It seems PR practitioners are trying to take stock of the tsunami of technologic changes that have emerged with the

Internet, re-evaluating traditional ways of reaching out to their desired audiences, revising strategy and creative practice, and searching for ways to measure effectiveness with a new bottom line which reflects the techno-realities. With its roots in ancient times, the practice of PR has a rich history in which waves of social change and political conflict provided the Petri dish for the advancement of the field. Today, the Petri dish is a satellite dish. The globe is the beat. And the demand for moving and influencing public opinion goes on.

BLOG, BLOG, BLOG

There's a consensus among the PR pundits and leaders in the PR arena—blogs are at the top of the list of fast-moving trends that are changing the very core of traditional PR practice. In their predictions for the PR industry, New Communication Blogzine editor and publisher Jennifer McClure [19], Richard Edelman [18], and consultant Joan Stewart [20] cited blogs as a major force in the transformation of PR today. McClure highlighted the magnetic power of blogs to attract advertising, their newfound niche in media companies and PR agencies, and the reality that in PR agencies, blogs are fast becoming "a basic service offering to fulfill demand for corporate blogging strategies." Stewart and others pointed out the practicality of blogs for PR professionals. "You no longer have to rely only on the media to get your message to the masses, you can create your own blog in an hour or two, and communicate with the masses," Stewart said [20]. Dawson [21] added that blogs also act as extensions of traditional media—through listings on online versions of newspapers and by the fact that they are increasingly being quoted as sources in newspaper articles.

Richard Edelman has suggested that in a communications landscape in which traditional media channels and media brokers are under siege and losing power, blogs are carrying real weight in terms of influence and credibility with clients and the public. As an example, Edelman cited [18] the huge commercial success of and the blogswarm swirling around Paramount Studio's niche film Hustle & Flow, which was promoted by music bloggers and fan online sites. Expert blogger Peter Blackshaw of Inteliseek has called blogs, "megaphones on steroids." In a talk to PR professionals, Blackshaw also emphasized the growing credibility of blogs with the public: "Whether you think bloggers are crackpots or not, many consumers trust them more than they trust you" [20]. Greg Sargent, creator and writer of The Horse's Mouth, a media and politics blog hosted by the American Prospect's website, agrees. In an interview on CBS News [22], Sargent said that that bloggers are becoming more obsessed with accuracy and have begun to establish real journalistic legitimacy. Although skepticism about blogging as an authentic journalistic source has been rampant among the mainstream media, Sargent said that readers recognize and respond to the journalistic achievements of today's bloggers.

One litmus test of the seriousness and power of blogs is the emergence of a new corporate executive—the chief blogging officer. In the C-suite of today's corporations, the CBO has joined the top ranks along with the Chairman, CEO, CFO, and COO. Master blogger Robert Scoble (available at http://scobleizer.wordpress.com) had predicted that the Fortune 500 would create this new position, and in 2004, master blogger Chris Locke made news by becoming the Chief Blogging Officer for High Beam Research, Inc. (see www.chiefbloggingofficer.com)—just another sign of the new blogging times.

RSS, SEO—MORE ALPHABET SOUP

Any talk about the blogosphere would be incomplete without talking about RSS—or Really Simple Syndication. Tech sites [23, 24] have detailed the evolution of RSS, which is actually an umbrella term for an evolving Internet format that syndicates news and the content of news-like sites and promotes the sharing of headlines and other Web content among diverse content providers such as news sites, corporate websites, and blogs. It's not just for news—"pretty much anything that can be broken down into discrete items can be syndicated via RSS—think of it as a distributable 'What's New' for your site" [24].

In non-techie terms, RSS works by developing a network of content-sensitive signals which are attached onto websites and blogs. When activated by new content, these signals send an alert to users with the critical identifying information such as title, authorship, content description, and links to the full content. Users can then simply note the new material or they can download it for future reference. Thus, while users work or sleep, RSS is working as a watchdog—an automatic environmental scan of the vast new news coming onto the Internet. This watchdog service gets high marks from PR professionals and journalists who find RSS a way to build reciprocal links with other sites and a way to save time obtaining information on specific industries and information websites by having it delivered to their e-box instead of spending valuable time surfing on the Internet.

In her predictions of the four top PR trends today [20], Stewart cited RSS as a "means of automatically sending your blog posts or new content at your website to those who ask for it—customers and shareholders to journalists who cover your topic." Stewart also pointed out that RSS is not simply a passive tech tool because RSS feeds can be used to do research. "It's a great way to check up on what your competitors are doing if you subscribe to RSS feeds from their sites and from blogs that keep you up to date on industry trends," Stewart said. Tech experts predict that the future of RSS is far more profound than simply serving as a helpful tool for media professionals: "RSS democratizes news distribution by making everyone a potential news provider. It leverages

the Web's most valuable asset, content, and makes displaying high-quality relevant news on your site easy. Soon we'll
see RSS portals with user-rated channels, cool RSS site of
the day, build your own topic-specific portal, and highly relevant search engines. A collective weblog would be another
intriguing possibility. May the best content win" [24].

Consider the growing importance of SEO or search engine optimization. In his review of the rise of marketing PR
[25], Elrond Lawrence reminds us that in the days of the old
media, "marketing and public relations professionals were
at the mercy of the news media. Journalists were the gatekeepers who decided which messages were worthy of print.
The business rewards for such exposure included increased
visibility and potential sales leads for companies that made
the cut. All others had to pay for their exposure through
advertising dollars."

Lawrence says that the growth of search engines has
dramatically altered that scenario because it has breathed
new life into the press release as a communication channel
that has been considered "dead" by media pundits. It's no
wonder considering the statistics. Today, more than 30 million Americans a month use Yahoo! News and Google News,
according to Nielsen/Net ratings from 2004. More than 70
percent of Americans use a search engine news portal, and
84 percent use a search engine to find information, products,
and services [25]. Marketing PR, which tries to reach buyers
directly and generate high-quality business leads, goes after this online power with a new-age version of the press
release designed with SEO in mind. According to Lawrence,
these marketing press releases are filled with embedded
hyperlinks, which precisely mirror keyword phrases and
terms that a sales prospect might use in an online search.
Lawrence says that these new-age releases regularly appear on the news sites of major search engines like Yahoo!
and Google, and it's not uncommon for them to continue
propagating in a viral-like way through the Internet where

they ultimately appear on other relevant news sites. It all adds up to a cumulative effect that steadily raises a search engine profile.

In its drive to increase search engine visibility, brand loyalty, and business, this process of the viral-like spread of ideas bypasses the gates of power in the traditional media outlets. In the old days, Lawrence says, a release was designed to generate media placements, and it would be read almost exclusively by reporters and editors. Today, the press release has become a viral tool that moves through the online world—generating sales leads with business prospects which use search engines to seek services or goods. The big difference today, as Lawrence points out, is that "whether a journalist actually finds the release or responds to it is secondary in importance" [25].

At first glance, it may seem strange to view SEO through the PR lens. Yet, in the Internet age, SEO has become a PR function because the underlying process involves publicity—obtaining media coverage by persuading media outlets to mention the name of a product, company, or person, and getting those names in the top rankings of search engines. Thus, SEO is the process of persuading a third-party media outlet (i.e., search engine) to mention the company (i.e., search rankings) at no direct cost the company (i.e., no payment for ranking) [23]. As noted on Knowthis.com, "SEO does what PR professionals do—namely obtain good placement in third-party media outlets"[26]. Add RSS to SEO, and the alphabet soup starts cooking.

CHANGING RELATIONSHIPS

In his overview of new directions in PR [27], Don Crowther joined Edelman and a host of other PR leaders in emphasizing the changing nature of client-practitioner relationships in the digital age. "Gone are the days of achieving success by appearing on a reporter's radar screen twice a year when you've got some news. Now you need to be carefully creating and cultivating relationships with key media sources which have the interest and the power to run your stories," Crowther said [27]. Ross Dawson put it another way—"Today, PR entails being involved with every aspect of how people encounter information and make sense of it. It is far more about being engaged in the flow of messages through an intensely networked world than it is about formal communication [21]. This is PR today in the world of "always-on" connections.

One of the keys to PR success in the future involves a simple concept introduced years ago by futurist John Naisbitt—high tech, high touch. Naisbitt suggested that "the more high technology around us, the more the need for human touch" [1]. In media-centric world of PR today, this means balancing the two sides of the equation and then building highly interactive, knowledge-based relationships with clients. These require:

Smart knowledge management techniques for wading through the overwhelming amount of information available today. John Paluszek, writing for PRSA [28], suggested that the information explosion of the last twenty years and the resulting expansion of intellectual capital provide the PR community with an unprecedented opportunity to "take the lead in showing how this knowledge can be used to improve the effectiveness of PR." This means giving clients a constant stream of real news, stories, leads, quotes, and statistics that they really need and can use. Given the huge amount of e-spam today, this also involves using e-mail carefully with descriptive subject lines, great lead sentences, and pitches that beg for more detail.

Ongoing collaboration and conversations in online spaces which allow clients and PR professionals to work together virtually on projects from conceptualization to implementation and to share real human interaction as well. In the era of new media, successful PR companies will embrace Naisbitt's concept of high tech-high touch. This requires moving beyond relics of the past such as formal press releases and corporate brochures and encouraging and engaging in more conversational relationships in which PR professionals share the story and don't own it. Edelman [18] suggested that PR professionals need to move away from a "pitching the story" mentality to becoming part of "conversations online."

Building an active online presence. Don Crowther [27] emphasized that PR firms must maintain a high-quality, highly functional online media room, a current lively blog, and leading-edge skill with search engine optimization that keeps their name circulating through the Internet. Those new media conversations, which take part within a wide and diverse network of channels and perspectives, are part of what Dawson [21] called the "new wave of citizen journalism." In this environment, the media is now a "participatory sport" in which journalists, PR professionals, citizens, and virtually anyone can play.

Speaking with video and audio as well as with words. With it roots in the "world of words" [21], PR firms are being forced to use other media to stay relevant in the world of podcasts, mobile video, vblogs, and the like. New Corporation's purchase of MySpace has sent a direct message to the communications world—play in the right space, speak the right language, or you simply cannot play at all.

Working with a new sense of openness. Tight control of information became extinct with the advent of the Internet. For PR firms, this means that transparency is the new norm in a wired world where blogswarms can send information around the globe in minutes and watchdogs monitor the Net. Trust, credibility, and "being smart about our subject and careful with our facts" [18] are a must because, as Bowman and Willis suggest, "participatory journalism uses a 'publish, then filter' model instead of the traditional 'filter, then publish' model" [29]. This new model, they suggest, reflects another sign of the digital times, a redefinition of credibility, who has it, what it takes to create it, and who the new experts are.

Doing PR for PR

So what can the field of PR do to ensure that it remains a vital contributor in the world of the new media? Regroup, say the experts. One place to start is by redefining PR's value and searching for new ways to measure success. As Stewart reminded us [20], "gone are the days when people measured the success of their PR campaigns by a bucket of clippings." Research [29] has shown that in the age of citizen journalism, "connections mean value." This includes creating organic websites, a mix of online and offline news sources, and social networking spaces which promote interaction among clients, colleagues, and community.

In this new media environment, retraining of PR professionals will be a must. John Plauszek [28] says that PRSA will be refreshing its training programs because "preparing for 2014" will require a new level of preparation among practitioners who need a portfolio of new skills. Those skills must equip practitioners to become experts at speaking the new digital language, creating new and different media forms,

and nurturing vast networks of connections. As Plauszek [28]
concluded, "every individual in our field will have to prepare
for a rolling decade."

Multiculturalism:
MARKETING WITH MULTICOLOR STRIPES
IN THE TWENTY-FIRST CENTURY

In his classic work Democracy in America [30], French historian and social observer Alexis de Tocqueville reported that "the surface of American society is covered with a layer of democratic paint." After a year's tour of the United States from 1831–1832, de Tocqueville worried that the rapid growth of the new country—with one hundred thousand Americans spread across forty states—might have a "disintegrating, decentralizing, and weakening effect on the bonds of the nation." Later this year, the United States will become a country of 300 million Americans—a country that is growing faster than any other industrialized nation in the world [31]. It is a diverse country that is richly painted with its signature stripes—the indelible, multicultural stripes laid down by America's long history as a country of immigrants.

America has a unique distinction of diversity—it's a land in which all Americans can trace their roots to other lands. Over the years, voyagers and waves of immigrants found their way to the new country.

The effects of the changing U.S. stripes are not without controversy. Some social critics, in the spirit of de Tocqueville, have expressed overt concern that the "multiplicity of cultures threatens our social fabric," as they long for "a more cohesive culture and a more homogenous America."[32]. These negative voices of the twenty-first century echo the ghosts of the "nativists" of the past—those Americans who were hostile toward new immigrants.

Yet, with an opposing point of view come the voices who have embraced the country's diversity as a source of great American strength and whose views push us past the American preoccupation with our demographic roots. It was historian Arthur Schlesinger Jr. who reminded us that the "old American homogeneity disappeared well over a century ago and will never return" [33].

Recent immigration debates in the U.S. Congress, the intensely emotional, nationwide protests of immigrants, and the new wave of anti-immigration books suggest that in 2006, immigration remains a lightning rod in the pluralistic society of today's America. The Small Business Administration says that multicultural pluralism of the United States has emerged as a gold mine for marketers.

THE EMERGING ETHNIC MARKET

Jedediah Purdy [34] offered a helpful reminder about one of the fundamentals from marketing classes. "The most successful marketing tends to pick up popular attitudes that are persuasive but not fully articulated, strongly felt by not yet painfully obvious—it shows people's desires back to them, made more beautiful and gracious, or wittier and more sardonic," he said, adding that "the American market is attuned to small differences in people's desires." For the millions of immigrants who have come to the United States from other lands, those desires combine a wish to live (and shop) with a dual identity—as Americans who stand with other Americans in "deep, horizontal comradeship"[35], and as hyphenated Americans who also wish to maintain their own cultural identity and integrity. And, says the Small Business Administration (SBA) [36], it is the growing numbers, growing affluence, and growing influence of these hyphenated Americans that are driving the enormous growth in America's ethnic markets today.

The SBA reports that the corporate giants in America were quick to sniff the sweet scent of this market and they have moved swiftly—pumping in big investments, reaping big profits, and leaving big lessons from this lucrative market not only for small businesses, but for those who market public programs as well. Find the ethnic niche, says the SBA, and make a long-term commitment to it, because short-term, one-shot promotions simply "don't cut it any longer." In the ethnic market, they concluded, "ethnic differences are opportunities, not obstacles," as illustrated by the successful examples taken from the retails sector.

A Carnival Cruise luxury line—the Fiesta Marina— dedicated in its entirety to the Hispanic market.

The creation of a wider selection of smaller sizes for women at Sears—in response to requests from Asian women.

Mainstream ads sponsored by corporate giants like McDonald's and AT&T on Spanish-speaking television stations.

New "Buneulitos" cereal produced by General Mills, the
first cereal company to produce a pre-sweetened
breakfast cereal especially for Hispanic families.

Olmec Corp's new black version of Barbie-like doll
named Imani.

Latin-oriented markets operated by Lucky Stores and
Food 4 Less Supermarkets, Inc.

IT'S ALL ABOUT THE CULTURE

The good news for those who market public programs is
they can share the lessons learned from the emerging ethnic market, and there's plenty of them because ethnic niche
marketing has been generating big buzz at national marketing conferences. Just as Jedediah Purdy had suggested [34],
marketers must be attuned to people's desires, and the SBA
says that this means building culturally sensitive programs
which revolve around language. The CEO of the Miller
Brewing Company said it well in a discussion about marketing for Hispanic populations [36]: "The desire to learn English
does not mean a desire to lose Spanish—it is not either/or—
it is both/and—Spanish remains the language in which they
discover, explore the world and dream." Hallmark Cards
has heeded this advice and now produces card lines in both
Spanish and Japanese. The scope of the bilingual market
is enormous when you consider that AT&T runs its ads in
twenty languages. Creating ethnic promotions and advertising programs by quickly adapting mainstream programs
is a big mistake, the retailers point out.

Language translators must be expert at language usage and the numerous, subtle cultural nuances that must
be taken into consideration. As Edward T. Hall, the guru
of intercultural communication, said years ago, "cultural
factors influence the individual behind his back, without

his knowledge" [37]. When cultural nuances are not taken into consideration, disaster is not far behind. In one case, a company offered promotional green baseball caps to Chinese men. Bad marketing move, said the local experts, who pointed out that green caps send a bad message—that the man's wife is cheating on him and that he wishes to bring her public scorn.

On the positive side, it is also important to utilize cultural informants who can help marketers identify who is truly the best target market for a particular product or program. For example, this could involve learning who the decision maker is in an ethnic family, and then designing the materials with that individual in mind. Another marketing basic is assuring that the target audience is able to identify with an ad. Thus, the ethnicity within the ad should reflect the target audience. Marshall McLuhan's idea that "the medium is the message" has gained some new traction in this surge of recent ethnic marketing programs. The SBA says that marketers generally recommend using foreign language newspapers and radio and television stations instead of the mainstream media, and as needed, seeking the help of minority marketing firms which can provide culturally specific advice on production and placement. And whenever possible, it's helpful to rely on staff who have firsthand knowledge of culturally specific practices.

Moving Away from "Monolithic" Thinking

While it may be tempting to view ethnic groups as homogenous, it's important to remember that cultural diversity varies within and across groups. It is clear that making culturally smart marketing decisions requires patience and a cadre of cultural informants who can lend their expertise as content experts and as gatekeepers who can prevent embarrassing gaffes. M.C. Tharp [38] has suggested that successful marketing in a multicultural society like the United States requires clarification of the values and beliefs of diverse groups, and customizing marketing strategies to match those beliefs.

WORKING ETHNIC MEDIA BECAUSE ETHNIC MEDIA WORKS

Both Lisa A. Gioun [39] and D.B. Stoy [39] suggest that becoming more culturally competent begins with conducting solid research on the target communities. This involves taking advantage of the large number of intercultural resources available in the community [40], participating in training programs, and developing relationships within ethnic communities. Uncovering tacit values and beliefs and learning about cross-cultural variations in non-verbal behavior can be challenging and time consuming. Nevertheless, the goal should focus on both knowing and understanding cultural differences, and then developing programs that are culturally relevant. Anthropologist Zeno Vendler [40] explained that knowing means you can describe something, tell how it runs, works, or operates. Understanding means that you can explain or interpret the "basis for action" which is not easily explainable. This can be accomplished by building relationships with key representatives from ethnic communities who can help unfold the cultural nuances that lie beneath the surface.

Why would professionals who market public programs invest their time and energy in building specific public marketing programs for multicultural groups? It's a matter of providing customer-friendly public service to major segments of the American public who are in need, who are under-served, or who have simply not been actively targeted in mainstream campaigns. It's a moving target that will never be fixed and final. Soon there will be 300 million stripes and we're still counting.

Skepticism:
WHO DO YOU TRUST?

Comedian Steven Colbert is getting a lot of laughs these days with his concept of "truthiness," but in these times of widespread skepticism and the backlash from Enron, WMD, and Katrina, it's no laughing matter. Although skepticism ebbs and flows with the times, plenty of it has been swirling around the American scene in the aftermath of 9/11. To name just a few...there's growing skepticism within both political parties about the Bush administration and its handling of the Iraq war and the missing WMDs [41, 42]; criticism of the United States press for its lack of skepticism in its reporting about the WMD issue [43]; post-Enron skepticism of the United States as a financial role model for the European union [44]; the clear-cut government failure immediately after the Katrina disaster [45] and one year later [46]; bad grades for Congress [47]; consumer distrust of the health care system [48]; and for the U.S. educational system, it is beginning to look like "no child left behind" may mean that many are [49].

In his preface to Edelman's "Annual Trust Barometer" [50], Leslie H. Gelb, Edelman's Counselor and the President Emeritus of the Council on Foreign Relations, says, "Trust in established institutions like government and the media remains shaky. How these institutions have responded to events such as Hurricane Katrina, urban riots in France, and the latest news-reporting fiascoes hasn't helped. All this jibes with other surveys, as well as anecdotal material that suggest people increasingly find government and the media to be self-serving and even untrustworthy."

WHO YA' GONNA TRUST?

In the communications world, PR giant Richard Edelman has earned plenty of industry awards and a reputation for providing insights into the steady decline of trust in institutions and authority figures and the rising credibility of average citizens. With its sophisticated version of "Who ya gonna trust?" Edelman has tracked the trust issue by picking the psyche of leaders around the world with its global survey of all-you-ever-wanted-to-know about trust. With the 2006 "Annual Trust Barometer," Edelman surveyed almost two thousand global opinion leaders—a sample of affluent, college graduates, age 35–64, who report being highly engaged in the media, or in economic affairs and policy issues. The Trust Barometer simply wants to know—which institutions, companies, and information sources the opinion leaders trust and how they rate the credibility of institutions.

In the latest report, there were a few surprises on the trust scale.

In the wake of the Enron and other corporate scandals, the diagnosis for CEOs may be "Enronitis." Corporate titans took a plunge in their credibility ratings on the most recent Edelman survey which showed that "lack of trust in established institutions and authority figures has motivated people to trust their peers as the best sources of information" [50]. The fact that rank-and-file employees were seen as more credible than CEOs and that there was a significant increase in trust in "a person like me" category prompted Richard Edelman to urge companies to "move away from sole reliance on top-down messages delivered to elites and toward fostering peer-to-peer dialogues among consumers and employees, activating a company's most credible advocates" [51].

Of special interest to marketers were the survey's findings on the modern media. As Internet use rose, television featured a show about big losers and became "the big loser in media trustworthiness." When asked where they turn first for trustworthy information, 29 percent of U.S. respondents cited television first, a figure that was down from 39 percent in 2003. The Internet was cited by 19 percent, up from 10 percent in 2003. Newspapers, whose demise may have been prematurely reported, were holding their own at 20 percent, the survey showed. When searching for credible information about a company, the opinion leaders turned first to articles in business magazines (66 percent) followed closely by "friends and family," a category which has grown very strongly in the United States from 35 percent in 2003 to 58 percent in the current survey [51].

A major highlight of the Edelman survey, and one of great interest to marketers, showed that in most markets, more than 80 percent of the opinion leaders said that they would refuse to buy goods or services from a company they didn't trust. And, in a confirmation of a classic marketing nightmare, more than 70 percent of the opinion leaders said they would "criticize (companies they didn't trust) to people they knew"—with 33 percent using the web to spread the bad news. The bottom line—trust matters, says Edelman. "Trust is the key objective for global companies today because it underpins corporate reputation and gives them license to operate," said Michael Deaver, Edelman's Vice Chairman, who advised that "to build trust, companies need to localize communications, be transparent, and engage multiple stakeholders continuously as advocates across a broad array of communications channels" [51].

SORTING OUT SKEPTICISM

As the focus of ancient philosophic debates or the daily buzz about ordinary current events, skepticism really is a mixed bag. Taken from the Greek word skeptomai—which means to look about and to consider—skepticism shouldn't be confused with cynicism which takes a firm stand against any claim that challenges the status quo. Skepticism, say the experts [52], is about suspending judgment and casting doubt as we search for truth; "Skepticism is the application of reason to any and all ideas—no sacred cows allowed" [53]. Skepticism, on the individual and collective levels, can be an intellectually rewarding way to establish or reestablish personal control. It is a way to protect against manipulation, improve decision-making, and push back from the minefields of advertising, political, and other types of extremes.

Astronomer Carl Sagan put the dichotomy of skepticism into a helpful, easy-to-understand perspective:

> It seems to me that what is called for is an exquisite balance between two conflicting needs: the most skeptical scrutiny of all hypotheses that are served up to us and at the same time, a great openness to ideas. Obviously these two modes are thought to be

in some tension, but if you are able to exercise only one of those modes, whichever one it is, you're in deep trouble. If you are only skeptical, then no new ideas make it through to you and you never learn anything new. On the other hand, if you are open to the point of gullibility, then you can't distinguish between the useful and the worthless [54].

In one of his lectures on skepticism and science, Sagan cited Henri Poincare, the French mathematician philosopher of science (1854-1912), who founded qualitative dynamics—the mathematical theory of dynamical systems. "We know how cruel the truth is, and we wonder whether delusion is not more consoling" [54], Poincare reminded us. These words from another century couldn't be timelier now when skepticism in the United States is rampant and trust in our institutions is steadily eroding. For those who market public programs, Poincare's words raise questions about how to best serve the public good in this age of skepticism, when truth and delusion compete for our attention. Interestingly, some answers can be found in the world of philanthropy.

FINDING FERTILE GROUND IN A SKEPTICAL WORLD

When Susan Berresford assumed the presidency of the Ford Foundation in 1997, she began her tenure by packing up and hitting the road. Berresford embarked on what might be called a listening tour—traveling around the United States and the world, listening to the concerns of people from many walks of life, including artists, business executives, university presidents, community and government leaders, and then linking these reflections about life in the twenty-first century to the philanthropic work of the Ford Foundation. During her many conversations, Berresford came face-to-face with the "deep seated feelings of uncertainty" experienced by citizens today, skepticism, the "loss of confidence in their ability to influence the powerful forces around them," growing doubts about the nation's political will to address issues such as poverty, and the "mourning of anchors" in people's lives during these times of unprecedented change.

In her reflections, which were published in Advancing Philanthropy [55], Berresford offered some practical advice about the work that lies ahead for the field of philanthropy. For those who market public programs, Berresford's advice—arriving at a challenging time when skepticism is high and traditional media have lost ground and public respect—feels fresh and hopeful. Consider the following ideas and their relevance to public marketing in today's time:

The power of real people. Berresford said [55] that it's important to spread the good news about the inspirational people who work in obscurity to build better communities against amazing odds—like those who are reclaiming their neighborhoods, helping troubled youth, and creating new and vital urban schools. Coverage of the Katrina one year anniversary identified some of these local unsung heroes. Couple Berresford's advice with the emergence of the power of the common man in the Edelman Trust Barometer [50], and you find a message for social marketers: Bypass the showcasing and showboating of powerbrokers and put your energy into highlighting the power of real people to bring about real change. Leveraging the success of real people speaking from real life spreads badly needed inspiration, Berresford said. Pam Talbot, Edelman's U.S. president and CEO said, "basically, a packaged message always comes across as packaged. Saying 'new, now improved' on a box doesn't mean much anymore. Companies must stop simply promoting products and start generating ideas that are worth talking about. You have to engage the audience in the brand process so that you are delivering something that's truly worth discussing, something that's genuine and relevant in highly specific and personalized ways. Smarter companies have already started embracing the new reality and are using it to develop strong relationships" [50]. Talbot cited the success of The Dove campaign as an example: "They used average women as models, took them to the media, and let them do the talking. They allowed the message to be about real people, delivered by real people. You identified with the women. That was 'people like me' at its best" [50].

The power of fairness and equal opportunity. Philanthropists, said Berresford, "must help to create the basic conditions that permit people to participate in the struggle for a better life—and that means ensuring safety, shelter, fairness and opportunity for all" [55]. For social marketers, there's another important message nested in this statement. As public servants, those who market public programs share a commonality with their colleagues who work in philanthropy. Both have an obligation to assure equal access to their programs, and both must expand and reach more people with their arms of good work. In this complicated, high-tech, multi-cultural age, actually providing this access and equal opportunity means that there needs to be plenty of soul-searching, networking, work, and re-work.. This also may mean adjusting the approaches used for measuring the effectiveness of public programs, from counting the volumes of outgoing communications, to looking for ways to truly assess access to and utilization of programs by individuals who live in under-served communities. As Susan Berresford stated, "At the end of the day, it is the energy and imagination of individuals working to improve their own circumstances that will change things for the better, not some grand scheme dreamed up from afar" [55].

The power of partnerships. Berresford said that "we must create systems and opportunities that draw people into the struggle for a better life, and we must foster educational systems that men and women might enter at various points in their lives; broaden their access to new information technologies, and advance community development and finance initiatives at the local level." For marketers, this translates into taking a hard look at our relationships with the communities we serve, extending them, and deepening them in new ways that empower individuals.

The power of multiculturalism. Berresford emphasized the pressing need for us to "develop ways for groups to coexist in mutual understanding and acceptance, and for us to celebrate the values we share with those different from ourselves" [55]. Working with community groups to design public programs that meet the unique needs of ethnic groups is one way that marketers can leverage multiculturalism for the common good. As it has been said so many times in the past, developing ethnocentric programming is not a simple matter of repackaging existing programs by changing some titles or some graphics. Instead, this requires making a long-term commitment of time and resources, learning about other cultures, and building new relationships.

Berresford said that in her business of doing good work, there's a case to be proven. In times of high skepticism, the work must be connected to the lives of ordinary people with real struggles who found real solutions, and it must be transparent. When making the case on behalf of marketing, we know that great marketing campaigns rely on testimonials from real people and not authority figures. The Edelman report suggested that it's best to reveal what you know, when you know it, while committing to updating as more information becomes available. But have government-sponsored programs really taken a look at their own transparency? Have they continued to keep the inner workings of programs and their effectiveness closed to the public they serve? Given the skeptics today who criticize government spending, have we willingly exchanged views with those who want to know what they are receiving from the use of their tax dollars in public programs?

Berresford concluded her comments about philanthropy with optimism that "the wealth accumulated by the few will help the many to improve their lives and communities." For those who market public programs, the marketing expertise of the few can improve the lives of many. Success depends on embracing skepticism, and using it to the public's full advantage.

Bi-polar Nation:
MARKETING IN DIVIDED TIMES

Who can remember a time when "red state-blue state" wasn't part of American-speak? In his blog written for AIGA, the professional association for design, Phil Patton reminded us that "we refer to the red states and the blue states so regularly now that the association seems long established, but the 2000 presidential election established the linkage of blue with Democrats and red with Republicans" [56]. No one predicted that in only a few years, the phrase "red state-blue state" would morph from its humble beginning as a simple graphics technique used for tracking election results into a divisive lightning rod for political spin, street chat, cultural angst, and what some see as a full-blown crisis of American identity.

Writing for George Mason University's History News Network [57], Timothy Burke said that dichotomies like "red state-blue state" are invented for "transitory premises for persuasive dialogues, social movements, and cultural conflicts." They can be novel forms of shorthand, simplifications, or downright crippling, high-stakes stereotypes, Burke suggests, and they draw from some very "deep wells." Patton also saw it from a wide lens: "The blue red opposition has come to stand for a wider sense of political and cultural polarization—between cultures, incomes and classes" [56]. In his book The Values Divide: American Politics and Culture in Transition [58], John K. White agreed that the "values divide" digs much deeper than cultural conflicts between Republicans and Democrats. Today, said White, "citizens are re-examining their own intimate values—including how they work, live, and interact with each other—while the nation's population is rapidly changing."

WHAT'S RED AND WHAT'S BLUE ANYWAY?

Wikipedia—the free, new-age, open-source dictionary—provides an interesting look into the zigzag path that led to the red state-blue state distinction [59]. Wikipedia says that the advent of color television and the increased use of color in newspapers in the 1980s and 1990s naturally led media outlets to use colorful national maps to designate which political party had won a state. Average viewers may not have paid attention, but prior to 2000, there was no consensus on color schemes among the television networks. Wikipedia reports [59] that from 1972 until at least 1992, NBC consistently showed Republican-won states in blue, and Democratic-won states in red. During two presidential elections, ABC had actually used yellow for one major party and blue for the other. But in a good example of groupthink, the media, including all major broadcast networks and cable news outlets, came together in 2000 and settled on a common color scheme—red for Republicans and blue for Democrats.

How did the current red-blue debate gain such deep traction in psyche of American current events? "It is neither the red nor blue alone where the meaning lies, it is in the combination—in the pairing with overtones of alarm," Patton warned. The contentious 2000 presidential election, with its controversial ending at the Supreme Court, sounded that alarm. The controversy about the election kept the colored election maps on television screens, and soon, Wikipedia says, the red and the blue became "fixed in the media and in many people's minds."

The feeding frenzy that surrounded the red-blue dichotomy soon became more than a simple who-won-what-state debate. Barone adds fuel to the fire with his well-known, oft-quoted 2001 article "The 49 Percent Nation" [60]. After extensive analysis of election patterns, Barone said that in 2000, the United States was closer to the decentralized, culturally divided, preindustrial America that Alexis de Tocqueville described in Democracy in America, than the culturally homogenous era in which reared Clinton, Gore, and Bush. He concluded: "The U.S. at the end of the century was a nation divided right down the middle. The two Americas in the 48 percent to 48 percent 2000 election are two nations of different faiths—one is observant, tradition-minded, moralistic— the other is unobservant, liberation-minded, relativistic"[60].

To this mix, Barone added differences on gun control, taxes, education, health care, abortion, and the environment, all of which "will continue to register the angers and the passions that are aroused when one of our nations seems to be threatening to use government to impinge on the other" [60]. Barone's bottom line prediction for the bi-polar nation? "The prospect ahead is for close elections, closely divided Congresses, bitterly fought battles over issues and nominations. The two nations with two different faiths will continue to live together, mostly peaceably—economically productive, militarily powerful, culturally creative, often seeming to be spinning out of control, but ultimately stable—as two nations united by the politics that seems to divide us."

A good demonstration of the vitriol involved with red-blue debates is the case of David Brooks, who published "One Nation, Slightly Divisible" in the December 2001 issue of The Atlantic [61]. Brooks, a Conservative pundit who lives the blue Montgomery County of Maryland, wanted to test Barone's view of the divided nation firsthand, so he traveled to red America to explore Franklin County, some sixty-five miles away. Brooks found that the red and the blue were divided by an "Ego Curtain" in which there's a battle between self, sensibilities, and common values.

Both Americas believe the differences are matters of choice, concluded Brooks, who saw that in the aftermath of 9/11, the United States was "one nation galvanized by what we shared in common" [61]. In the following years, Brooks and his search for a crack in the union were frequently quoted. He was later accused in the blogsphere of "propagating the myth—reinforced by a Washington media living amongst Montgomery County liberals—that Democrats are the party of elite, new age yuppie professionals and Republicans are favored by the poor," and of fueling Republican hope that they might be able to gain working class votes" [62]. In the afterglow of his newfound visibility, Brooks was eventually skewering in the blogspohere [63] for not checking his facts, making false generalizations, and drawing caricatures of the bi-polar nation rather than collecting real data.

SEEING SHADES OF RED AND BLUE

The shade of red or blue you see in this current debate depends on the lens through which you're looking at the country. In 2004, academia weighed in on the debate. Writing in the LA Times [64], Princeton professor Sean Wilentz concluded that the red-blue divide "isn't between the coasts and the heartland—it's between cities all over the U.S. and

the rest of the country." Wilentz said that what we are really experiencing is a city-country divide. Cities are home,
disproportionately, to wage earners, civil service employees,
racial minorities and immigrants—the traditional Democrats who are still hoping to cash in on the American dream,
pray and work, and to enclaves of liberal elite. He also says
that there is another aspect that is usually "mentioned only
in code"—divisions of race, as seen by the high proportions
of African Americans living in America's cities.

That perception of cities was refuted, however, by researchers at Wayne State University. A review of the research concluded that:

> There is no culture war convulsing America, at least
> among regular folks outside the political profession-
> als. And in the big metropolitan areas where demo-
> graphic change happens first, a nation that is sup-
> posedly engaging in a voluntary political segregation
> turns out to be mixing and changing in other ways
> in a surprisingly dynamic fashion. In that sense, the
> true future of the nation may well be Red and Blue
> in some places, but it will also surely be brown and
> beige and black and many other colors unanticipat-
> ed. Like San Francisco [65].

The pummeling of the political spinmeisters continued
when an august trio of well-known professors published
Culture War? The Myth of a Polarized America in 2002.
Most Americans, they said, were actually standing in the
middle of the political landscape. There they preferred centrist candidates from either party to the extreme partisans
who often emerge from the primary process. It has been the
political parties and the media that have ignored this fact
and distorted public perceptions, the professors claimed.

The bottom line, they said, is that the political class—of-
fice-holders, activists, and pundits—have been the forces

that have shaped "the public face of American politics" and "have distorted the reality of most Americans actual views about the social, political and economic issues of the past 30 years." Under the microscope, the professors concluded, Americans were much more "moderate, centrist, nuanced, and ambivalent than extreme, polarized, unconditional and dogmatic" [66].

In 2006, the weighty arm of Harvard added some more brawn to the pushback on red-blue debate. New research conducted by Harvard economists [67] called the red-state dichotomy misleading. "Along most dimensions, like political orientation, states are on a continuum—by historical standards, the number of swing states is not particularly low, and America's cultural divisions are not increasing," the economists said. There were, however, "two profound truths" within the debate. First, the Harvard trio emphasized what so many others have said—"the heterogeneity of beliefs and attitudes across the U.S. is enormous and has always been so." Second, "political divisions are becoming increasingly religious and cultural. The rise of religious politics is not without precedent, but rather returns us to the pre-New Deal norm. Religious political divisions are so common because religious groups provide politicians the opportunity to send targeted messages that excite their base" [67].

Thinking, Talking Purple

As politicos are salivating at the thought of the next red state-blue state fight at the polls, marketers just might need to take a step back and re-examine their role and responsibility in reinforcing the much-ballyhooed red-blue split in the United States today. In 2004, David Potorti, Co-Director of "September 11 Families for Peaceful Tomorrows," [68] issued a clarion call for an end to promoting polarity and for more civil engagement in which conversations might lead to a better understanding of "the other." "How would it change the perspective of everyone to realize that we all have values, and that those values, however differently expressed, are almost identical?" he asked. Potorti then concluded: "That the politicians and their dutiful press have already divided us into red and blue, suggests the true sources of our polarization and tells us that any common ground will have to be found by us, not them"[68]. In a recent piece about the "red and blue states of mind," Robert Brustein, the theater critic for the New Republic, made a similar case. "Today a mindless dogmatism has overwhelmed healthy skepticism along with a numbing predictability—both our political right and our political left are deeply red in their desire for unconditional certitude," he said.

Those who market public programs are obliged to search for common ground as they serve the public in midst of the red state-blue state mania. Those looking for some new spin can find some in the blogsphere courtesy of the popular blog "the daily kos." In a piece called mental gerrymandering [69], "Cool blue reason" says what may seem obvious, that in the political world, the red/blue split serves the interests of incumbents on both sides of the aisle, aids in fundraising through the increased self-identification of constituent bases, and facilitates the redirection of resources away from "safe" areas. That may not be healthy for our democracy, Cool states.

Depending on the color you wear, you might not agree with Cool and the other critics' spin on the red-blue debate. But in the search for common ground in what feels like a bi-polar nation, Cool has offered some practical ideas which are worth considering:

Don't talk about politics in terms of "red" and "blue." Cool says that we feed right into the hands of partisans when we insist on using red/blue terminology about the "culture war." Avoiding generalizations might actually improve the level of discourse.

Talk to others when they use the terms. Another
practical suggestion is to take every opportunity to
discuss why you don't like to talk about "red states"
and "blue states" and to drive the discussion deeper
to the real issues at hand.

Put quotes around the terms if you reference them
online and in other writing. Cool offered a reminder
about the power of the blogosphere: "The way we
frame ideas—even in an insular online community
setting—can have a significant impact."

Think purple. In a recommendation from the edge,
Cool says that challenging convention might be in
order. Purple is symbolic of the mix between red and
blue—it's what we really have in this country today—so perhaps we need to start thinking purple.

Other writers suggest that in addition to thinking purple, we might need to simply start talking purple—or more
simply, talking with one another—red to blue, and blue to
red. Such a simplistic idea seems increasingly out of reach
in this era when the intensity of the red-blue differences
has escalated to a point where people have stopped talking
to "the other side." Cate Malek [70] suggested that the country needs to start by increasing civility, resolving misunder-
standings, reaching out to the other side, and then using
dialogue as a way to move away from extremes and toward
the center.

Dialogue—derived from the Latin word "dialogus" which
means to have a conversation or discuss—is just what the
country needs at times of extreme polarization. In his 2004
article "House Divided," Jeffrey Rosen advocated for more
dialogue with purple groups. This, he said, was "consistent
with studies of group polarization, which suggest that, when

politically mixed groups deliberate, they move toward the middle, whereas, when like-minded people deliberate, they become more extreme" [71]. Daniel Yankelovich, the chairman of Public Agenda, put it this way: "Dialogue forces participants to reconcile their views with their most basic values, it obliges them to confront their own wishful thinking, and it exposes them to a variety of ways of seeing and framing issues—an indispensable way to escape polarization and gridlock" [72].

Just as David Potorti has suggested [68], Cate Malek says that the red-blue conflict needs to be reframed so that common ground can be the foundation for solving the complex issues that confront the nation. This complexity cannot be trivialized, squeezed into thirty-second sound bites, or smoothed over by superficial politeness. As Yankelovich suggested, "democracy does not wear dainty white gloves and speak in polite murmurings" [72]. Yankelovich explained:

> Democracy requires space for compromise, and compromise is best won through acknowledging the legitimate concerns of the other—we need to bridge opposing positions, not accentuate differences. Each partial framing of an issue, taken alone, sheds an imperfect light on the larger picture. Only by approaching both with an open mind can we begin to understand what we must do. Serious consideration of both positions leads directly to the kinds of questions the nation should be pondering [72].

Malek summed it up this way: "A civil society cannot avoid tough but important issues, simply because they are unpleasant to address—constructive debate needs to focus on the solutions that are most likely to be successful, and not upon personal attacks leveled by adversaries against one another" [70].

The bottom line may very well be that a more constructive way to address the red-blue conflict is by thinking and talking purple. Who will be leading the drumbeat for dialogue and promoting the purple cause remains history as yet to be written.

Terror, Terror, Terror:
LIVING IN A WORLD WITH A SHORT FUSE

Five years after the September 11 attacks on the World
Trade Center and the Pentagon, terror seems to have etched
a permanent place in the American way of life and in our
lexicon. We're talking terror 24/7 in the United States today—on television and radio—in the blogosphere, the print
media, and the halls of Congress—as we grapple with a host
of terror topics. Day in and day out, we're working to recover
from the horrors of the 9/11 terrorist attacks—predicting
and preventing future attacks, surrounding ourselves with
the latest anti-terror technology which we hope will keep

us safe from harm, and trying to figure out which of our political parties is the best equipped to handle the terror turf. Frightened, exhausted, anxious, determined, detached or numb—we're living in a world filled with relentless repetition of media messages about terror and its very short fuse. Add the threat of bird flu, disasters like Katrina, the steady wave of violent crimes in the United States, and the Iraq war and you have a growing mega-business of terror.

Terror in the Hearts and Minds

Terrorism is a beast of its own kind, with two mighty tentacles that have the power to kill and cripple the masses. One reaches into communities and disrupts the essential rhythm of daily existence by destroying life, limb, property, and economic welfare. The other "targets the social capital of a nation—cohesion, values, and ability to function" [73] as it surrounds its victims like a python and suffocates them with fear, anxiety, depression, and anger.

Prior to 9/11, much was known about the devastating effects of terrorism. One review [75] found that shootings and terrorism are the most disturbing types of disaster, with as much as two-thirds of those who are directly affected experiencing some type of psychological impairment such as post-traumatic stress disorder (PTSD) with persistent flashbacks or nightmares, extreme irritability, anxiety, depression, or substance abuse. In the wake of the 9/11 attacks, researchers concluded that these reactions occurred in the cities where attacks occurred and throughout the country, and they have continued over time [76, 77, 78]. On the fifth anniversary of 9/11, the National Mental Health Association [79] published statistics about the mental health problems that continue in the country. In its assessment of the attacks' impact on survivors and rescue workers, the Association found that:

Two to three years after September 11, 64.7 percent
of building survivors reported experiencing a new
onset of depression, anxiety or other mental health
problem.

Two to three years after the attacks, 10.7 percent
of building survivors were experiencing serious psychological distress—twice the prevalence of serious
psychological distress within the general New York
City adult population during the same time period.

13 percent of rescue and recovery workers evaluated between ten to fifteen months after the attacks
met criteria for PTSD. The three most common issues cited were problems with social life (15 percent),
work (14 percent) and home life (13 percent).

The effects on the general population showed, "17%
of Americans, despite where they lived, had symp-
toms of PTSD two months after the attacks. The
Association also found a high level of concern about
terrorism and its consequences among Americans of
all demographics. Half of Americans (50%) and two
in three parents (65%) were concerned that members of their family will experience fear and distress
about the threat of terrorism" [79].

Terror as Big Business

Travel through any U.S. airport today and you step—
sans shoes—right into the new business world of anti-terror terrain. There's the uniformed staff of the new federal
agency, the Transportation Safety Administration, which
was established by the Aviation and Transportation Security Act on November 18, 2001, to strengthen the security
of the nation's transportation systems [80]. There are warn-

ings about items not allowed on board, and depending on the airport, you may be subjected to "puffers, chemical scanners, biometric devices, or backscatter x-rays" [81]—all part of the government's growing arsenal of post 9/11 antiterrorism technology.

Below the radar screen lays an enormous emerging business market with a cast of investors, venture capitalists, and entrepreneurs who are scrambling in their search for the next holy grail of anti-terror technology and their next big investment in homeland security. Among the vast array of new world of anti-terror products, there's "brain fingerprinting," which measures brain recognition of familiar words or photographs [81]; anti-terror bluegill fish in use by San Francisco water treatment plants as modern day "canaries in the mine," which can detect non-biological threats to the water supply such as pesticides, mercury, cyanide and heavy metals [82]; green, leafy, genetically engineered "sentinel plants," which thanks to a $3.5 million dollar grant from the Defense Advanced Research Projects Agency, are being tested as the latest living sensors for detecting chemical warfare agents or animal pathogens such as anthrax [83]; "sky watch" sentinels with radar and thermal imaging that can stop bullets from an AK-47 and sniff bombs as well [84]; and BlastWrap, a product which can smother bomb explosions in trash cans [85].

Recent estimates from the brokerage firm Morgan Keegan [84] suggest that the demand for security spending is growing at 16 percent per year, with spending on technology and systems to track people, protect assets, and prevent terror attacks estimated to reach some $65 billion. Experts predict that along with this growing budget will be increased pressure on companies to prove that their technologies actually deliver what they promise [84].

TERROR AS POLITICAL CAPITAL

Although terror has found a dual niche as both a killer and a big business opportunity, it's also found new traction on Capitol Hill as the central political issue of our times. On the days after the fifth anniversary of the terrorist attacks of 9/11, media reports saturated the airways and the online world with stories about the rising political tensions in the United States surrounding terror. CNN reported [86], "Democrats and republicans have struggled for the upper hand on what has become the main issue of the midterm campaigns—the war in Iraq with the broader battles against terrorism." CNN said that the unity experienced in the country immediately after the terrorist attacks five years ago has long since morphed into a high-stakes political war. The battle lines are clearly drawn. The Republicans believe that President Bush's leadership has made the nation safer from terrorist attacks. The Democrats, on the other hand, argue that the country is less safe. They accused Republicans of failed policies that have cost thousands of American lives, and they have criticized the President for politicizing the 9/11 anniversary. The bottom line, said CNN, is that "partisanship has rarely been more in-your-face, and old saws like 'politics stops at the water's edge' have been discarded."

TERROR—MEDIA IN THE MIDDLE

The media and its role in assuring freedom of the press, influencing public opinion, and protecting national security have also come under attack in the political battles swirling around the administration's approach to terror and its use of surveillance techniques which keep skirting the legal edge. The president recently condemned news outlets for revealing details of a program that used the Internet to scan bank statements for evidence of terrorism financing while other administration officials labeled reports from major media outlets as "disgraceful" [87]. Media gurus defended their actions, said that the "legitimate public interest outweighed the potential cost to counter-terrorism efforts" [87]. This current clash between elected government officials and the press is not new news, of course, but the battleground has been changed by technology, which has created greater opportunities for government surveillance and a blurring of lines between informing the public and keeping intelligence secrets.

Beyond the controversy about the media's role in censoring sensitive content lies another concern—the harmful effects of 24/7 terror coverage on the American psyche. American experts who study media psychology agree about the negative impact of U.S. terrorism coverage, which they suggest leaves viewers in an emotional bind. After watching horrific scenes on television, viewers can feel helpless because there is little they can do and there is simply no place to hide. Experts say that citizens react by "freezing" parts of their normal lives. They stop flying or shopping, may feel fearful about going out or doing much of anything, drink more alcohol, function less productively at work, worry about threats, which lead to higher levels of stress hormones and real illness and sometimes lose confidence in society or government [88, 89, 90].

Repetition of traumatic images, the chronic "rehashing" of events and the increasingly graphic nature of the coverage make it hard, especially for children, the experts concluded. Images seen from the media coverage "get forcibly embedded in memory" and have a very negative effect on well-being. The dilemma, said Michelle Slone, author of Responses to Media Coverage of Terrorism, rests in balancing the media's right to freedom in reporting uncensored events vs. the need for restraint "to avoid fertilizing public panic and serving the aims of the terrorists who depend on propaganda and media dissemination of their activities" [88].

Terror threats, when coupled with the ill-fated, oft-paro-
died color rating system promulgated by the Department of
Homeland Security, and the continual feed of "news alerts"
that flash during cable television programs, may no longer
have the shock value they once did. This may be caused by
the "crying wolf" phenomenon, which, according to research
[74], is caused by an imprecise alert system that keeps people
constantly on edge and contributes to complacency as the
public views the threats as non-credible and overly common
and routine. And there seems to be some resignation about
the inevitability of dealing with terror threats as a part of
regular life. Tom Goodman, president and CEO of Goodman
Media, a public relations firm in New York, said, "there's always the idea it could happen again—this is the world we
live in and it's going to be like this for a long, long time" [89].

BOUNCING BACK, PUSHING BACK

Reports on the 9/11 anniversary events showed that as
heated political rancor about the war on terror raged on,
there were hopeful, mixed signs that the country is bounc-
ing back, but changed by the 9/11 experience. In addition
to expressions of grief and loss, it was reported that the
"season of fear" that followed 9/11, "seems more than just
a bad dream and less than the advent of a 'new normal'" [91].
Polls show that Americans think people have permanently
changed the way they live although fewer than one in four
actually have [91].

However, in this new age of terrorism, optimism seems
to be tempered by anger and fear. One study [92] found that
some Americans are still coping with an exaggerated sense
of fear of terrorism and other risks such as flu, while others continue to suffer from post-traumatic stress syndrome.
There are reports of growing community anger in New York
City about what is seen as the "slow-footed" government response to caring for the thousands of Ground Zero workers

who helped with the rescue and clean-up work at Ground Zero, and who are now suffering severe respiratory problems and other ailments [93].

Helping the country to live with terror, terror, terror has kept the psychology experts busy since 9/11, and they say there is plenty we can do. Leaders can foster a sense of psychological resilience, while communities—including schools, employers and religious organizations—work on providing information about terror attacks and coping mechanisms, reassurance, and improved local mental health support, emergency response, and security surveillance systems [73, 90].

Local efforts must also be closely coordinated with federal efforts, which ideally should help us predict, prevent, prepare, and recover from terror attacks and disasters. This work involves a broad spectrum of activities that include both consequence management—the operations needed to soften an attack's adverse effects and facilitate the community's recovery; and "fear management," which focuses exclusively on reducing the public's fear, panic, and anxiety after an attack [74]. Public experts suggest [94] that effective disaster relief depends on public confidence in the "reliability of information from official sources, the capacity of government to perform effectively in a crisis, and the capability of response systems, particularly the health systems and first responders."

Absence of confidence in either response systems or leadership may undermine crisis plans, and may lead to unnecessary panic and excess loss of life, the experts concluded. A no-confidence vote should be a great national concern because, as research has shown:

Confidence in the federal government to protect the homeland from terrorism has steadily declined since 2002. Barely half of Americans (53%) are confident in the ability of government to protect the area in which they live from a terrorist attack. This is down from 2002 when 58% expressed confidence, and far below the 62% level of confidence in 2003 [94].

For those who work in marketing, media and public relations, the post 9/11 statistics provide plenty of food for thought about the state of the nation and role of the media in times of terror. In its report "Combating Terrorism"[95], the National Science and Technology Council suggested that those responsible for developing effective risk communication plans need to be educated about the roles of public trust, designated spokespersons, and the media. They must understand the effects of living with long-term threats and uncertainties, and to the extent that is possible, assure that media messages do not traumatize nor desensitize the citizenry.

Most of all, the Council said that it's important to remember the mass media have great potential to influence the quality of people's responses to terror. The demands of the media can be a hindrance to effective disaster response, and there can be the spreading of rumors which bias the nature of the response. The bottom line, say some terror experts [74], is that the media must remain mindful that it has the power to "alter the reality of disaster."

Nervous Energy:
HOW THE UNITED STATES IS GRAPPLING
WITH ITS ADDICTION TO OIL

With the war on terror, Katrina, the country's dependence on oil, sticker shock at the pumps, and national worry about a disruption in our oil supply, it's easy to understand the buzz about energy security in the United States. Forget easy, immediate solutions that can rally the entire country. Forget the short-term optimism when prices at the pump drop a bit. Finding a long-term solution for what President Bush called our "addiction to oil" is going to be anything but easy. The Department of Energy [96] says that our national fleet of SUVs, minivans, and other gas guzzling vehicles currently uses almost 20 million barrels of oil a day.

Our cars use more than 40 percent of the total oil we consume—at an estimated cost of $186 billion per year [98]. Add to this some of the realities from the supply side of the oil issue—a outstripped domestic refinery capacity, the reduced ability of oil suppliers to respond quickly when a sudden disruption in supply occurs, and high prices based on fear that the global oil supply chain will be disrupted [99]. It's no wonder that any talk about America's energy policies touches the very core of our lifestyles, special interests, politics, and our pocketbooks.

A CASE OF BAD NERVES

There's seems to be a growing nervousness in the United States about the country's oil dependence in the current world climate. In 2004, the Natural Resources Defense Council (NRDC) said that the United States, with only 2 percent of the world's oil reserves, relies on the Middle East for one-fifth of all its imports, and it concluded that "America's oil habit not only pinches our pockets and fuels OPEC's rising profits, but it also threatens our economy, national security and the environment" [99].

The damage to oil refineries after hurricanes Katrina and Rita provided an unsettling and realistic glimpse into the impact of a major oil-supply disruption and yet another painful reminder of the country's oil habit [100]. In June 2006, at his first Congressional appearance after retiring, former Fed Reserve Chairman, Alan Greenspan, said the balance of world oil supply and demand "has become so precarious that even small acts of sabotage or local insurrection can have a significant impact on oil prices" [101]. In August 2006, an oil spill, pipeline problems, and the ultimate shutdown of a BP oilfield in Alaska were seen as more unnerving. In an oil-dependent country like ours, four hundred thousand fewer barrels of oil every day really matter.

The inevitable solution to American nervousness about our country's oil dependence may seem simple—reduce demand for oil. Stop the delicate dance with the oil cartel leaders, and break America's oil habit. But that's a solution that is easier said than done by a controversial industry, which digs deeply into the ground and into our politics as well. The recent furor in California over Proposition 87 is a case in point about the tensions associated with energy costs, oil dependences, and air pollution [102]. Also known as the Clean Alternative Energy Act, the initiative has the potential to raise $4 billion via a tax on oil production in the state, while also lowering use of petroleum by 25 percent. Whatever the fate of Prop 87, the give and take related to energy and oil dependence in California is sure to be newsworthy.

LOWERING OIL USE BY RAISING THE BAR

The NRDC says that the "the most crucial step on the path to independence is to raise the bar on energy efficiency of our cars, pickups and minivans" [99]. It's not new news, but the NRDC has said [98, 99] that there are easy, readily available options, such as:

Buying electric-gasoline hybrid cars which achieve double the mileage of today's cars.

Expanding use of renewable, non-petroleum fuels such as ethanol made from corn wastes and increasing requirements for renewable content in gasoline.

Keeping tires properly inflated.

Using fuel-efficient engine oil.

In addition to promoting changes in fuel efficiency for passenger cars, the NRDC says that we could reap additional oil savings through national efforts aimed at reducing heavy duty truck idling; weatherizing homes that use heating oil; making improvements in technology that reduce the amount of oil used in industry; requiring tire manufacturers to sell fuel-efficient replacement tires; improving mass transit systems; improving air traffic management, which can reduce wasted waiting time for take-offs and landings; offering tax incentives for fuel efficient cars; supporting smart growth initiatives instead of suburban sprawl; and exploring the production of fuel cells and hydrogen fuel, whose only byproduct is water.

WILL WE HAVE THE WILL?

Will we or won't we succeed in breaking our oil habit? Can we save the planet from lethal global warming? Predicting the outcome is risky in such a controversial arena filled with inconsistent federal policies on energy, eternal optimists about energy conservation and green causes, and the ever-present voices of doom-and-gloom. The NRDC keeps watch over the administration's energy activities (available at www.nrdc.org/bushrecord/airenergy_policy.asp) — the interpretation of which depends on politics and special interest. One recent example is the Bush administration's September 2006 proposal for a renewable fuels standards (RFS) program, which would double the use of fuels such as ethanol and biodiesel [103].

The RFS program, which was authorized by the Energy Policy Act of 2005, has been billed as an energy solution that yields good results for farmers, for energy, and for the environment as well. Estimates predict that the RFS program has the potential to cut petroleum use by approximately 3.9 billion gallons a year by 2012 and reduce greenhouse gas emissions by up to 14 million tons annually. Administration critics point out [104] the current administration's patchy record energy policy, and the fact that it was only three years ago that the Bush administration sided with auto manufacturers and proposed changes that would make it easier for auto companies to qualify SUVs and other "light" trucks for weaker fuel economy standards.

Speaking to a very small audience, Greenspan said that although the country is slowly disengaging from petroleum, the process is slow, "like watching grass grow" [101]. In an editorial in the Washington Post [97], Samuelson pointed out that Americans talk a lot about driving less, taxing oil heavily, and raising fuel economy standards but, in reality, we have taken little real action because the remedies for our oil dependence are wildly unpopular with the public, have political consequences, and are slow to show any real benefits. "Because Americans want painless salvation, our politicians proffer visions that promise just that: a shift to hydrogen fuel or a surge in ethanol. The first may be futuristic thinking; the second is mainly a costly giveaway to farmers. Both are deceptions, new excuses not to do the 'right thing,'" said Samuelson [97].

In the midst of such continuing cynicism, however, there's a growing wellspring of optimism and new entrepreneurial energy about energy. The NRDC believes that improving energy efficiency and decreasing oil dependence are realistic goals that, with the American spirit, the country can rally around and achieve. The Environmental Protection Agency's continuing success with it Energy Star Program (profiled later in this book and available at www.energystar.gov), is another indicator that there is real progress being made on the energy conservation front. And there are other interesting developments on the national scene.

Consider the case of Al Gore, the former Vice President of the United States and Democratic presidential candidate in 2000. After being handed his historic defeat by the U.S. Supreme Court, Gore disappeared from sight as he reset his life's compass after a painful public loss. Stints as a professor and journalist were preludes to the public reemergence of Gore as an unlikely movie star and the leading green spokesperson in the feature film An Inconvenient Truth, which was released in May 2006. In the movie, which has been called Gore's "traveling global warming road show" about our "planetary emergency" [105], Gore makes a convincing case that the global warming situation is so serious that it's a moral issue which has to be seen beyond the confines of politics. The film, Gore's message, and his relentless, high-profile campaigning have hit a big nerve and have put the issues in the news and catapulted Gore to film star status at the renown Sundance Film Festival [106], and as an international adviser on green concerns [107].

In September 2006, Wal-Mart, the world's largest retailer with close to 2 million employees, launched its "Embrace the Earth" campaign, a massive program designed to "encourage sustainability of the world's fisheries, slash energy use and reduce waste, push its 60,000 suppliers to produce goods that don't harm the environment, and urge consumers to buy green" [108].

Wal-Mart plans to cut gasoline use by its trucking fleet. They plan to use more hybrid trucks as strategies for increasing efficiency by 25 percent over the next three years, and double that in ten years—measures that will save the company $310 million a year by 2015. In addition to cutting energy use in its seven thousand stores worldwide, the company is also experimenting with wind power and permeable asphalt that allows rainwater to seep through parking lots to help refill underground aquifers. Given the scope of the Wal-Mart effort, it's hard not to take the company's efforts seriously.

The company has formed fourteen "sustainable value networks" which include groups of employees, suppliers, and environmentalists who focus on figuring out how to find and buy environmentally friendly products. There's a new emphasis on using less packaging, saving energy in stores with new, energy efficient LED lighting systems and "skylight harvesting," and promoting the purchase of compact fluorescent light bulbs produced by GE. Wal-Mart's many critics, such as WakeUpWalMart, have criticized the new green campaign as a clever cover-up designed to re-tool the corporate giant's somewhat tarnished public image. But others such as TransFairUSA, which markets fair-trade coffee, and the environmentalist group Environmental Defense say that they are taking Wal-Mart's green efforts seriously, while reserving judgment until the program's results can be evaluated.

In addition to the news from Wal-Mart, Richard Branson, the British billionaire and business brain behind the Virgin brand, announced at the meeting of the Clinton Global Initiative in NY [109], that he was donating all the profits from his transportation businesses to combat global warming, which is estimated to be about $3 billion. In interviews [110], Branson said the money will be invested in projects which find renewable, sustainable energy sources, and help "wean the world off of oil and coal," fossil fuels that are linked to global warming because of their carbon dioxide emissions. Branson cited the direct influence of green luminaries, Al Gore and Ted Turner, in his decision to dedicate such large funds to the green movement. As with Wal-Mart, critics state that his "donation" wasn't totally altruistic because it may pay off with large dividends for Branson and his company.

A MECCA FOR MARKETING

Amidst all the nervous energy that surrounds our national energy woes, one thing is certain—the ongoing energy debate—with all its complexities, controversies, and competing points of view—will continue to be a Mecca for marketers. One walk through EPA's Energy Star website provides some hard, fast evidence of the immense, diverse marketing efforts involved in marketing energy related issues. There are Energy Star qualified products, programs, partnerships, and public education programs—all of which depend on strong, competent marketing strategy and partnerships with the private sector.

ICF International [111] is a prime example of the wide swath of marketing activities related to energy work. As one of Energy Star's partners, this for-profit firm has been involved in using multimedia to reach stakeholders of public programs like Energy Star. The company provided marketing and communication support for Energy Star's Building and Green Lights Program and produced two videos which were used as a means of reaching high-level managers of prospective partner companies. The company also supports Energy Star by providing outreach support for Energy Star's Commercial, Institutional, and Industrial Sectors, which seek to reduce operating costs associated with energy. The company also works on raising the profile of renewable energy investments and environmental commitments through community outreach and on developing local solutions to energy issues such as the energy initiatives in California. Those initiatives involved partnering with Energy Star and the eighteen-month statewide Renewable Energy Consumer Education campaign (RECE) for the California Energy Commission. ICF International also works with the Homeland Security Council and provides chemical hazard consulting to Canadian districts, search engine optimization support for energy giants like ConEdison, and assistance for the Philippines government in launching a national climate change mitigation awards program for a joint U.S. Agency for International Development (AID)-EPA program. Thus, ICF International provides a good example of the strategic combination of energy industry expertise with public relations and marketing know-how in a complex and nervous marketplace.

Volunteer Nation:
CONTINUING THE AMERICAN TRADITION OF LENDING A HELPING HAND

From colonial days to modern times, volunteerism has been as American as apple pie and motherhood. Helping one another in the new America, however, was driven by necessity and circumstance, rather than pure altruism: "The hardships of the early settlers to North America, where government was then weak and distant, forced people to join together to govern themselves, to help each other, and to undertake such community activities as building schools and churches and fighting fires" [112]. In 1736, Benjamin

Franklin organized the first volunteer firefighting company in Colonial America [113]. Colonial life also featured a volunteer fighting force with its ranks filled by citizen volunteers whose goal was to win the Revolutionary War. Citizens in the colonies opened their homes to care for the wounded soldiers because medical hospitals did not exist [114]. The Bank of North America, America's first organized bank, was created by a group of Philadelphia citizens who focused their efforts on sending supplies to the destitute Revolutionary army [114]. After the colonies won their independence, they often met the new challenges of self-government by relying on the support of citizen volunteers.

John Winthrop, the first governor of the Massachusetts Bay Colony and one of the first Puritans to arrive in the colonies, saw the helping hand of the new land as a sign of its character: "We must delight in each other, make others conditions our own, rejoice together, mourn together, labor and suffer together, always having before our eyes our community as members of the same body," Winthrop said [115].

The Underground Railroad, considered to be one of the largest organized volunteer efforts in this history of our country [114], is a good example of the generosity and willingness of Americans to work together toward a common goal. Volunteering—lending a helping hand to others—thus became the "hallmark of the American character" [114], one that evolved into a longstanding tradition of citizens coming together to meet the needs of their community.

DOING GOOD FOR YOUR COUNTRY

During World War II, when the U.S. Department of Agriculture urged American citizens to plant their personal "victory gardens" to help alleviate wartime food shortages, the country rallied behind the cause. By 1943, over 20 million citizens had planted personal victory gardens, which in turn produced 40 percent of the vegetables grown in the

United States [116]. In 1963, when he created the Peace Corps, President John F. Kennedy issued the most famous call for volunteers to serve their country when he said: "Ask not what your country can do for you, ask what you can do for your country" [116]. Since that clarion call from President Kennedy, more than one hundred eighty-two thousand Peace Corps volunteers have served others in 138 countries [117]. By 1971, in response to the growing interest in volunteerism within federal agencies, Congress mandated the creation of an independent private-sector agency, the National Center for Voluntary Action (NCVA), which focused on educating the public about benefits of volunteerism and supporting the development of volunteer programs to assist in program development. At this time, the American business community began to embrace the idea of corporate social responsibility.

Kennedy's successors in the White House have supported volunteer programs, although their views of the government's role in sponsoring volunteer programs vary with their political views. President Lyndon B. Johnson created the Volunteers in Service to America (VISTA), which is sometimes called the "Domestic Peace Corps" and the Retired and Senior Volunteer Program (RSVP), which matches senior citizens with volunteer opportunities; while President Bill Clinton created AmeriCorps, a network of local, state, and national service programs that connects volunteers with nonprofits, public agencies, and faith-based and community organizations. President George H.W. Bush created the USA Freedom Corps, which focused on strengthening the non-profit sector, while Ronald Reagan established the White House Office of Private Sector Initiatives, which encouraged businesses and the private sector to get involved in organizing volunteer projects [114–118].

Giving by Many

Recent data from the Bureau of Labor Statistics, U.S. Department of Labor [119], show that more than 60 million Americans or about 28 percent of the population over age sixteen do some volunteer work each year, and that number has been steadily rising. The most likely volunteer group by age was the 35–44 range, with 45–54 year olds following close behind. Teens also logged in plenty of volunteer hours—primarily though volunteer activities in their schools. The median number of hours spent on volunteer activities was fifty-two per year, with senior citizens devoting the most numbers of hours per year—a median of 88 hours. Women traditionally volunteered at a higher rate than men, a trend that held across age groups and education levels; volunteer rates were higher for college-educated individuals than for high school graduates; and whites volunteered at higher rates than African Americans, Asians, or those of Hispanic origin [117]. The Bureau also [117] follows a trend that is of interest to those who market volunteer programs—two out of five volunteers used their own initiative to find volunteer work, while two in five were recruited as volunteers by someone inside the organization.

In 2005, the outpouring of a vast army of volunteers during the Katrina disaster brought these statistics to life, as Americans kept the tradition of lending a helping hand alive and well by collecting and preparing food, providing general labor, raising funds, and serving as guides for disaster relief and recovery efforts.

Giving—Good Business, Big Business

Although volunteering has always been a cultural tradition in the United States, in today's America it's good business and big business. It was in 2002 that President

George H.W. Bush sent out a call to all Americans to devote at least two years to community service. The U.S. business community responded by organizing "Business Strengthening America" (BSA)—a massive, nonpartisan, peer-to-peer business network designed to involve small and large business in civic engagement through volunteer service [120]. The premise of BSA is really a throwback to colonial days—when a commitment to volunteering was viewed as a path to building relationships and a stronger society. The group's work involves increasing the number of businesses who encourage and support their employees as community volunteers, improving the effectiveness of volunteer efforts in the workplace, and building more partnerships between businesses, community service organizations, and local communities.

The twenty-first century spin on volunteering, however, is not grounded in pure altruism. Promoted by groups such as BSA, the modern view of lending a helping hand positions volunteer programs as simply good business with mutual benefits for both the citizens they serve and the sponsoring businesses. In both small and large businesses, supporting employees who volunteer on work time gives the business community a tangible way to "do well by doing good." Part of that "doing good" translates into tangible business benefits such as an enhanced business image in the community, improved relationships with employees, consumers and shareholders, a feeling of pride within the company, new skills and new networks developed through the volunteer service, and enhanced employee morale and retention, which are major challenges and concerns in any business. In addition, helping the community is good public relations and the work is sweetened by tax breaks from the federal government [120].

It has been said that "if there is a need in the community, across the country, or around the world, someone in the U.S. is trying to address it, and if there is a resource, someone is trying to match it to a need" [121]. In cities all over the country, employee volunteer programs serve the community in just about every area of community need such as health, homelessness, poverty, public safety and disaster preparation, literacy, arts and culture, community development, housing, and education. Innovative business programs cited by BSA [120] include:

Samaritan Technologies—a small company with fewer than ten employees; provides full-time, permanent employees with four hours paid leave per week for community service.

Wachovia Corporation in Charlotte has instituted a "Time away for community service," which provides four hours of paid time off for employees who volunteer.

Triple A Containers, Inc. has employees who regularly work at a local California food bank where they sort, package, and distribute food for the hungry.

BSA members in Charlotte joined forces with the national non-profit organization KaBoom! to build a playground which served three hundred neighborhood children, while a similar group in Atlanta built a basketball court, garden, picnic tables, and an outdoor classroom.

While these stories represent only a small sample of the massive employee volunteer programs available in the United States today, they provide a look into the business strategy of using volunteerism as a competitive strategy. According to the Allstate Foundation [122], employee volunteer programs provide America's corporations with a strategic resource for retaining skilled workers, functioning more efficiently, and staying competitive in the global marketplace.

In a survey commissioned by the Points of Light Foundation [122], the Allstate Foundation collected data from diverse businesses, which varied in geographic location, size, years in business, and industry sector. The survey found a significant increase in the number of businesses using employee volunteer programs to support business functions through volunteering in education, hunger programs, elderly needs, welfare to work assistance, diversity, racism, and programs in arts and culture.

Almost half of the businesses had incorporated the volunteer program into their company's business plan, and more than half had incorporated a commitment to community service in the corporate mission statement [123]. The survey also found that corporations were using volunteer programs to fulfill the company's business goals by incorporating public relations (83 percent); marketing and communications (64 percent); employee skill development (60 percent); employee recruitment and retention (58 percent); and valuing diversity (56 percent) [122]. Recognizing the work of the employee volunteers has become an important corporate function via stories in company publications, awards and certificates, volunteer recognition events, and letters of commendation to volunteers.

The Allstate survey also found that today's corporations were spending more effort and resources on evaluating the impact of volunteer programs on the company, the employees, the community, and the company's partnerships within the company. A smaller number of companies are collecting data that assess the specific effect of volunteer programs on employee morale, team building, employee turnover, absenteeism, and productivity [122]. The survey also identified corporate concerns about the future of employee volunteer programs such as: the cost and the challenges of maintaining support for employee volunteer programs; high turnover in staff who manage the programs; the need for more sophisticated measurement techniques for evaluating program impact; the challenges of involving small businesses in volunteer programs; and the need to align employee volunteer programs with business goals.

MARKETING VOLUNTEERISM TODAY

A single Google search on volunteerism provides clearcut evidence that marketing volunteerism has become an enormous American industry in the twenty-first century. There are thousands of websites devoted to the art of attracting, managing, training, and thanking volunteers; educational programs, which specialize in volunteer management; and, according to the giant blog-watcher Technorati (www.technorati.com), close to five hundred thousand blogs talking every day about some aspect of volunteerism. Other signs of the times include:

Virtual volunteers — In this era of the Internet, it's no surprise that volunteering would find a niche in cyberspace. Founded in 1996 by Steve Glikbarg and Cindy Shove, co-founders of Impact Online, The Virtual Volunteering Project "encouraged and assisted in the development and success of volunteer activities that can be completed via the Internet, and helps volunteer managers use cyberspace to work with ALL volunteers" [123]. By combining volunteerism with information technology, virtual volunteerism allows citizen with Internet access to contribute time and expertise to organizations in need of volunteer services. Volunteer assignments can be exclusively virtual or they might include a mix of virtual and onsite activities.

Matchmakers — The enormity of the volunteer industry, in combination with the Internet, has also spawned a new generation of matchmakers such as VolunteerMatch, which serves as an online connector between nonprofit organizations and Americans who are ready to "help feed the hungry, tutor children, care for the environment, inspire our artists, strengthen our communities and prepare for our future" [124]. VolunteerMatch sought to build "a marketplace for civic engagement" when it built its online recruiting service for the nonprofit world. VolunteerMatch currently supports over thirty-seven thousand organizations and a large network of active volunteer opportunities that average more than thirty-five thousand a day throughout the year. Another match maker is the 1-800-Volunteer.org, a "bilingual volunteering portal where volunteers can find volunteer opportunities in their community and can register to use their skills to assist in disaster recovery efforts or to address year-round community based needs" sponsored by the Point of Light Foundation [125].

New age niche marketing— According to the Corporation for National and Community Service, "the world of senior volunteerism is undergoing a transformation of unprecedented proportions driven by the baby boomer generation" [126]. After a series of conferences focused on senior volunteers, the Corporation created a blueprint for recruiting baby boomer volunteers who "will have education levels higher than that of previous generations, are individualistic in their thinking, and are looking for meaningful roles" [126]. The many recommendations offered by the Corporation include: Refining the volunteer experience to reflect a more challenging, meaningful set of experiences that can make a definable difference in the community; removing many of the distinctions between the paid and unpaid workforce, thereby fo-

cusing on the work to be done and the skills needed
rather than remuneration; designing and managing
volunteer positions in ways more like paid positions;
placing new emphasis on the needs and characteristics of the future volunteer; keeping bureaucratic
tasks to be minimum in order to attract volunteers
with high skills; using high-profile media and technology; and working with corporations to develop
programs who support corporate volunteer release
time for pre-retirees, as well as second career preparation and training through volunteer education and
work [126].

Sharpening the saw — In both the non-profit and
business sectors, this involves conducting ongoing
research on volunteerism in the twenty-first century,
and leveraging this knowledge to recruit and maintain the right volunteer force, which is working to its
fullest potential. Such research can further identify
the various motives of volunteers, which can range
from leisure, skill development, material rewards,
ego needs, family traditions, and commitment to a
cause [127], and then using care to align the skills of
the volunteer with the needs of the organization [128].

The power of partnerships — There's no doubt that
leveraging the great power of America's volunteers
requires consummate skills in developing and nurturing partnerships across a number of groups, agencies, and organizations. Just as citizens of Colonial
America knew that they had to lend a helping hand
in the process of self-government, today's federal
agencies know that the successful outcomes which
serve the public good are achieved by the work of
many. The Alaska Department of Natural Resources
in its ten year strategic plan for 2006–2016 states

that "many successful partnerships have been established and nurtured to improve the division's programs and promote outdoor recreation statewide. For this agency to survive, it must transition further toward seeking assistance from other agencies, volunteers, local constituency groups, the private sector and individuals through partnerships" [129].

As the Points of Light Foundation states, the bottom line for volunteering today is that "together we can make a difference" [130].

Self-Health Nation:
THE AGING UNITED STATES BATTLES WIDER WAISTLINES AND CONSUMER CONFUSION

Today, Americans are living longer than ever. In 2003, the Centers of Disease and Prevention (CDC) said that life expectancy was at an all point high of 77.6 years [131]—thanks to control of infectious diseases, improvements in motor vehicle safety, research and technology breakthroughs, and massive budgets devoted to public health programs, research, health care, and health education. The CDC tells us that the overall health of the nation is improving, although these benefits are not equally shared by all Americans. And, it's no surprise that the United States spends more money on health per capita than any other country in the world, with much of this spending associated with the care of chronic diseases and an aging population that is growing larger each day as the baby boomers reach retirement age. And when you add the billions spent by consumers on "self-help," it is clear that our national obsession with health is a reality in the American landscape.

In today's marketplace, we are bombarded with non-stop news about losing weight, eating better, looking younger, and living longer. Being masters of our own health doesn't come cheaply however—the price tag we pay for the latest self help advice was estimated to be worth $8.5 billion in 2003, and may be as high as $11 billion by 2008 [132]. The American Obesity Association [133] estimates that consumers spend roughly $30 billion per year trying to get slim or stay slim. This includes money spent for diet sodas, diet foods, diet drugs, diet books, commercial weight loss programs, and fitness clubs. Spending just on weight loss programs is estimated at $1 to 2 billion per year [133].

But, despite plenty of talk, millions of dollars spent, and the best of intentions, there's evidence that the United States may be losing not only the battle of the bulge but years of life as well. Reports from scientists at the National Institute of Aging [134] suggest, "the U.S. could be facing its first sustained drop in life expectancy in the modern era." The researchers said that these concerns apply not only to older Americans but also to younger generations who are also experiencing weight problems earlier in life.

Being Fat

Take a stroll through any of America's public places and it's easy to see why the medical establishment is concerned—today's citizens have grown wider than ever. According to the CDC [135], obesity in the United States has risen significantly in the last twenty years. Statistics from the Harvard School of Public Health [136] show that in 2002, 28.7 percent of adult men and 34.5 percent of adult women in the United States were just too fat; that's over 60 million people. Our children have grown fatter as well—with 16 percent of America's kids between the ages of 6–19 now considered overweight. Recent news reports [137] have suggested that fast food consumption has increased fivefold among children since 1970, and that every day in the United States, almost one-third of American children aged four to nineteen eat fast food, which is the cause of six extra pounds per child per year.

How did we ever grow so fat? The CDC says it's easy to understand. Today, we have an amazing abundance of food choices and food is simply everywhere. There's plenty of pre-packaged food-to-go, home delivery of take-out foods, and drive-through restaurants. There are plenty of food choices—healthy and not so healthy alike. There's the growth of high-end "organic" mega-grocery stores like Whole Foods (available at www.wholefoodsmarket.com), the world's largest retailer of natural and organic foods, which now dot the American landscape. And, in contrast, our streets are lined with fast food restaurants that have transformed the United States into the ultimate "Fast Food Nation" [138]. Wherever we eat, Americans eat BIG in a "super sized" world of Big Macs, big gulps, big bagels, big chocolate bars, big fancy coffee drinks, and big portions of just about everything [139].

In addition to eating too much, we exercise too little. The CDC says that Americans have become sedentary with the help of technology designed to save us time and labor such as remote controls, cars, elevators, computers, dishwashers, and televisions. Today's workforce is primarily a workforce of knowledge workers who spend most of their workdays sitting at their desk, rather than working in the fields as in days past. We ride to the mall instead of walking to the corner store. According to the CDC's Behavioral Risk Factor Surveillance System [135], in 2000 more than 26 percent of adults reported no leisure time physical activity at all.

There's a physical cost to being super sized and sedentary in the United States today—the dangerous risk of high blood pressure, high cholesterol, heart disease, arthritis, diabetes, and stroke. According to the National Institute on Aging [134], life expectancy for the average American could decline by as much as five years unless the rising rate of obesity in the country is slowed. And, there are personal and collective financial costs in terms of medical care, loss of productivity from illness, and premature death. The CDC has estimated that the cost of medical care associated with obesity is over $100 billion per year; the FDA's 2004 Working Group on Obesity [140] calculated the costs at about $117 billion per year, with more than $50 billion in avoidable medical costs. Other sources [141] say that costs of excess weight account for 5 percent of all health care costs.

An Expanding Marketplace

The growing waistlines in the United States are creating a whole new marketplace that didn't exist at the turn of the last century, when waistlines were smaller and life expectancy was shorter. Consider the new medical specialty of bariatric surgery—the twenty-first century world of gastric bypass, gastric banding, and other types of stomach surgery designed to decrease the size of a person's stomach, their caloric intake, and their weight. In the United States, the number of bariatric procedures increased 600 percent in ten years [142]. In 1995, there were twenty-thousand weight-loss surgeries; by 2004, the number had risen to one hundred forty-four thousand surgeries—including a number of high profile cases such as weatherman Al Roker, television personality Star Jones, pop singer Carnie Wilson, and opera diva Deborah Voigt.

Stomach surgery has costs and can be deadly—the average procedure costs $30,000 and has a death rate of 1 percent. The National Institute of Diabetes, Digestive, and Kidney Diseases has also reported [143] that the surgery is no piece of cake for the patients—up to 20 percent need

additional surgery because of complications, and an estimated 30 percent develop problems such as malnutrition,
anemia, and bone thinning. For plastic surgeons, the enormous weight loss from stomach surgery has created a new
surgical niche—removing the large amounts of excess skin
which simply get in the way of regular physical activity [144].
The American Society of Plastic Surgery says that each year
more than fifty-thousand body-contouring procedures are
performed for massive weight loss patients [144].

In addition to the expanding bariatric specialty, there's
evidence that America's growing girth is causing a domi-
no effect in a number of other industries. Transportation
experts now say that it takes more fuel to transport overweight passengers, and that the extra weight is adding an
additional burden to our nation's fuel crisis [145]. Growing
body size has also had an impact on the fashion industry
which is adapting women's sizing for today's more ample
figures, a change that is replacing the Department of Agriculture guidelines of the 1940s. The plus-size reality of today is affecting furniture manufacturers, medical suppliers
who must provide sturdier X-ray tables, larger ambulances,
stretchers, and needles to accommodate a larger population.
The Ford Motor Co. has also begun recalibrating engineer-
ing standards to accommodate heavier drivers, and in 2004,
the Federal Aviation Administration revised its passenger
weight standards for the first time in sixty-six years [145].

CONSUMER CONFUSION

Consumers who wish to eat a better diet and lose weight
share a common bond with other citizens who are barraged
on a daily basis with massive amounts of information about
diet and health issues. In one study by the National Health
Council [146], consumers reported that they simply "didn't
know what to believe" because of conflicting reports about
health in the media. This confusion causes anxiety and

frustration about being able to sort out the reliable from the unreliable health information, and making the best health-related decisions. Consumer confusion is not limited just to public health recommendations about nutrition and weight loss—there's confusion that cuts across the full spectrum of health topics such as:

The connection between salt intake and high blood pressure [147]

The oversimplification of the "energy-in/energy out" equation as a way to understand obesity [148]

The safety of arthritis drugs in the wake of the withdrawal of Vioxx [149]

The benefits of hormone replacement for menopausal women [150]

The interpretation of current food labels, particularly nutrition content and serving size [151]

The benefits and dangers of taking vitamin supplements [152]

The nutritional advantages of fish vs. the dangers of poisoning [153]

"Health consumers face numerous challenges as they seek health information, including the complexity of the health systems, the rising burden of chronic disease, the need to engage as partners in their care, and the proliferation of consumer information available from numerous and diverse sources," states a 2004 report by the Institute of Medicine [153]. The report summarized findings from over three hundred studies, which showed that there is varying and sometimes inadequate levels of consumer knowledge; that most consumers lack skills for using and applying health information; and that health information cannot be understood by most of the people for whom it was intended [153].

The concern about consumer confusion with health recommendations was so great that the Department of Health and Human Services included "health literacy" as a focus of its Healthy People 2010 initiative (www.healthypeople.gov/Document/pdf/uih/2010uih.pdf). In this long-term government project, health literacy was defined as "the degree to which individuals have the capacity to obtain, process, and understand basic health information and services needed to make appropriate health decisions" [154]. The Healthy People 2010 initiative cited numerous studies which showed that low levels of health literacy were associated with lower levels of knowledge about health, disease, and self-management. This concern is especially important in this era of "consumer-centric" health care in which individual citizens are expected to take an active role in making their own health decisions. Making those decisions requires finding information from a number of sources and wading through complex facts and often-contradictory health recommendations. Poor decision-making ultimately means poor health.

It is believed by some that the popular media have played a role in consumer confusion about health recommendations. A report on "good science" by the Dairy Council [155] found that the most important factor that contributed to public confusion about healthy eating was lack of sufficient context in media stories. This included catchy phrases about "breakthroughs" that oversimplified or dramatized the research results, limited discussion about the flaws of a particular research study, provided an incomplete description of the meaning of "risk," and failed to emphasize that a single study is not the final word on any given health-related subject [155]. The Dairy Council report also pointed out the perspectives of some special interest groups, with political and ideological agendas, may cause additional confusion by publicizing misinformation, which conflicts with national health recommendations put forth by government regulations and credible scientific organizations. This tactic can scare the public away from the advice of the established scientific community and can cause "nutrition backlash," which makes the task of educating the public even more difficult.

Some additional causes of consumer confusion, as stated by the Dairy Council report [155], comes from conflicting information about whether a food is healthy or not, recommendations that perpetuated misperceptions that some foods should be eliminated from the diet entirely, reversals of previous recommendations, and the public's lack of familiarity with the process of science, which can be filled with inconsistencies. Research [154] has also shown that scientific findings may be viewed by consumers as "intrusions" on the pleasure of eating, which then leads to the unwillingness to follow health recommendations and ultimately, a less healthy diet.

So what's a health-conscious consumer to do in the midst of all the current confusion about health? The answer may ironically lead to the Internet. The Internet now has resources designed specifically to help consumers wade through the tsunami of conflicting claims, guidelines, and recommendations. Those seeking advice on nutrition can find help with consumer advocates or intermediaries like those at Tufts University. The University's nutritionists offer expert online guidance at the Nutrition Navigator (http://navigator.tufts.edu). At this site, consumers can find expert assessments of the best and most trustworthy nutrition and diet websites. Another similar site is the Food Marketing Institute (www.fmi.org). This site has a consumer section with a variety of topics related to food choices and food safety. Also, the Food and Nutrition Information Center (http://fnic.nal.usda.gov) website has a "consumer corner" in which consumers can find information on nutrition, ask questions, and get current information on food topics.

"UNMIXING" MARKETING MESSAGES

Those who market public health programs today may find themselves working in a challenging marketing environment. On the plus side of the equation is the insatiable consumer demand in the United States for the latest scientific know-how and practical do-it-yourself health advice. On the negative side are consumer confusion about health recommendations and the growing backlash against the medical establishment and the media, which are increasingly seen as inconsistent and sometimes prone to sensationalizing new medical news. The growing presence and power of the Internet as a source of easily accessible health information is a factor [156], although accuracy can also be a concern.

So how can marketing experts "unmix" their messages about health and be more effective in helping the public understand health information? The Dairy Council [155] suggested that when publicizing new scientific findings about nutrition, marketers should be sure to emphasize the context of the study being reported, the study's limitations, the review process undertaken by the researchers, and the clear risks and benefits for consumers. This type of information can help consumers identify "junk" science with results that are simply too good to be true or sweeping claims that are based only on a single research study. The best guidelines are those that avoid over dramatizing, overstating, or oversimplifying new studies. As other research reports have suggested [151], the current confusion about food labeling in the United States has generated insights that can now be used to improve consumer understanding of nutrition. These include providing nutrition information for the entire container of food or drink as opposed to a serving size;

removing information that is known to be difficult to understand; and simply highlighting the most critical information needed by consumers.

Another area in which marketers can meet their obligation to the public and extend the reach of their public education campaigns is by improving health literacy. The National Library of Medicine suggests that this can be done by "ensuring that educational materials are multi-lingual, culturally appropriate and easy-to-read; developing methods and materials to teach consumers how to evaluate health information resources, especially those found on the Internet" and by developing partnerships with community-based organizations which can facilitate the development and outreach activities of public health educations programs [154].

The Fight Against Fat

Who will win the American battle of the bulge? Research conducted by The Trust for America's Health [157], a non-profit, non-partisan organization funded by the Robert Wood Johnson Foundation, says that the country faces big barriers in the battle. These include inadequate funding for health initiatives, the political view that obesity is a matter of personal responsibility rather than public policy, and sheer lack of will to solve the obesity problem. In its report on the American obesity epidemic [157], the Trust stated that individual behavior change will not work by itself. The country must develop a comprehensive approach that involves families, communities, schools, employers, the food industry, health professionals, as well as state and federal governments. To overcome the obesity crisis, the entire country must mobilize its policies, energy, and will.

The good news from the National Institute of Aging is that the negative forecast for a reversal in our improved life expectancy is not an absolute given. According to the researchers, there is room for optimism—"government and private sector efforts are mobilizing against obesity, and increased education, improved medical treatments and reduced smoking can tip the balance in favor of reduced mortality and continued improvement in life expectancy" [134]. But, will we have the willpower to eat less and exercise more? Will we increasingly turn to surgeries that let us "pig out and still lose weight" or will we continue to search for the holy grail of "guilt-free gluttony," as some scientists have suggested [158]. In the battle against wider waistlines, one thing is certain—the controversies swirling around "girth control" in the United States are no flash in the pan.

Mine, Yours, and Ours:
THE NEW FAMILIES OF THE TWENTY-FIRST CENTURY

Writer Anna Quindlen said that she writes about families because "they are a metaphor for every other part of
society" [159]. Today, that means that the families of the twenty-first century and the society they live in have changed.
Demographers' state:

> The demise of the "traditional" married-with-chil-
> dren family is nearly as old a story as the 1950s-era
> Ozzie and Harriet plots that promoted this image of
> hearth and home in America. In 1960, nearly half of
> this country's households fit the mold of a married
> couple with at least one child under age 18. Fast-
> forward to today, when, according to Census 2000,

less than one-fourth of households conform to this family model [160].

It's interesting to wonder what Ozzie and Harriet Nelson might think of the variety of today's family units. There are stepfamilies with many and varied steps, gay families with known and unknown donors, singles choosing to go solo, unwed mothers who may be in their thirties and forties, and seniors who are living longer and thus spending more time living alone as empty-nesters, widows, and widowers. What can be said is that marketing campaigns today that are targeted to "families" must be savvy about the present-day family form. Whatever the form, families say a lot about the United States and their influence on the marketplace today.

STEPFAMILIES

In 1969, it was television's "Brady Bunch" that represented a modern version of the family unit—the stepfamily. According to the National Stepfamily Resource Center [161], a stepfamily is "a family in which one or both of the adult partners bring children from a previous relationship." Today, the Brady Bunch looks like a simple family form compared to new-age configurations of stepfamilies. These might include a combination of siblings (biologically related; from the same parents); stepsiblings (not biologically related; parents are married to each other); half-siblings (partially related biologically, i.e., share one parent); mutual child (a child born to the remarried couple); residential stepchildren (live in the household with the remarried couple the majority of the time.); and nonresidential stepchildren, who live in the household less than half of the time [161].

Just how many stepfamilies there are in the United States today is not certain. The Stepfamily Foundation [162] says that the data from the 1990 census states:

1,300 new stepfamilies are forming every day.

Over 50 percent of U.S. families are remarried or re-coupled.

The average marriage in America lasts only seven years.

One out of two marriages ends in divorce.

75 percent remarry.

66 percent of those living together or remarried break up when children are involved.

80 percent of remarried, or re-coupled, partners with children both have careers.

50 percent of the 60 million children under the age of thirteen were currently living with one biological parent and that parent's current partner.

50 percent of all women are likely to live in a step family relationship, when "living-together" are included in the definition of the stepfamily.

Suffice to say, many children today will grow up in stepfamilies (or "blended" families as they are sometimes called) because divorce is so prevalent in the United States. In the wake of this trend, psychologists have been actively studying the effects of divorce on children. The Stepfamily Foundation [162] reports somewhat conflicting results on the development and resilience of children who experience divorce and reconfiguration of their family unit during their formative years. While this research continues, it is safe to say that like other social trends, the growth in stepfamilies has created a large, diverse market of products and services related to the needs and interests of stepfamilies. There are ministries devoted to stepfamilies' educational programs; books and other resources; therapists and other mental health counselors who specialize in working with stepfamilies [163]; newsletters and magazines [164,165] written especially for stepfamilies; a host of professional organizations devoted to the exclusive needs of these families such as the national Stepfamily Resource Center [166]; and web brokers like "The Positive Way" [167], which provide links to web-based information sources for stepfamilies. For those who market public programs which are targeted to "families," accessing the extensive stepfamily network that exists today can open up a vast web of critical connections to the stepfamily community.

GAY AND LESBIAN FAMILIES

The U.S. Census Bureau did not start tracking same-sex households until 2000, although we know that for many years, gay and lesbian parents have been starting (or restarting) families with children, many of whom were from previous heterosexual marriages that ended in divorce. Now, with the help of new-age reproductive science, artificial insemination by known or unknown donors, egg donation, in-vitro-fertilization, and surrogate mothers, there are new and different forms of gay families on the American scene. These possibilities of parental combinations, like the Rubik's cube, are redefining our traditional notion of family and parenthood.

Estimates of the numbers of these new families vary. One report from the Urban Institute [168] used figures from the 2000 Census to estimate that there are one hundred thousand female same-sex couples; sixty-seven thousand male same-sex couples with at least one child under eighteen in the home; and two hundred fifty thousand children are being raised by same-sex couples. Other sources [168] put the figure at four million gay and lesbian parents raising eight to ten million children. Thus, there is somewhere between 1 to 12 percent of America's children with gay parents. This phenomenon, called a "gayby boom" by some [169], represents a major redesign of the American family with gay fathers, gay mothers, single lesbians, known and unknown gay male donors, married and unmarried couples, part-time and full-time parents, and biological and adoptive parents in the amalgam of family forms.

There are plenty of legal issues swirling around these new types of families. According to a recent article in the New York Times, the law has been slow to catch up with this trend—partly because this phenomenon is fairly new and also because there is "a reluctance to offend socially conservative voters" [169]. The gray legal areas overlap with the personal side, where gay parents grapple with the challenges about parental rights, visitation, and divorce in ways that are similar to straight divorced parents. Yet, gay families are different in their own right. One gay mother said, "Our families are designed. They're conscious. They just don't happen by happenstance. We had to sit down and say… 'Ok, what's your relationship to the kid going to look like? What's our relationship to each other going to look like? What's this family going to look like?'" [169].

While the debate about same-sex marriages continues at the state level, it's clear that gay families are fast becoming a marketing niche in today's twenty-first century marketplace. In 2003, Volvo featured a gay family—complete with two fathers, a child, and a dog—in its XC90 SUV campaign. This campaign was reported [170] to be the first campaign in which a new vehicle was introduced simultaneously in the gay and mainstream media. Volvo had taken a position that it was natural for the company to address the needs of gay families. Thomas Anderson, executive vice president of Volvo Cars North America said, "We're targeting people with modern family values. It's a value set and the Volvo-minded consumer is very diverse. 'Family' is much more than the traditional family" [170]. Advertising research [170] has reaped benefits for Volvo and Jaguar, which are both owned by the Ford Motor Company. Research from gay focus groups has shown that gay families prefer direct messages that "show who they are" rather than general ads targeted to traditional families.

There's other evidence of the growing potential of marketing to gay families. There are now gay television networks that cater to the growing gay market. There was television star Rosie O'Donnell's "R Families Vacation" 2004 cruise for fifteen hundred gay people and their families. With the cruise's huge success and its debut two years later as an HBO documentary [171], O'Donnell fulfilled one of her dreams to provide a discrimination-free vacation for gay families. O'Donnell's successful sold-out cruise exemplifies what the business world now sees as the growing market of selling travel, financial advice, and wedding services to same-sex couples and families. "It's not surprising that as the gay family market comes of age, marketers want a piece of that," said Bradley Johnson, Advertising Age's editor at large [172].

SINGLE MOMS

Unmarried mothers and their children have long been part of the American family scene and our national preoccupation with love, marriage, and children. The furor that emerged in 1992 when then Vice President Dan Quayle criticized television star and single mom Murphy Brown was evidence of the emotionally charged "values" debate that revolved around the rights of women to have their babies out of wedlock. The debate took a new turn in 2005, when a new report from the National Center for Health Statistics confirmed suspicions that the United States had hit a record high for the number of babies—1.5 million—born to unwed mothers [173]. More specifically, the Center reported that there were 1,470,152 babies born to single women in 2004, a figure that accounts for 35.7 percent of all births in the United States.

Newspaper reports [173,174] speculated that the rising numbers of unwed mothers, and the increase in unwed mothers in their twenties, thirties, and forties, may be a result of a number of factors that reflect larger changes in U.S. society in the twenty-first century. These include the growing numbers of high-visibility celebrity single moms; greater numbers of couples who have chosen to cohabitate and may be delaying or totally avoiding marriage; and more tolerant societal views of unwed motherhood that doesn't match the prototypical expectation that marriage come first and then children. Unwed motherhood is not the source of shame and condemnation as it was in the past. Finally, greater career options for women may also be another factor that has caused so many women to delay child rearing.

Whatever the root cause, the new statistics are stimulating plenty of buzz about the impact of out-of-wedlock births on the long-term welfare of children. Concerns about the statistics show that half of unmarried women who gave birth in the last year lived below the poverty level [175] and that women who bore children out of wedlock are "less likely to marry and when they do, they do not marry well"—and calls to re-evaluate so-called "marriage promotion programs," which have received millions of federal and state subsidies in 2006 to promote family formation and healthy marriage among low-income Americans [176].

GOING SOLO

No discussion of the American family landscape would be complete without including what has now become the most common type of contemporary American household—citizens living solo. According to the U.S. Census Bureau [177], in 2000, there were 27 million American households with individuals living alone, as compared to 25 million house-holds with a husband, wife, and child. In the Census Bu-reau survey, "Examining American Household Composi-tion: 1990 and 2000," demographers found that one in four American households consisted of an adult living alone (25.8 percent). Other reports [178] have shown that in 1970, women living alone represented 67 percent of the one-per-son households. By 2003, however, there were more men living alone, although women still represented 58 percent of the solo households.

Like the increase in out-of-wedlock births, the growth in solo households is thought to be a result of a variety of so-cial factors such as delays in the marriage age, the growing acceptance of being single as a "lifestyle," and longer life expectancy. And it may well be a bad sign for a country, says Robert Putnam, Harvard Professor and author of the 2000 best selling book, "Bowling Alone" [179]. After more than five hundred thousand interviews, Putnam concluded that Americans are not only bowling alone, but are also suffering some collective signs of civic disengagement—signing fewer petitions, belonging to fewer organizations, knowing our neighbors less, meeting with friends and even families less frequently. Putnam suggested [179] that these signs of new single times in the United States have resulted from myri-ad of changes in American life— in work, family structure, age, suburban life, television, computers, women's roles, and other factors. But while social scientists debate the di-lemmas presented by "Bowling Alone," and health care ex-perts analyze the pros and cons of living alone on health and longevity, marketers are starting to sense a new marketing bonanza in the singles scene.

Beyond the growth in the food industry of "solo" serv-ing sizes, there's a growing single women's market [180]. Some marketing experts suggest that the marketing industry may be behind the curve in responding to this evolving market.

Marketers are having trouble even acknowledging there might be something other than couples and perfect nuclear families out there. So, when we hit the estimated point in 2008 when a majority of households will be headed by an unmarried person, the majority of brands might be living in a time warp. Remember how the 50s housewife used to be the icon of womanhood? There was some serious lag time before brands figured out the vast majority of women no longer looked, acted or thought like Harriet Nelson. Now, we may be facing a similar tortoise-slow reaction to western world trends in the women's market: solo-hood [181].

For those who market public programs, the message about "family" is clear—family in today's United States, whether straight or gay, old or young, has many forms. Each family form represents a specialized marketing niche that can be artfully studied and then leveraged for a wider reach to those who are blended, bowling alone, or living solo.

COMMON THREADS AMONG THE TRENDS

In this final section on trends in the United States today, we've taken a look at the changing form of the family in America. The Census Bureau [177] tells us, "changes in the number and type of households are influenced by patterns of population growth, shifts in the age composition of the population, and the decisions individuals make about their living arrangements. Shifts in social norms, values, laws, the economy, and improvements in health also influence how people organize their lives." Yet, in each of the diverse trends we have discussed, from the World Wide Web and public relations to our bipolar, self-health nation, we've seen some common threads—the erosion of traditional sources of power, more divergent social norms, and an "open source spirit" in the America of today. In this environment, trends serve us as road signs for the future, although the map of the new frontier of marketing has yet to be drawn.

Part Three

LEARNING FROM SUCCESS:
AN IN-DEPTH LOOK AT FOUR CAMPAIGNS THAT CHANGED AMERICAN LIFE

TABLE OF CONTENTS

Used with the permission of the Forest Service, U.S. Department of Agriculture

*Photo courtesy of The Heart Truth, National Heart,
Lung, and Blood Institute*

THE HEART TRUTH:
A NATIONAL AWARENESS CAMPAIGN FOR WOMEN ABOUT HEART DISEASE

How does a federal marketing campaign about women's health become a national movement? Take an urgent health issue that is "past its time" and add a little red dress. Bring together the fashion world, the First Ladies, and countless crusaders for better health for America's women. Add savvy public marketing strategy, research and execution, and you have The Heart Truth, the landmark marketing campaign of the National Heart Lung & Blood Institute (NHLBI).

ROOTS IN EQUAL OPPORTUNITY

The roots of The Heart Truth campaign go back to the 1980s—a time in the United States when female baby boomers were beginning to experience menopause, breast cancer, and heart attacks—a time of growing awareness that "protection" of women in the past had excluded them from participation in clinical research—and a time when advocacy groups began to pressure the federal bureaucracy to focus on women's health concerns. As a result, the National Institutes of Health created a new policy in 1986 that required the inclusion of women in federally funded research studies. In 1990, the Women's Health Equity Act was introduced with twenty-two bills related to research and care of women. In this context, researchers began conducting new research studies on women's health and quickly learned some difficult lessons about messaging and marketing.

George Washington University Medical Center in Washington, DC was a case in point. The long-awaited recruitment of postmenopausal women for clinical studies in the nation's capital had begun at a disappointingly slow pace. The recruitment telephone lines were quiet. If women were clamoring for equal opportunity in clinical research, why were they not responding to advertisements for participants in the new women's studies? Faced with this dilemma, Diane Stoy, the Recruitment Director at the University's Lipid Research Clinic, set out on a quest to explore the world of the women, figure out the dilemma by conducting field research, and turns the situation into a success.

In private sessions at a small downtown hotel, Stoy successfully engaged the leaders of Washington's notable women's groups in lively discussions about women's perceptions of health, aging, menopause, health care, and illness. Menopause, the leaders said emphatically, was a negative term in America's youth culture. Stay away from that word, the leaders suggested. Women simply do not think that they can have a heart attack. Rewrite your marketing messages and make your purpose clear—put your focus on improving awareness that heart disease is a concern for women as well as men. Send out a compelling call to arms that women needed to help improve our collective understanding of heart disease in women, and they will respond, the leaders said.

Stoy moved quickly to revamp the recruitment program by creating a new slogan—"Women have hearts too!" with a new icon (the queen of hearts), and new promotional materials. "This was followed by one of those Eureka moments," Stoy now says, "when I knew that the campaign needed a big voice—perhaps from Hollywood—and who else should it be but NBC's 'Golden Girls' who had recently broken barriers on national television by talking about getting older and having hot flashes?"

Facing plenty of skepticism from colleagues, Stoy persisted in her pursuit of help from Hollywood. After one call to Golden Girl Betty White, Stoy and Claudia Dominitz, her colleague from the University's public relations office, were on their way to the Golden Girls' set in Hollywood to tape the public service announcements. Thus was born the award-winning, groundbreaking national campaign, "Women have hearts too," with the voices of Betty White and Rue MacClanahan urging women on television stations around the country to give their time to participate in studies of women and heart disease, and massive print and broadcast coverage of this Golden Girls' appeal.

Yet despite the great national success of the Golden Girls' campaign and other health campaigns geared toward women's health, national surveys conducted in 1991 showed that only 34 percent of women recognized that heart disease was the greatest threat to their health. Women's advocacy groups continued their considerable pressure on the NHLBI to act. In March 2001, the Institute responded by convening a strategy-development group, which recommended creating a national awareness campaign to address the low level of awareness among women that heart disease was the number one killer of women. In October 2001, Ogilvy Public Relations Worldwide was awarded the contract to develop the campaign. After a year of intense research and development, The Heart Truth campaign was launched in September 2002. Five months later, the founding partners (NHLBI, the American Heart Association, and WomenHeart: the National Coalition for Women with Heart Disease, the nation's only patient advocacy organization that represents women living with heart disease), announced the partnership between the campaign's founding partners and the American fashion industry, and the debut of the red dress as the symbol for the emerging campaign.

Four years later, the campaign has grown into a groundbreaking, multi-faceted, award-winning women's health movement. According to Terry Long, Director of Communications for NHLBI, The Heart Truth represents "a perfect fit between the problem, concept, strategy, and execution, which came together perfectly."

*Photo courtesy of The Heart Truth, National Heart,
Lung, and Blood Institute*

RESEARCH FIRST

According to Long, research played a central role in the campaign's ability to define, describe, and profile the appropriate target group. Research also played a central role in developing and testing a variety of campaign messages, testing creative concepts for use in campaign materials, and conducting environmental scanning of the media and communications environments. This six-month process involved a variety of research methods, such as:

Comprehensive analysis of mid-life women—including attitudes, socioeconomic factors, knowledge, behaviors, and demographics;

Archival analysis of print media coverage of women and heart disease;

Literature review of research articles on women and heart disease;

Comparative analysis of NHLBI's complementary and competing women's health programs;

Focus groups and message testing with women in four cities;

Review of all materials by the key campaign partners.

AN URGENT MESSAGE OF LIFE AND DEATH

Most women believe that heart disease is a man's disease, when in reality heart disease is the leading killer of American women and a major cause of disability and a significantly decreased quality of life. Because one of every three women in the United States dies of heart disease, the campaign's challenge was to increase women's awareness of this reality, change their belief that heart disease was a health concern for men and not women, and urge them to take the appropriate actions to reduce their personal risk of developing heart disease.

According to Long, women who participated in the prelaunch focus groups and message testing felt very strongly that the campaign's message must be direct and serious. The women recommended that personal stories of women with heart problems be used as a channel for "putting a face" on the campaign's message. The decision was made to frame The Heart Truth campaign message as a direct, edgy, emotional life or death message—a wake-up call—that women must take their own personal risk of heart disease seriously by making the connection between risk factors (such as high blood pressure and high cholesterol) and heart disease. But it doesn't stop there. The campaign sends an urgent message for women to act—to talk with their doctor, assess their personal risk of developing heart disease, and then to take action to reduce those risk factors for heart disease.

TARGET, TARGET, TARGET

The primary target for The Heart Truth campaign is women forty to sixty years of age (a time of life when the risk of heart disease increases), who have at least one risk factor for heart disease and are not taking action. Secondary target audiences include women aged 18–39, and health care professionals who can carry the campaign message through their own channels of influence with women. For younger women, the messages focus on preventing heart disease, which can begin in the early years of life. For senior women and those with heart problems, there's the hopeful message that it is simply never too late to begin taking steps to reduce cardiovascular risk. The campaign has also targeted women of color, who have been found to have low levels of awareness of heart disease risk. The Heart Truth Communities of Color initiative includes partnerships and activities with leading organizations that represent and reach women of color.

Defining and keeping loyal to a narrowly defined target audience is essential in a complex marketing campaign such as The Heart Truth. Yet, program planners charged with using federal funds to benefit the public work in an environment in which public advocacy plays a major role. In the planning stage, Long and other campaign leaders experienced significant public pressure from interest groups that wanted the campaign to include teenagers and much younger women within the target audience. Long says that the campaign repeatedly pushed back on the public pressure because it was critical "to focus like a laser on the audience that could benefit most from the message." This is a critical lesson in marketing.

THE RED DRESS—A POWERFUL SYMBOL

Early in the planning stage, designers of The Heart Truth campaign recognized the importance of using a powerful, positive symbol (like Smokey the Bear, Rosie the Riveter, and the pink ribbon for breast cancer awareness) to carry the clear, compelling urgency of the campaign's message. The campaign needed an appropriate, recognizable icon that could achieve widespread recognition and adoption by potential corporate and community partners, and a message that would stand out from the myriad of messages competing for space in the crowded public health marketplace.

After conducting focus groups to test a variety of options, the campaign selected the red dress and the slogan "Heart Disease Doesn't Care What You Wear—It's the Number One Killer of Women." Women in the focus groups saw the red dress as a real attention-getter, a symbol of the seriousness of heart disease, and an ideal way to change public perception that heart disease was not just a man's health concern. The red dress was viewed as a strong link between a woman's focus on her outer self and the need to focus on her inner self—particularly the health of her heart. The color choice was also critical. Red not only represented the heart, but also the symbol of a stop sign or urgent alert for women to pay attention to risk factors for heart disease. And the red dress was seen as a brand that would apply to women of all shapes, sizes and backgrounds.

Photo courtesy of The Heart Truth, National Heart, Lung, and Blood Institute

REACHING OUT THROUGH FASHION

The Heart Truth campaign is a great example of leveraging a small symbol for great impact. The campaign linked the symbol of the red dress to the fashion industry, its traditional fashion week in February each year, corporate partners, and the country's First Ladies. During Mercedes-Benz Fashion Week in 2003, the first Heart Truth national event, nineteen top designers (including Vera Wang, Donna Karan, and Oscar de la Renta) contributed red dresses to the "Red Dress Collection." At annual fashion week, "runway" events funded by corporate sponsors such as Johnson & Johnson, Celestial Seasonings, and Swarovski, the fashion industry now highlights red dresses created exclusively for The Heart Truth campaign. According to the NHLBI, the estimated value of the campaign's linkage to the fashion industry is estimated conservatively at $6 million.

In 2005, the First Ladies of the United States further extended the reach of the campaign with their donation of red gowns and suits for the "First Ladies Red Dress Collection." Some of these ensembles have become part of The Heart Truth Road Show, which spreads the campaign message and offers health screenings in cities throughout the United States. The campaign also created "National Wear Red Day," an event that takes place on the first Friday in February of each year. This activity gives female and male citizens a way to show their support for greater awareness of heart disease in women by wearing red clothing and the campaign's red dress pin.

The campaign also includes outreach activities to health professionals with the Heart Truth exhibit, which travels to health professional conferences. The exhibit urges health professionals to become part of the campaign by talking to women about their risk of heart disease, assessing their risk, and urging them to take actions to reduce their risk.

POWER THROUGH PARTNERSHIPS

The Heart Truth campaign has demonstrated the tremendous power of ongoing partnerships and cross-programming to extend the national and local reach of marketing campaigns. The reach of the campaign can then move through the distribution and promotional channels of the partners. In addition to alliances with the giants of the fashion industry, the campaign has built lasting partnerships with:

The First Lady of the United States, who serves as the campaign's national ambassador. Mrs. Bush has made numerous media appearances on behalf of the campaign and hosted an event at the White House when President Bush announced campaign activities and declared February 2004 as American Heart Month.

Media organizations with female readers such as Woman's Day and Glamour that have published articles about the campaign. Corporations such as RadioShack, General Mills, Wal-Mart, Albertsons, and Johnson & Johnson which have underwritten the costs of community events, promotions, advertising, and products.

National and community nonprofit organizations such as, the American Heart Association, Women Heart, the National Black Nurses' Association, and the General Federation of Women's Club, whose diverse Red Dress activities further extends the reach of the campaign to diverse audiences.

MEDIA AND MATERIALS EXTEND THE REACH

The savvy use of the media has also played a central role in extending the reach of The Heart Truth campaign. The goal of the national media relations outreach was clear—position NHLBI as a leader of the renewed women's heart disease awareness movement by capitalizing on and leveraging all national and local events, promotions, products, and activities. From February 2003 to March 2005, the core Heart

Truth public service multi-media advertising campaign generated major events such as national press conferences, high visibility press events at the White House and Fashion Week events, observances of the first National Wear Red Day, and events announcing new campaign partnerships. On the local level, there were hundreds of targeted Heart Truth events created and led by local community partners such as rallies, health fairs, celebrity teas, power breakfasts, walks, and red dress fashion shows. There were advertisements in national newspapers, print and broadcast public service announcements, a multitude of campaign-related products distributed through partner promotion, and wide distribution of the Healthy Heart Handbook for Women and the campaign's signature red dress pins.

The Heart Truth's media campaign was grounded in the campaign's web suite, or online shopping store, where organizations, communities, and individuals could access and order a myriad of educational and marketing materials such as:

The one hundred-page Healthy Heart Handbook for Women

The Heart Truth online toolkit with ideas and materials for use in community activities

The Heart Truth for Women speaker's kit with an easy-to-use speaker's guide, PowerPoint presentation, and ten-minute video

Print, radio, and television public service announcements in both English and Spanish

Fact sheets, infographs, brochures, and posters

Red Dress pins and note cards

Patient wallet cards

Partnership directory of community, government, and nonprofit partners of The Heart Truth

Heart healthy cookbook

A Heart Truth activity registry, which provides a forum for campaign partners to share stories of successful campaign activities and ideas

The web site, which supports The Heart Truth, is another great example of a good marketing technique. The web suite becomes a rich public health resource, with easy access for reviewing all the diverse campaign materials and ordering materials through a safe, secure, centralized fulfillment system. The rich, user-friendly repository of campaign materials is a public domain site designed to increase the use of the campaign materials and to assure consistent, nationwide branding and messaging. The materials also allow for flexibility in local programming, a feature that was recognized early in the campaign as essential to the campaign's long-term success.

The campaign also recognized the importance of developing guidelines for partner participation so that the NHLBI could assure partner adherence to messaging and branding. This combination of flexibility and standardization was viewed as critical to extending the reach of a campaign, which involved many competitive partners. Terry Long says that one of the important lessons learned is that the campaign focus must remain on the issue rather than the NHLBI or the other campaign partners.

Metrics for Success

Another hallmark of The Heart Truth campaign is the sophisticated use of research to evaluate and demonstrate the campaign's impact. Success with the campaign has been evaluated through two lenses. From the program perspective, all the diverse media and event activities sponsored by the campaign have been monitored, recorded, and analyzed. To assess the campaign's impact on the target group, the campaign has relied on its partners to collect ongoing survey data on the awareness and action campaign objectives.

Program Success

The campaign planners designed a data collection system that scanned the country and the media, and recorded all campaign events and activities. Four years after The Heart Truth was launched, the NHLBI conducted an extensive analysis of the campaign's activity and its reach, such as:

Targeted campaign activities such as Single City Stops, Road Show Stops, First Lady Events, and Health Professional Conferences. From February 2003 to March 2005, there were fifty-six national events and hundreds of local community events.

Assessment of the financial value of partnerships. This metric was based on the estimated value of in-kind investments from the fashion industry, as well from designers, models, and celebrities. Over the two-year period with three major Fashion Week events, the total value has been estimated at $6,591,900. This does not include national newspaper advertisements; copies of the Healthy Heart Handbook; four hundred fifty thousand red dress pins promoted and distributed through partner promotion; and color public service ads in partner publications.

Media impressions and media coverage. A total of 1 billion media impressions were identified. Broadcast, newspaper, magazine, and online media coverage totaled more than 604 million placements over the two-year period.

Media coverage specific to major print publications, defined as top U.S. newspapers, business magazines, and general interest magazines, totaled seventy-five.

Television public service announcements equaled 206 million media impressions, while radio gained 187 million.

Airport dioramas, with educational and promotional materials, have appeared in twenty-two major U.S. airports and have generated a reported $7 million equivalent in paid advertising.

Distribution of campaign materials was also tracked. A total of 466,268 red dress pins were distributed by corporate partners and three hundred twenty-eight thousand by NHLBI. Other campaign materials that have been distributed equaled 816,059. Distribution by type of materials was also analyzed by sources.

SUCCESS WITH THE TARGET GROUP

The NHLBI depends on its partners like the American Heart Association to monitor the direct effects of the campaign on consumer awareness, beliefs, and actions. Surveys now suggest that The Heart Truth campaign has begun to have an impact on women's perceptions of heart disease. In one survey conducted by the American Heart Association in 2005, 55 percent of American women knew that heart disease was the leading killer of women. This was an improvement from the 34 percent in 2000. The survey also showed improvement but persistently lower levels of awareness among African American and Hispanic women, groups at a higher risk of heart disease.

In 2005, campaign planners received some good news from a survey commissioned by one of its founding partners, WomenHeart: the National Coalition for Women with Heart Disease. In this survey, conducted by Harris Interactive®, the selection of the campaign's red dress symbol was validated by the finding that 77 percent of women surveyed saw the red dress as an appropriate symbol for women and heart disease awareness; and 60 percent of U.S. adult women were stimulated by the red dress to learn more about heart disease. The red dress symbol was recalled by 25 percent of the women surveyed. A total of 45 percent of the women also agreed that the red dress was a good prompt to seek the advice of their physician about their heart disease risk

Two indicators of the public health challenge that still lies ahead were identified in other studies. A 2005 survey of two thousand seven hundred women, conducted by the Preventive Cardiovascular Nurses Association, found that over 80 percent of the women surveyed did not know their cholesterol numbers. Cholesterol is considered a risk factor for heart disease. Another study published in a 2005 journal called Circulation, found that there are gender differences in the way physicians provided preventive care about heart disease; more physician education about women's risk of heart disease was needed.

One survey conducted in 2006 by the NHLBI and Lifetime Television, demonstrated some improvement in women's awareness of heart disease and their acknowledgment of personal risk. Greater than 50 percent of women correctly identified heart disease as the leading cause of death among women, although this was only 4 percent greater that the previous survey in 2003. A total of 31 percent of women stated that they saw themselves as personally at risk for heart disease. Another survey by the Society for Women's Health Research showed that the fear women associated with heart disease had doubled since 2002, although most women still had the greatest fear of breast cancer.

KEEPING MOMENTUM

The Heart Truth campaign has been an overwhelming success and may have set a new gold standard for federal marketing campaigns. Terry Long, NHLBI Communications Director, says that the campaign has been an "amazing journey" that demonstrated the power of marketing strategy and execution; the power of an idea—the red dress; the importance of developing a clear, appropriate message, testing it, and then staying on it; the value of clearly defining the campaign's metrics at the beginning of the campaign; and the power of partnerships with external public relations experts, corporations, nonprofits, health care professionals, and citizens.

Looking to the future, the work of The Heart Truth campaign remains unfinished, although women's health experts and advocacy groups feel that real progress has been made. Some even believe that the campaign has created a "tipping point" for a health issue that badly needed the public's attention. The savvy decision to link the campaign's signature event to the annual ritual of Fashion Week was a smart, strategic way to sustain and perpetuate the campaign's momentum. Obtaining multi-year commitments from corporate sponsors has helped to ensure a high level of ongoing corporate involvement. In the years to come, the campaign will focus on expanding community action activities in communities of color and growing the campaign in a smart way. That will include searching for new corporate partners in the retail and cosmetics markets.

Wherever The Heart Truth campaign goes, the little red dress is sure to follow. And along with it will be some important lessons from the past for those involved in marketing public programs. Every successful campaign begins with the right idea. And, as we learned from the Golden Girls' campaign, one big idea, lots of persistence, and a single telephone call can change the direction of a national campaign forever.

ENERGY STAR®:
PARTNERSHIPS, PRODUCTS,
AND PROTECTION OF THE ENVIRONMENT

Fifteen years after the first Energy Star was introduced by the Environmental Protection Agency (EPA), Energy Star has become a marketer's dream that has it all—a big mission, name recognition, plentiful partnerships, and real power to move the American marketplace toward improved energy efficiency, cost savings, and enhanced protection of the environment. With thousands of diverse national and international partners and a well-recognized Energy Star label on products and buildings, the Energy Star story is savvy strategies for success, using product endorsement and education to leverage government funding for global impact, developing a brand identity with enduring clout, and busting barriers to energy efficiency in the commercial and industrial marketplace.

Source: EPA
ENERGY STAR is a registered trademark of
the U.S. Environmental Protection Agency

LOOKING FOR LEVERAGE

Energy Star is a good business story with roots in the tradition of Archimedes, the great Sicilian mathematician and scientist credited with discovering the principle of the lever. Archimedes' famous quote, "Give me a lever and I can move the world" [1], has become a basic business principle that can be found at the heart of Energy Star's success. Faced with strategic decisions about where and how to leverage federal funds for the greatest good, the architects of Energy Star decided against investing directly in equipment, products, or services that would be limited to short-term energy savings typically associated with demand-side programs. Instead, the program began with public awareness "missionary work" on behalf of environmental protection, issued a call to action for consumers, and then moved forward with a market-based strategy, which was centered on solid, research-based information about the benefits and cost savings associated with energy efficient products or equipment. This information was used to influence corporate and consumer decision-making in the marketplace by reducing transaction costs and investment risks, and improving the attractiveness of energy efficient products or projects.

The Energy Star program has made smart use of leveraging in a number of other programmatic decisions. According to EPA, the program was careful in its early years to certify products such as computers, which had definite high growth potential in the marketplace, and to target "flagship" corporate partners that would serve as exemplary models for other companies. The program's search for leverage on Wall Street led to CEOs who must listen to shareholders and to groups of socially responsible investors who ultimately put pressure on companies to support improved energy efficiency. EPA planners realized early in the campaign that "you can't sell the program to the Fortune 500 companies by appealing to their altruism—you have to appeal to the cost benefit side instead." All of these strategies were high-leverage approaches that helped to "direct private capital toward energy efficient investments" and provide "a large environmental and economic payback for the government investment" [2].

BUILDING A BRAND WITH CLOUT

The Energy Star experience illustrates how a government program can overcome one of the major challenges in marketing programs that focus on complex societal issues— making the case for the cause. Energy Star is complex. The objectives of decreasing greenhouse gas emissions and protecting the environment are lofty—both literally and figuratively. The objectives are not daily concerns for average citizens such as gasoline prices might be, or for businesses in which decisions are driven by the financial bottom line. And, the objectives do not offer consumers immediate, obvious personal rewards.

Making the global local was a major lesson for the Energy Star planners. EPA planners recognized that they simply could not sell the issue of global warming to average citizens. This overarching reality of the nature of environmental protection leads to the incorporation of a hybrid marketing model into Energy Star. Driven by a socially conscious message about environmental protection, Energy Star's path to connecting personally with consumers has centered on reducing air pollution at the local level, and on motivating product purchases that would direct national attention and local buying habits to energy efficient products, practices, and homes. This movement in the marketplace would ultimately lead to less greenhouse gas and greater protection of the environment. This market-based, product-driven strategy is evident in Energy Star from its earliest roots.

In 1992, EPA launched the first Energy Star label on computers and computer monitors. Since that time, the agency has worked steadily to build a massive product evaluation system and a credible, well-recognized brand that carries weight in the marketplace. The credibility of such a system and its success rested on assuring the scientific integrity, reliability, accuracy, and transparency of the program's product testing processes. In 1996, EPA partnered with the U.S. Department of Energy (DOE) on the Energy Star program and DOE oversees 6 product areas within the Energy Star portfolio. EPA works to assure that products which are awarded the Energy Star label are truly energy efficient and can produce real savings for the consumer. Important features of the product evaluation process include identifying energy efficient usage patterns of products (such as the stand-by mode for computers), quantifying energy efficiency in standardized terms, and determining if higher up-front costs (such as those for energy efficient appliances) actually produce reasonable return to the consumer over the product's life cycle.

According to EPA [3], the Energy Star label is now recognized by 65 percent of the public. The branding effort has become a real enterprise which now includes thirty-five product categories in six major product areas—office equipment (computers, copiers, and fax machines); home electronics (televisions, VCRs, radios); heating and cooling systems (central air conditioning, furnaces, thermostats); appliances (washers, dryers, dishwashers, refrigerators, room air conditioners); lighting (fixtures, bulbs, exit signs); and building supports such as windows. Extensive product information is provided for direct public access through the Energy Star website (www.energystar.gov) and hotlines are maintained by EPA. Through these channels and Energy Star's ongoing public education campaign, citizens can learn about the expected energy savings and environmental protection from products, stores that carry the products, and additional ways to improve the energy efficiency of their homes. The underlying message continues to reinforce the connection between improved energy efficiency, cost savings, and improved environmental protection.

Another central feature of Energy Star's brand development is the program's commitment to taking product information to the local consumer's point of purchase. Through partnerships with retailers and state energy groups, EPA offers training materials and a centralized tool kit as a way to avoid replication of effort and to encourage integration of Energy Star's core educational resources into local outreach efforts. The Energy Star program also works closely with more than two thousand homebuilders and the Army Corps of Engineers to promote the construction of new homes that are energy efficient, comfortable, and affordable. These homes are built with Energy Star qualified products, such as heating and cooling systems, appliances, lighting, and windows. Another major focus is working to improve the energy efficiency of the existing homes that need cost-effective energy improvements. Energy Star and its partners in the home-building industry offer unique training programs for contractors and homeowners on home sealing and insulation techniques and for retrofit specialists who conduct energy audits and assist homeowners with making smart, cost-effective home improvements.

Because a government brand as large and visible as Energy Star cannot afford to rest on its reputation for accuracy and integrity, EPA has built a number of quality control mechanisms into the Energy Star program to ensure the integrity of the label. This includes:

A monitoring system which assures that the label is used only on products that have truly qualified for the distinction;

Random product testing which re-tests and re-confirms a product's qualifications; and

Regular updating of product specifications as market conditions change

Light the way.

*Source: EPA. Advertisement encouraging people
to purchase Energy Star lights.*

BUSTING BARRIERS

Another key factor in Energy Star's success is the program's laser-like use of force-field analysis to drive the program's environmental agenda forward. Taken from the classic work of Kurt Lewin [4], this approach suggests that successful large-scale change initiatives, such as environmental protection, involve driving forward the forces pushing for change as well as removing any restraining forces or barriers that can impede the change effort. Within the sizable commercial and industrial sectors, EPA recognized that product endorsement and energy efficient labeling were simply not enough to achieve the program's long-term objectives.

The ultimate success of Energy Star would require identifying, addressing, and removing barriers to improved energy efficiency. To address the lack of corporate commitment to increasing energy efficiency, the program enrolled the support of top-level executives through Energy Star partnerships available for organizations of all types and sizes. These partnerships, which now include more than twelve thousand public organizations, as well as large and small businesses, center on what EPA considers the proven elements of model energy management:

Strong commitment from the top of the organization, which assures that energy efficiency work will be adequately supported;

Routine evaluation of energy use within and across organizations that provides a mechanism for benchmarking and continuous improvement;

A whole-systems approach to upgrading buildings to improve energy efficiency, which recognizes that many inter-dependent components are intricately involved in improving energy efficiency.

The Energy Star program [2] cites some statistics that support the use of these management principles. For example: The efficiency of building components such as windows has improved more than 30 percent in the past twenty-five years although building energy use has not improved as much.

The best energy efficient American buildings use 75 percent less energy that the worst performing buildings. This difference was not attributable to climate, building size, building age, or particular technologies.

The Energy Star experience also illustrates the critical importance of linking the campaign's message directly to the target market's concerns and priorities. For the commercial and industrial sectors, this meant that the program needed to make a clear, compelling financial case for energy efficiency. This required refining the campaign's message and recasting energy savings in terms that were specifically matched to core business objectives. Examples [2] include, "a commercial building owner can generate $2–3 of incremental asset value for every $1 invested in energy performance improvements" and "a full service hotel can realize the equivalent of increasing its average daily rate by $1.45 (about 1.6 percent) from a 10% improvement in energy performance." A central activity within this recasting process involved the production of robust, well-designed, credible financial analyses that provided tangible, bottom-line proof that effective energy management goes hand-in-hand with strong performance on Wall Street.

Another barrier overcome by EPA was the lack of standardized, reliable measurement tools for assessing the energy performance of commercial buildings and industrial facilities. In 1999, EPA launched its new national energy performance rating system, which offers building owners a rating that can be used as a recognized factor in negotiations of real estate assessments or real estate leases. Since 1999, this rating system has been used in thousands of buildings such as retail, office buildings, food services, lodging, education, hospitals, post offices, and waste treatment facilities which now carry the high-visibility Energy Star label. For building owners, this label represents a standardized yardstick for assessing energy performance, a symbol of the cost savings gained from improved energy efficiency, and name recognition for the business owners who have proactively invested in energy management.

The critical role of barrier busting to Energy Star's success was reiterated in its 2005 annual report, which stated:

> The continued success of the Energy Star program is a result of its focus on practical strategies to remove market barriers. These barriers can hinder investment in cost-effective, energy-efficient products and practices that help individuals and organizations realize significant savings.

WHAT'S AHEAD FOR ENERGY STAR

The program's 2006 report leaves little doubt that the Energy Star's effort has had significant impact:

> Americans, with the help of Energy Star, prevented 37 million metric tons of greenhouse gas emissions in 2006 alone—equivalent to the annual emissions from 25 million vehicles—and saved about $14 billion on their utility bills. They also saved a significant amount of energy in 2005—150 billion kilowatt hours (kWh) or almost 5 percent of total 2005 electricity demand. In addition, Energy Star helped avoid 35,000 megawatts (MW) of peak power, equivalent to the generation capacity of more than 70 new power plants. These benefits have grown yearly and now total more than twice the benefits achieved in 2000. Savings are on track to nearly double again in

10 years as more households, businesses, and organizations rely on Energy Star for guidance on investing in energy-efficient products and practices. The
2006 Energy Star results represent about one-third
of the total greenhouse gas emissions reductions
from EPA's climate change programs [3].

The 2006 report[3] also demonstrates the extraordinary
reach of the Energy Star program, which includes:

More than nine thousand Energy Star partner organizations;

About seventeen hundred manufacturers using the
Energy Star to label and differentiate more than
forty thousand individual product models, many of
which carry the brands that today's consumers prefer.

More than nine hundred retail partners bringing
Energy Star qualifying products and educational information to their customers

More than thirty five hundred builder partners con-
structing new homes in every state and the District
of Columbia that qualify for the Energy Star—saving homeowners money while maintaining high levels of comfort.

About thirty two hundred private businesses, public
sector organizations, and industrial facilities investing in energy efficiency and reducing energy use in
their buildings.

More than 40 states and more than 500 utilities and

other energy efficiency program sponsors leveraging Energy Star to improve the efficiency of government buildings and of their customers.

Hundreds of energy service providers, energy raters, architects and building engineers, and financial lenders partnering with Energy Star to make energy efficiency more widely available and to provide exceptional value to consumers and businesses.

International partnerships with Australia, Canada, the European Union, Japan and Taiwan.

Yet, beyond this amazing network, the Energy Star story is also a good example of a mature marketing program's quest to move forward by building on the past and embracing the future. The program's website (www.energystar. gov) is filled with news of new endeavors, new successes, new partnerships, and new challenges. In 2006, more than thirty two hundred office buildings, schools, hospitals, and public buildings earned Energy Star status for superior energy and environmental performance. The program has just recognized over eighty organizations as winners of the 2006 Energy Star Partner-of-the-Year Awards. And the program has recently adopted new guidelines for federal buildings that included integrated design, energy performance, water conservation, and indoor environmental quality.

With this focus on the future, Energy Star is similar to the visionary businesses cited by Jim Collins and Jerry I. Porras in their best-selling business book Built to Last [5]. According to the researchers, visionary companies see "no ultimate finish line" because continuous improvement is "an institutionalized habit—a disciplined way of life—ingrained in the fabric of the organization and reinforced by tangible mechanisms that create discontent with the status quo"

For the Energy Star program, the work of the future will focus on four major targets:

1. Expanding public recognition of the Energy Star label beyond the current 65 percent

2. Increasing consumer confidence in the Energy Star label by reinforcing that the program is government sponsored and is committed to providing accurate, unbiased, credible information about energy efficiency.

3. Using peer review and additional methods of assessing the environmental and economic benefits from the program. The EPA estimates that 50 percent of the current benefits come from citizens using Energy Star products at home, with the other half from the commercial and industrial sectors.

4. Expanding the program so much that in 2012 the impact of the program will double in terms of greenhouse gas emissions avoided and energy bills reduced by $15 billion annually.

Making these goals a reality will require a programmatic focus on maintaining the strong value of the Energy Star label, assuring consistently high quality product data on energy efficiency, and maintaining a high level of transparency with the business community as the program moves forward with continuous improvement in the decade ahead. As the findings from Built to Last suggested, "good enough never is."

THE GREAT AMERICAN SEAT BELT SAGA:
A LOOK INTO THE MARRIAGE OF MARKETING AND LAW ENFORCEMENT

Has using seat belts become a way of life in the United States? Government reports say it has since the most recent data [6] from the National Highway Traffic Safety Administration (NHTSA) show that the use of seat belts by front seat passengers is at an all time high in the U.S.—82 percent in 2004 as compared to 71 percent in 2000, and 58 percent in 1994. Statistics from NHTSA (available at http://www.nhtsa.gov) also showed that in 2004, forty-nine states and the District of Columbia have safety belt use laws in effect, with New Hampshire as the exception. According to NHTSA, seat belts are believed to have saved 195,382 lives from 1975–2004, with 15,434 lives saved in 2004 alone. An estimated 7,472 lives were saved by child restraints from 1975–2004. Yet, a deeper look into the slow success of this public safety is one filled with controversy, conflict and ultimately, cooperation among some unlikely allies.

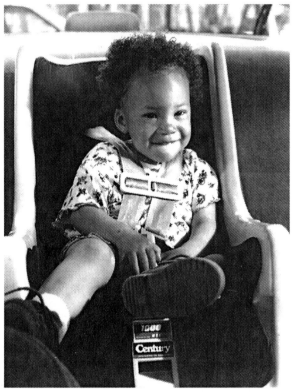

Source: U.S. Department of Transportation

Why Seat Belts?

The seat belt dates back to 1885 when New York inventor Edward J. Claghorn received the first U.S. patent for a safety-belt for tourists, described in the patent application as "designed to be applied to the person, and provided with hooks and other attachments for securing the person to a fixed object" [7]. Since Claghorn's invention first appeared in automobiles around 1900, the design of seat belts and public perception of their use have changed. Cartoons spoofed the rough rides in early automobiles, but they didn't show that seat belts were being used to literally keep the passengers in their seats. In the 1920s, seat belts were added as protective devices in racecars. But it was not until the 1930s that modern advocacy on behalf of seat belts as lifesavers began when American physicians installed lap belts in their own cars and began lobbying auto manufacturers to provide seat belts in all passenger cars [8]. Twenty years later, the first factory-installed seatbelts appeared in the 1950 Nash Statesman and Ambassador models [9], and the Yellow Cab Company became the first fleet of American taxis to install seat belts [10]. Throughout the 1950s, seat belts began appearing in cars produced by Volvo, Ford, and Chrysler [9], although auto safety was not viewed as a priority by the auto industry or the government.

The 1960s brought new activism on the American scene— and with that came the highly visible efforts of legislators and consumer advocates like Ralph Nader who propelled seat belts and car safety into the public consciousness. In 1966, the passage of the Highway Safety Act and the National Traffic and Motor Vehicle Safety Act created the National Highway Safety Bureau (which later became the National Highway Traffic Safety Administration or NHTSA), and a tsunami of auto safety regulations, were designed to improve auto safety. The improved illumination of highways and new features in automobiles, such as headrests and the mandatory installation of seatbelts, were just a few of the improvement made for road safety. Since then, despite extensive research, which has proved that seat belts prevent injuries, save lives, and reduce the costs of highway accidents and lost productivity, convincing citizens to use seat belts has been an uphill battle. This has produced a Mecca of opportunities for those who work in marketing public programs.

Availability Does Not Equal Use

The concept of the seat belt goes right to the heart and soul of the need for marketing—government mandates and the mere availability of useful products, devices, or services do not assure public awareness or behavior change. In the late 1960s, advocates soon realized that they faced some monumental obstacles in changing the public's perception about seat belts. Some people believed that it was better to be thrown from an automobile than to risk being trapped by a seat belt and then burned or drowned after a car crash. There were researchers who suggested that wearing seat belts encouraged risky driving behavior because the drivers would be protected by the seat belts [9], although studies did not support this claim. And there were civil libertarians who argued that the decision to use seat belts was an individual decision that should not be forced on individual citizens by the harsh hand of government mandate.

What followed was a contentious period of debate in which public vs. private interests became the centerpiece of legislative battles. These battles pitted legislators and safety advocates against American auto manufacturers. Advocates and legislators came to view the advent of automatic restraints as the possible answer to increasing public use of seat belts, while auto manufacturers resisted because of costs. Court battles continued until 1984 when a compromise was reached with a proposed mandatory seat belt law that would shift the primary responsibility for safety from auto manufacturers to the public. The compromise was strengthened by the passage of child restraint laws, which had begun appearing on the legal scene in 1975 [7]. This was a time of reckoning for the American highway safety surveillance system, which grew in scope and complexity in the years ahead.

VINCE & LARRY — DUMMIES IN THEIR OWN TIME

The lessons learned in the great American seat belt saga include some early insights into the public marketplace. Vince and Larry, the Ad Council's crash dummies, are good examples. The Ad Council has been involved in highway safety since 1945, but in 1985, the group partnered with NHTSA in a national seat belt education program. Vince and Larry became the icons of the public service advertising campaign, which targeted general consumer awareness of the dangers of not wearing seat belts. Crash dummies, Vince and Larry, carried the campaign message—"You can learn a lot from a dummy.... Buckle your safety belt."

©1985 U.S. Department of Transportation

A retrospective on the Ad Council campaign (provided by the Advertising Educational Foundation (AEF) at (www.aef. com/exhibits/social_responsibility/ad_council/2434) shows how icons like Vince & Larry can meet an early demise when they land in the middle of public controversy. After Vince and Larry made their television debut, new commercial television ads for toy crash dummies, produced by a NJ toy company, sparked concern about possible public confusion about Vince and Larry's motives. Were Vince and Larry spokesmen for a good cause like wearing seat belts or were they pitchmen for toys? Uncertainty led to the demise of the two crash dummies from the airwaves. Five years later, Vince and Larry were officially retired and were replaced by "a new series of more realistic PSAs designed to target part-time seat belt users with the slogan, "Buckle Up Always." This new campaign illustrated a new segmentation of the target market for seat belt campaigns, the official demise of Vince and Larry, and the beginning of a new phase in the evolution of American seat belt campaigns.

VINCE AND LARRY—A SUCCESSFUL CRASH?

The AEF retrospective on the Vince and Larry campaign also provides an interesting case study about the challenge of assessing the impact of a public education campaign. Similar to The Heart Truth campaign, the Ad Council's Seat Belt Education campaign with Vince and Larry, measured their success by the amount of media exposure and industry awards received. In its first six years, the campaign garnered more than $337 million in donated media time and space, and a prestigious award from the New York chapter of the American Marketing Association. However, the evaluation appears to be less objective in the assessment of the campaign's impact on seat belt usage:

In the first six months of 1986, a DOT survey in 19 cities reported that 39% of drivers reported using their seat belts as opposed to 23% a year before. Overall, between 1982 and 1988, seat belt usage by all vehicle passengers nationwide increased from 11 to 47 percent. **While the campaign was not the only factor, it was definitely a significant one as statistics reported before the launch indicated that while 80% of Americans believed seat belts work, only 11% regularly used them.**

This illustrates one of the fundamental challenges in evaluating the impact of specific public programs with outcomes that are influenced by other factors. As NHTSA later learned, the best approach to assess program impact is a carefully controlled research design with pre and post campaign data collection. Thus, marketing specialists must use caution in taking direct credit for improvements, which may have resulted from a number of highway safety factors.

A HELPING HAND FROM CANADA

In 1984, seat belts were only being used by 14 percent of American drivers despite early public education campaigns. This reality stood in stark contrast to highway safety programs, which were developed and refined in Canada and a few areas in the United States such as Elmira, NY. These areas were reporting astounding success rates of 80–90 percent from new "selective traffic enforcement programs" (STEP), which combined public education, legislation, and strict law enforcement with waves of publicity [11].

The STEP approach, which had its roots in programs focused on reducing speeding and drinking while driving, includes three primary components: 1) intense data collection from a number of sources pre-campaign and throughout the entire campaign period; 2) strategic, high visibility publicity which warned the public about the high daily levels of enforcement throughout the campaign; and 3) regular media events to inform the public about the campaign's impact. In 1987, seat belt use increased in the United States to 42 percent after thirty-one states passed seat belt use laws. By 1989, there were mandatory seat belt laws in thirty-four states. In 1991, NHTSA launched "Operation Buckle Down," a two-year program based on the Canadian STEP model. The success of this experimental program showed that the most effective design for a seat belt initiative combines legislation, public education, and primary enforcement of the seat belt laws. Primary enforcement laws allow police to stop and ticket a driver who is not belted just like any other routine traffic violation, while secondary enforcement laws permit an officer to issue a citation only after the driver is stopped or cited for some other traffic offense. These laws zero in on one of the major challenges of the seat belt enforcement—the cover of darkness. According to Dr. James Nichols, former Director of the Federal Office of Research and Traffic Records and a seat-belt historian, there was simply no way to enforce seat belt use in the darkness without enforcement laws. The reality, said Nichols, was that "the problem didn't go away at night" and to counteract this required high visibility enforcement.

BUCKLE-UP... OR ELSE!

In 1997, President Bill Clinton issued Executive Order 13043, which put the presidential stamp of approval on a massive, national seat belt campaign that exemplifies the marketing marriage of public education and law enforcement. This order required all federal employees to use seat belts while on official business. It encouraged tribal governments to adopt and enforce seat belt policies. Federal contractors, subcontractors, and grantees were also encouraged to adopt and enforce on-the-job seat belt use policies and

programs. Federal agencies conducted widespread seat belt
education campaigns on the importance of using seat belts
and the consequences of not wearing them. Clinton encouraged primary enforcement of seat belts in national park
areas and on Defense installations, and instituted new Department of Transportation reporting requirements on seat
belt use rates, safety statistics, and agency programs, which
exemplified best practices in seatbelt campaigns. The goal
of the campaign was to increase seat belt use to 90 percent
by 2005.

The new national "Buckle Up" initiative was based on
a "four point plan" which could serve as a primer for those
who are designing federal marketing campaigns:

> The "Buckle-up" campaign was built on a central
> premise—using seat belts is an individual respon-
> sibility, but it is also "the responsibility of a great
> many to encourage, enact, enforce, and inform." The
> campaign's emphasis on public-private partnerships
> is similar to NHLBI's The Heart Truth campaign
> in its reality-based thinking and call for continued,
> cross-sector collective action. Highway safety had
> become an issue far too complex, too big, and too
> challenging for any single group to tackle. The Heart
> Truth and Buckle-up campaigns both illustrate that
> the federal government is an enabling role in which
> the government facilitates partnerships, provides
> guidelines and tools which can standardize the
> messaging of local campaign efforts, identifies and
> publicizes exemplary models and best practices in
> community service programming (such as "Click-It-
> or-Ticket'), and offers financial incentives for state
> and local program initiatives.

The experience of the "Buckle-up" initiative also illustrates a reality drawn from the past and relevant to the fu-

ture of public education programs. Success with a seat belt campaign would require more than marketing and public education. Simply making citizens aware of the personal benefits of using seat belts was not enough. To be successful, public education campaigns needed to be tied to legislation and strong, primary law enforcement. Thus, the campaign called for the enactment of primary seat belt laws and closing the gaps in child passenger safety laws for all children up to age sixteen. The campaign then linked the legislation to "active, high-visibility enforcement" as a means of increasing public compliance with buckling up. This included a number of techniques, such as safety checkpoints, child safety seat clinics, and police officers serving as role models and public advocates for seat belt use. Greater enforcement also had other benefits in terms of increased apprehension of criminals and greater recovery of stolen property. All of these efforts require massive public education efforts with community events, paid and public service media advertising, and promotional events to assure that all citizens knew about the benefits of using seat belts and the practical, personal consequences of not following the law.

A WINNING EXAMPLE

"Click-It-or-Ticket" is a clear winner on the seat belt campaign landscape. This national safety campaign is conveyed through a clear, catchy message focused on enforcement, not the health benefits of seat belts. Simply stated, state laws empower the primary enforcement of seat belt laws by police officers. To avoid traffic tickets and possible jail time, all motorists need to do is click their seat belt into place. North Carolina's "Click-It-or-Ticket" campaign, with NHTSA and all North Carolina law enforcement agencies as partners, has been cited as not only the first program of its kind in the United States, but also the most successful, ongoing state-wide, seat belt enforcement programs in the nation.

Modeled after the successful STEP program in Canada, the program began in 1993 with a blitz of television, radio, and print advertising about the state's new enforcement law and the legal consequences of not using seat belts. According to Don Nail, the public affairs representative for the North Carolina Governor's Highway Safety Program, having the state's primary seat belt enforcement law in place was a huge help in launching the "Click-It-or-Ticket" program. Nail cites that the support of the Governor, who sent word about the program from the top to the state's highway patrol, the aggressive media campaign designed to increase name recognition for the program, and the fact that the highway patrolmen were really serious about writing tickets are all factors that were critical in the program's success.

After two years, evaluation of the program showed that seat belt use rose from 65 percent to 83 percent in North Carolina. Fatal and serious injuries were reduced by 15 percent, and there was an estimated $100 million saving in health care related costs. In the early years of the North Carolina program, tickets were $25 but four years ago, the fees were raised to $75. This stiffer penalty, says Nail, has proven to be successful in further increasing North Carolina's rates of seat belt usage.

Source: U.S. National Highway and Traffic Safety Administration

Nine years later, NHTSA's evaluation of "Click-It-or-Ticket" programs reported that the ten states that implemented full-scale "Click-It-or-Ticket" campaigns had increased safety belt use overall by 8.6 percentage points, to 77.1 percent. The campaigns used paid and earned media in conjunction with high-visibility state-wide law enforcement for four weeks. In the states that used only the increased enforcement method, without publicizing the effort through paid media, seat belt use increased an average of only half a percentage point.

On its "Buckle Up America" online headquarters (www. buckleupamerica.org), NHTSA maintains a centralized

"Click-It-or-Ticket" toolbox for local agencies that are starting their state-wide campaigns. Planners can select ready-to-use or easily adapted fact sheets, news releases, banner ads, letters-to-the-editor, op-ed articles, television and radio spots, television billboards, posters, and proclamations. Like The Heart Truth campaign, this centralized toolbox approach serves the national and local interests by improving campaign partners' access to a variety of promotional materials, helping standardize the campaign messages, and also allowing flexibility in local programming. NHTSA also maintains "communication calendars" that provide details on the agency's year-round messaging strategy as well as new ideas for developing state programs.

One of the major lessons learned from campaigns like North Carolina's "Click-It-or-Ticket," and one of the key concepts from marketing, is the need to use "waves" of publicity to intermittently reinforce consumer behavior and sustain the campaign's momentum. Don Nail says that in the North Carolina program, they have always recognized that use of constant media is not effective, although law enforcement can continue to "keep the pressure on." North Carolina participates in NHTSA's annual seven-week "Click-It-or-Ticket" Memorial Day campaigns (www.buckleupamerica. org) in which state campaigns participate in a well-organized national research and demonstration project. Data on seat belt use are collected before and after media blitzes and increased law enforcement. Without carefully controlled research or carefully conducted follow-up research, it is difficult to identify specific cause-and-effect relationships between programming and improvement in seat belt use.

LOOKING TO THE FUTURE...

There seems to be little doubt that the most effective seat belt campaigns are hybrids that integrate the critical components of education, legislation, and primary law enforcement with sophisticated data collection and use of public service and paid media. A 2001 Harvard University study [12] demonstrated that that seatbelt usage increased an average of 11 percent after the passage of secondary enforcement seatbelt laws and 22 percent after the passage of primary enforcement laws. When states switched from secondary enforcement laws to primary enforcement laws, usage increased an average of 13 percent as fatalities decreased. In 2002, NHTSA's National Occupant Protection Use Survey also showed a differential impact of primary vs. secondary enforcement laws. Seat belt use in states with primary laws were at 80 percent, where as states without primary laws were at 69 percent.

As of April 2003, NHTSA reported that only eighteen states, Puerto Rico, and the District of Columbia had primary safety belt laws (Alabama, California, Connecticut, Georgia, Hawaii, Indiana, Iowa, Louisiana, Maryland, Michigan, New Jersey, New Mexico, New York, North Carolina, Oklahoma, Oregon, Texas, and Washington) with New Hampshire remaining as the only state that has no adult safety belt law. Use of seat belts varies across the United States with statistically similar rates in the South, West, and Midwest and lower rates in the Northeastern United States. Differences are thought to be related to the varied types of enforcement and public education programs and public attitudes.

The next chapter in the great American seat belt saga may be the era of market segmentation for targeting marketing efforts to riders of different ages and drivers of different types of vehicles. NHTSA is working on a new campaign—"Buckle up in your truck." North Carolina is focusing new programming on improving seat belt usage in rear seats. And the Ad Council is working to increase the use of restraints with children riding in booster seat and with "part time users"—those citizens who only use their seat belt intermittently.

Policy makers suggest that the American experience with seat belts is a real success story given the country's weak seat belt laws at the state level.

A FEW GOOD MEN:
THE MARKETING CHALLENGES OF MILITARY RECRUITING

John Paul Jones, generally considered the "father" of the U.S. Navy, was a Scottish merchant marine who sailed the sea as a boy, fled England as a fugitive after killing a mutinous crew in the West Indies, and gained international fame as a victorious commissioned officer in the Continental Navy [13]. With recruitment of Continental soldiers underway for a year, historical records [14] suggest that even in 1777, Jones clearly understood the challenges of recruiting men to serve their country in circumstances that were typically stressful, unhealthy and often deadly. Jones also knew the of the difficulty in recruiting 140 men for a cold, difficult November voyage on his sloop, the Ranger, to France and the battle with the British Royal Navy that waited there.

In what is now believed to be one of the earliest military recruiting advertisements [15], Jones showed a flair for flamboyant public relations as he distributed posters all over New England. Referring to the "glorious cause" of the country, the posters issued an invitation to "any gentleman volunteers who have a mind to take an agreeable voyage in this pleasant season of the year." There were offers of "great encouragement," the opportunity for sailors to see the world, and promises of cordial treatment, kind entertainment, good pay, and potential prize money. Jones successfully lobbied U.S. President John Hancock and the Congress for financial incentives for the prospective sailors and then placed the following notice in The Freeman's Journal in Portsmouth, NH on July 26, 1777:

Whereas the seamen of these States have for some time past been discouraged from entering into the navy, by thinking they have hitherto been unfairly dealt with in respect of prize money, and the regular

payment of wages: Therefore, to remove all cause of
future complaint, I will be answerable to every person who may enter to serve under my command, for
the punctual and regular payment of wages. And I
will also, with the consent and approbation of officers and men, appoint an agent for the prizes, whose
duty it shall be to see the captors part sold to the
best advantage, and to make punctual, just and regular payments to every person concerne'd.

Every seaman in the navy is entitled to eight dollars
per month wages, with an advance of forty dollars
at entry on board. Every marine or landsman is entitled to six dollars & two thirds per month wages,
with an advance of twenty dollars at entry on board.
Every private person, who may loose a limb or be
disabled in engagement, will receive two hundred
dollars smart money; if kill'd, his wife or family
will receive it. Every person, who may be disabled
in engagement, will receive half pay during life or
an allowance proportioned to the injury sustained.
The pay is extended to persons in captivity, provided
they return to the service as soon as possible [15].

Sources [14] suggest that the Ranger's crew of 140 and six
officers that finally sailed with John Paul Jones in 1778 was
paid a total of $713; Jones paid $542 to recruit them. This
colonial price tag for military recruitment would become a
harbinger of today's military recruiting enterprise. Two
hundred years later, the U.S. Department of Defense is the
country's largest employer. Military recruiting has been called
one of the "most challenging human resources staffing operations conducted by any large-scale organization" [16]. Monthly recruitment goals [17] for all active duty services (Army, Navy,
Marine Corps, and Air Force) and reserve forces (Army National Guard, Army Reserve, Navy Reserve, Marine Corps

Reserve, Air National Guard, and Air Force Reserve) now exceed twenty-five thousand recruits per month. Armed with a combined military recruitment and advertising budget of $1.4 billion [18], and a well-stocked arsenal of marketing strategies, today's military recruiters face immense challenges as their search to find a few good men (and now women) continues. The combination of the massive scale of the military's recruiting goals, growing alternatives to military service, and eroding support for the war in Iraq, has created a tough recruiting environment—one that has forced recruiters to search for new techniques, new message channels, and a new spin on what John Paul Jones called the "glorious cause" of the country.

TARGETING THE "INFLUENCERS"

The launch of the Defense Department's "Today's Military" campaign [19] in 2003 is a powerful example of a marketing campaign's direct response to current social realities and their potential influence on a campaign's primary target group. In comments related to the Army's recent recruiting challenges, one Army General [20] suggested that the influential adult's negative perceptions of military service and that person's lack of information about the benefits of service were the greatest challenges facing Army recruiters who have needed to contact as many as one hundred young adults for every person willing to sit down and talk about the career possibilities offered by the Army. Another report on the parent problem in the New York Times states, "Two years into the war in Iraq, as the Army and Marines struggle to refill their ranks, parents have become boulders of opposition that recruiters cannot move" [21]. The article said that parents had grown increasingly concerned that their children might be killed in an unnecessary, unending war; that they resented the aggressive recruitment tactics used by the military recruiters; and that they were discouraging their children from considering the military as a career option.

In the military's new "make it a two-way conversation" campaign, which is part of the Joint Advertising Market Research and Studies program, the military clearly acknowledges the direct role of "influencers"—adults such as parents, relatives, teachers, guidance counselors, clergy, and coaches—who exert substantial personal power on a young person's decisions about their future and their potential enlistment in the military. And, the military tackles the issue head-on by offering a menu of educational resources that have been designed to help influencers and young adults avoid one-way conversations and prepare for the type of tough, stressful conversations that take place when a young person suggests the possibility of enlisting in the military.

So what's the Army's strategy for influencing the influencers? In addition to public service announcements and magazine ads in twenty-seven national publications, the "make it a two-way conversation" campaign provides online educational materials (available at www.todaysmilitary. com/app/tm/parent) that clearly reflect the Army's belief that more informed influencers will lead to greater encouragement for young adults who are thinking about enlisting in the military. Thus, each of the numerous links on the site contributes a different perspective on the lesser-known benefits of military service, such as:

Career options: To combat the perception that military jobs are limited in their scope and applicability to the civilian workforce, the site describes the fifteen job categories and forty-one hundred different job paths available for enlisted personnel and officers. The site emphasizes that military jobs are similar to many civilian jobs, and that those who exit the military are often considered highly qualified candidates for jobs in the private sector.

Path to education: To emphasize the practical benefits of military service, the site details the diverse educational options, tuition support, and educational assistance provided to members of the military.

Qualities for life: To reinforce the importance of developing character, the site provides real-life examples of role models who developed "qualities for a successful life" while serving in the military. These included focus, determination, total commitment, sense of mission, devotion to duty, and unselfishness.

Myths vs. realities: In an effort to bust the typical myths associated with military service, this section counters each of the main myths with facts about military service.

In addition, the site includes a self administered career inventory, detailed discussion guides that helps facilitate difficult discussions about military service, and links to additional resources.

Pitching with Pizza

It's no secret that the prolonged war in Iraq has created a challenging recruiting environment for military recruiters. During tough times, marketers often have to come up with their most creative strategies for reaching their target audience. Just ask the Army National Guard. In March 2005, the Guard was facing a significant short fall in its goal of recruiting sixty thousand new soldiers each year. This impending reality loomed large over the military, which has come to depend heavily on Guard members for frontline troop strength in Iraq. As suggested in Newsweek [22], the

Guard's lagging recruitment statistics reflected "a sobering reality for the entire military—the longer the war in Iraq drags on, the harder recruiters will have to work to keep the enlistment up" (p. 30). Identifying the causes of the shortfall (rising casualties and long tours of duty) was easy for the military recruiters, but the solution was not. Given the current realities of the war in Iraq, how could Guard recruiters breathe new life and renewed success into their recruiting campaign?

Source: United States National Guard

With the help of a bigger advertising budget, a ramped-up recruiting staff, and an enlarged pool of bonus cash, the Guard seems to have found the answer. Launch an eclectic, multi-faceted campaign, mix in new age Net promotion, hang out where your target group really is, not where you think their attention might be, add old traditional incentives like hard cash that have survived the test of time, and use unexpected channels to send your message with tempting aromas and appealing offers as well.

In 2002, the Army's monumental success in drawing more than a million to the Internet to play "America's Army"—its free computer game with high action rifles, obstacle courses, snipers, and parachute jumps—left no doubt that the Net represents a powerful cyber-age recruiting tool for the military [23]. Guard recruiters used a different spin on Net attraction in 2006 by drawing potential recruits to the Army National Guard online recruitment site by offering free iTunes downloads as an incentive. This strategy had real drawing power—over a year's time, two hundred thousand eighteen to twenty-five year olds responded to the offer, and from that group nine thousand eventually talked personally with a Guard recruiter.

Instead of spending advertising dollars on expensive magazine ads with questionable return on investment, the Guard recruiters went right to the source by setting up recruiting booths at recreational events frequented by large numbers of young adults—rodeos and NASCAR events. After the decision was made to use pizza as an unlikely promotional channel, small pizzerias throughout the country received free pizza boxes. Consumers ate pizza from boxes emblazoned with Guard recruitment slogans and reminders about tuition reimbursements offered by the military. And, to sweeten the campaign even further with additional financial incentives, the Guard added a number of new $1,000 recruitment bonuses. Newsweek [22] says the Guard's "pizza offensive" reflects "a trend in advertising—less Old Media, more Net, more niche."

Source: United States National Guard

The results? As the marketing world took note of the Guard's catchy campaign, Newsweek [22] reported that the Guard was "back on track.". Yet, below the radar screen, there's controversy smoldering within the military and in the court of public opinion. Were recent peaks in recruitment numbers truly a response to new recruitment strategies? Or, were the improved numbers a result of lowering standards such as waiving the high school requirement? As debate continues, marketers agree that the success of the Army National Guard's new recruitment campaign is a helpful reminder that new promotional channels may be just a meal away.

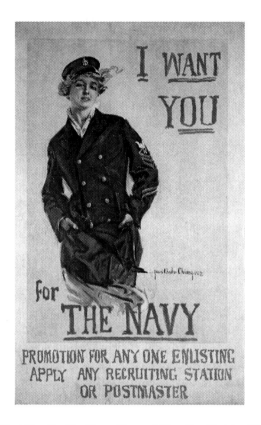

I Want You For The Navy. Howard Chandler Christy, 1917.
Source: Library of Congress

GETTING SMART

Can a marketing campaign, a catchy acronym, and real cash extend the reach of military recruiters by turning regular soldiers and civilians working on Army bases into successful military recruiters? The U.S. Army Recruiting Command (USAREC) is hoping that Operation SMART (Sergeant Major of the Army Recruiting Team) and its $1,000 referral bonus program will infuse Army recruiting with new energy and new recruits (available at www.usarec. army.mil/smart). Based on provisions set forth in the 2006

National Defense Authorization Act, Operation SMART
provides lump-sum bonuses to soldiers who refer a potential
soldier that visits an Army recruiter, and then enlists in the
active Army, Army National Guard, or the Army Reserves.
Early reports [24] suggest that the SMART program was off
to a good start with soldiers cashing in on their new role as
recruiter, the financial boost, and the official recognition of
their help finding recruits in tough times.

RETURNING TO PATRIOTIC VALUES

In his 1777 sales pitch, John Paul Jones offered would-be
sailors a double-track, recruitment "package." On one hand,
Jones referred to the "glorious cause" of the country as a motivation to serve in military service. According to a National
Research Council report on youth and military recruiting
[16], one approach to military recruiting involves emphasizing patriotic values and obligations such as "duty to protect
the country, self-sacrifice to maintain a free society, and the
noble virtues of an effective military service." In contrast,
Jones also linked service on the Ranger with more personal
benefits that could be realized by military service but were
not exclusive to it. These included such tangible benefits of
service such as seeing the world and being well paid.

Since the U.S. Army began recruiting soldiers for the Revolutionary War in 1776, two centuries of military recruiting
campaigns have utilized both approaches—the powerful imagery of patriotic duty in concert with the personal benefits
to be gained from military service. Analyses of recruiting
strategies over time [16] have shown that environmental factors such as war, the size of the youth population, the extent
and focus of media coverage, and employment trends, influence the imagery of military recruiting campaigns and their
ultimate success in meeting recruitment goals. The surge in
patriotism and military enlistment that occurred after September 11, 2001, is a prime example of values-based recruit-

ing. In the challenging recruiting environment of today's Iraq war, the pendulum seems to have swung toward the benefits side with large enlistment bonuses and an intense focus on educational benefits.

Recruiters who work on the streets of New York think the pendulum may have swung too far. In a 2005 report from the Times Plaza Recruiting Station in downtown Brooklyn, Army recruiters reported 12–14 hour work days, lots of competition from plentiful civilian jobs, mounting concern about the Iraq war, a large high school drop-out rate, and a "lukewarm" response from the community to ramped-up military marketing efforts [25]. Lots of hype and creative marketing events such as hosting basketball tournaments and blasting hip-hop music out of a Humvee didn't help the recruiters, who failed repeatedly in 2005 to reach their goals for both active duty and reserve soldiers.

The recruiters agree with military decision makers who believe that influencers have become a stumbling block in the recruiting process because they fear for their loved one's safety. Although deployment to a war zone is a possibility, it isn't a guaranteed outcome, the recruiters emphasize. They increasingly rely on telling their own personal stories about military service, and they are rejecting the idea of "selling" military service by primarily pitching tangible, material benefits. The recruiters believe that these sales pitches eventually lead to disillusionment among the new recruits. The alternative is "a whole new approach to recruiting"—promoting the classic Army values "attributes such as loyalty, duty, selfless service, honor, integrity, and personal courage." The NY recruiters have seen that this values-laden message resonates with potential recruits who like "the idea of values, traditions and service to country" [25]. This recent experience suggests that old-fashioned values may not be old after all.

Bringing Tattoos to the Rendezvous

Survey today's military recruiting landscape and it's easy to see that the American military recruiting enterprise is running on 24/7 alert for new recruits. Recent policy changes in the Army have been a help in bringing a larger potential pool of recruits into the rendezvous or recruiting stations. In January 2006, the Army announced [26] that it had raised the maximum enlistment age from 35 to 40 years, and had doubled the cash enlistment bonuses—up to $40,000 for the active Army and $20,000 for the Army Reserve. As a sign of the times in which an increasing number of young adults are sporting "skin art," the Army has also changed it policy on welcoming prospective recruits who have tattoos. According to a March 15, 2006, press release [27], tattoos that are "not extremist, indecent, sexist, or racist are permitted on the hands and neck."

Tattoos on the head and face are prohibited, although female recruits are allowed to wear permanent eye liner, eyebrows, or lip-liner. The policy allows recruits to have a tattoo that is in good taste on the neck below an "imaginary line straight down and back of the jawbone." These changes in the Army's inclusion criteria are a clear attempt to "bolster recruitment of highly qualified individuals who might otherwise have been excluded from joining." In marketing lingo, this means widening the target group and looking to tattoos for some help.

Moving into New Space

But for military recruiters, the big question remains—will a wider potential pool of recruits and the increasing sophistication of military recruiting campaigns be enough to meet the current demands? Because the U.S. Marine Corps can't be sure, the Marines have recently taken a big leap into the new, controversial territory of new media such as MySpace.com, reported [28] to be a "sort of a cyber combination of a yearbook, personal diary, and social club" for more than 94 million members.

The Marines are entering this new world at an interesting time [29]. As one of the fastest growing websites in the country, MySpace has garnered lots of media attention as the hot new place for cyber-savvy young people to connect and make friends. But growing concern about the privacy and personal risks associated with social networking sites has tempered the military's embrace of MySpace. In response to the investigative efforts of NBC's "Dateline" [28], which exposed MySpace as a possible hunting ground for sexual predators, the U.S. Army withdrew its ads on MySpace.

Assurances about the revamped safety protections within MySpace have apparently convinced the Marines that the space has real potential as a hunting ground for few good men. And, so far, about twelve thousand digital natives have signed up as friends of the Marines on MySpace, and over four hundred of these have requested time to meet with a recruiter. Critics [29] point out that "the Iraq war has forced the military to search 'under every bush' for recruits." But, in this era of new media, those bushes are planted firmly in the soil of cyber space. The bottom line—the Marines, the Army, and the Air Force have been forced to start plowing some new ground.

Part Four:
Planning Your Campaign

So the easy part is over. You've thought of your next campaign or project idea. Now all that's left is to get started. The 16 worksheets in this section are the perfect tools to help you give life to your campaign. These worksheets will help you create and execute a plan for your next public campaign. Whether you are creating a brochure or planning a multi-year national effort, having a foundation can help steer your activities. You can download a copy of the actual worksheets at www.trackg.com/trackworksheets.pdf. The following information in this chapter helps explain each of the worksheets. Whether you use all sixteen worksheets, or just a few, they are designed to guide and assist you through the whole process of a campaign- from planning to evaluation. They are designed to help you identify and manage all the parts that make a successful project- from a simple brochure to a complex campaign with multiple stakeholders. The worksheets are living documents for government use, and can be modified and adjusted to suit your needs. You can make alterations, duplications and deletions as you see fit. The worksheets break down the actions to take and the questions you should ask yourself before, during, and after a campaign that will help you stay on TRACK.

Worksheet 1 gives you an easy, practical framework to start thinking in depth about the message you are trying to convey. It asks you to consider the 6Ps- Product, Price, Place, Promotion, Partnership, and Policy.

Worksheet 2 covers the SWOT (Strengths, Weaknesses, Opportunities, Threats) Analysis Grid, which is an analytical tool that will help you assess the marketing environment that may impact your message.

So what do you want to accomplish? What are your agency's objectives? **Worksheet 3** will help you figure out how to align your agency's goal to the goals of your campaign.

Do demographics really matter? In marketing, absolutely! **Worksheet 4** will help you ask the why, who and how questions.

You've discovered who your target audience is. Now you need to develop a campaign that will resonate with their needs. **Worksheet 5** will help you figure out what stimulates and appeals to your target audience's needs.

How will you craft your message so that it will appeal to your target audience? **Worksheet 6** will help you decide what is right for your audience.

Now it's time to take action. **Worksheet 7** will help you develop a campaign that will incite your audience.

Wait! There are other competitors? Yes. And because you must consider the competition, **Worksheet 8** provides ways to help you analyze, compare and contrast competing actions.

Besides competitors, there are other barriers you must consider. **Worksheet 9** will help you identify factors that will make it easier for your audience to take advantage of your marketing efforts.

Worksheet 10 asks you a couple of questions that will help you begin planning and designing an evaluation plan for your campaign or project.

Now you need direction. **Worksheet 11** will help you create a research plan that will answer some critical questions, which will direct you to a successful program.

Worksheet 12 will help you think of different channels you will use in order to reach out and connect with your audience.

After you begin your campaign, there are a number of things you should consider. **Worksheet 13** provides four areas- funding, staffing, training, and technology- that will help you prepare some major details when your audience begins to respond to your marketing efforts.

Developing partnerships is important in helping you "extend the reach and impact of a public program". **Worksheet 14** lists potential partners to help you reach that goal.

Worksheet 15 helps you identify strategies in keeping the momentum of your campaign moving forward. These will help you answer the question, "How can I keep the excitement and the interest in my campaign?"

Worksheet 16 helps you measure the success of your campaign. It allows you to identify what needs to be changed and what had a good impact in conveying the message in your campaign.

WORKSHEET 1: THE SIX PS

In this first section, the TRACK method gives you an easy, practical framework to start thinking in depth about your issue or message. Here are the six Ps and a description of each:

Product: What's the "product" at the heart or center of your message? This is an essential first step in campaign development because if you are not clear about your product, the messages you create will be fuzzy and unclear as well. A product can take a number of forms. If the campaign was related to reducing blood cholesterol, for example, it could be knowledge (of the cholesterol content of foods); an attitude (such as believing that research has proven that cholesterol lowering is beneficial); or a behavior (such as actually reducing the cholesterol intake of one's diet).

Price: This includes the price (in monetary and non-monetary measures) of getting involved in the issue. To return to our example of lowering cholesterol as a means of preventing heart disease, the price in this case may include the actual cost of eating healthier, non-processed foods and more fresh fruits and vegetables. The price may also include the time it takes to prepare healthy food versus purchasing less healthy fast food.

Place: This places the issue in some location within the community. With cholesterol awareness, this involves grocery stores, restaurants, hospitals, physicians, and the entire health care system.

Promotion: With this "P," you will identify the possible communication channels or vehicle which can be used to create a higher level of awareness about the issue. The National Cholesterol Education Program utilized a multitude of multi-media channels to communicate the new guidelines for cholesterol management in the United States.

Partnership: It's important to identify potential partners in the issue because partnership can increase the reach of the campaign, tap the available expertise in the community, and stretch the program budget. With the example of cholesterol awareness, the federal agencies responsible for the program built an extensive network of partnerships with organizations such as the American Heart Association and a number of food producers.

Policy: There is no issue or message that exists outside of the rule of law or the governance by federal policy. Thus, you must think through what laws or policies affect your target issue and what changes will need to be made. With cholesterol awareness, much policy work was needed to update and refine the food labeling laws in the United States.

Before proceeding to the next step, ask yourself: *Have I considered each of the six Ps?*

WORKSHEET 2: SWOT ANALYSIS GRID

Now that you've looked at your issue through the lens of the six Ps, you can continue analyzing the marketing environment that can affect your message or issue. This worksheet gives you a framework—the S (strengths), W (weakness), O(opportunities), T(threats) grid—which is a well-established analytic tool for assessment of the marketing environment. Using seat belt use in trucks as an example, the following four sections ask you to identify factors in each of the four areas that you will consider as you actually design your campaign:

Strengths: There's plenty of research that shows that use of seat belts saves lives. Seat belt campaigns are well established and they are linked to law enforcement in most states. Truck manufacturers are supportive of seat belt campaigns.

Weaknesses: Seat belt use in trucks conflicts with the freewheeling culture of truck driving in some areas.

Opportunity: A new seat belt campaign directed specifically at truck drivers would provide a new "spin" on seat belt campaigns: "Buckle up in your truck."

Threats: The impact of seat belt campaigns such as "Click-It-or-Ticket" may be weaker than in the past because the campaigns are so well established.

When you have completed your SWOT analysis, ask yourself: *Have I identified all possible factors that may influence the environment in which I will launch a new campaign?*

WORKSHEET 3: AGENCY & PROGRAM OBJECTIVES
(TARGET)

The first step of the TRACK framework asks you to list your agency's and your program's objectives related to your issue. Think of it this way—this step is like "beginning with the end in mind." Why? Because all your program development activities related to your marketing campaign—from conception to implementation to evaluation—must first be aligned with your agency's strategic objectives related to the issue at hand. After all, your agency's objectives are the engine that is driving your work in marketing public programs. The agency's objectives spell out the results that are expected from the work of the agency. These objectives set forth the vision of what might be possible, and they clarify how the issue is related to the agency's mission to serve the public good. The objectives also provide critical direction for the journey's destination which lies ahead on the horizon—this helps to assure that your program does not become "sidetracked" by going down a side road or a path that might move the program too far away from the central mission.

The program objectives are equally important because these critical statements detail the linkage between the program and the mission of the sponsoring agency. These objectives can be written in a number of ways—as a public problem to be solved; as a statement of the program's desired results; as a hypothesis to be tested; or as questions to be answered. The program objectives also serve as critical guideposts for all the steps that will be involved as you develop your marketing campaign. They specify what citizens should know, feel, or do as a result of the campaign and the output or desired effects of the program's efforts, rather than the specific activities that you are planning to help them achieve those results.

So in this first step of the TARGET phase, your work is to focus on mission—the agency's and the program's. If you need help, take another look at the successes of public programs of the past. As a case in point, remember the clear and simple charge of the National Highway Safety Administration to make road travel safer and save lives. Revisit how the "Click-It-or-Ticket" campaign linked the use of seat belts to highway and personal safety. It's all about mission, and alignment of purpose and results.

So ask yourself at this point: *Have you clearly articulated the objectives of your program or campaign, and how those objectives align with your agency's objectives?*

Worksheet 4: Target Audience Demographics
(*Target*)

Why, who, and how... these are the small, but critical questions you will need to answer at this stage of the "Target" phase. In marketing, demographics really matter. Why? It's a simple answer—not all citizens are alike. Knowing your audience is critical in marketing because demographics—the vital and social statistics that define us—influence your audience's needs, interests, incentives, viewpoints, and ultimately, its lens on life. The distinctive differences among Americans can make a real difference in marketing campaigns because these differences directly affect if and how the members of a group will respond to a campaign. And, the response of the target audience is directly linked to the bottom-line success of your marketing efforts. Taking the time and effort to gather crucial statistical information about target groups is important in all marketing programs. But for those who market public programs, knowing your audience is critical. It helps you avoid the time and effort involved in sending inappropriate information to a particular group or the mistake of omitting information that is critical to another group. Knowing your audience helps you meet your obligation to use federal funds wisely and to leverage those funds for the greatest public good. It's a matter of fit—knowing your target group so well that the program fits well and sells itself.

Who is your audience? This might appear to be a simple question, but in reality, knowing your target audience requires that you devote careful thought and detailed research to identifying market segments. You will need to paint a detailed picture of your target audience, and this means identifying all the relevant statistics and characteristics of the group most likely to benefit from your marketing campaign. Depending on the campaign, you may focus your research on describing the typical, normal, or average person in the target group. This focus on the average person is a means of assuring the broad appeal of your campaign messages. Or, in other campaigns, you may be focusing on an atypical and narrower segment of the population with very specialized and more narrow needs and interests. Possible consumer demographics you may need include statistics, which describe characteristics of individuals such as age, gender, geography, marital status, education, occupation, income, children, home ownership, and health status; special skills, knowledge or attitude; or specific experience. Other demographics may be specific to businesses such as number of employees, industry, and revenue. Some statistics may be related to situations, while others may involve making a decision, as opposed to individual characteristics such as age. A good example of a decision-making scenario is the military's new campaign (available at www.todaysmilitary.com/app/tm/parent), which is designed for parents who are helping their children make a decision about enlisting in the military.

How do you identify the demographics of your target group? Collecting demographic information may require using a number of research techniques such as accessing relevant databases, talking with key informants, conducting interviews and focus groups.

All data collection methods, however, are driven by one key question: *Who is my target audience?*

WORKSHEET 5: UNDERSTAND YOUR AUDIENCE
(*RESONATE*)

In the previous step of the TRACK process, you worked to identify your target audience and describe that audience with a variety of vital and social statistics. But as we all know—numbers are only one part of the human story. In this second step of the TRACK formula, you will begin developing a campaign that resonates with your target audience. This means that the campaign relates to their needs and has the appeal that can stimulate the desired behaviors or actions.

The first part of this process involves getting to "know" members of your target audience by learning more about them and their current beliefs about a certain topic. You will do this by analyzing data on trends and conducting new research with members of the potential target audience. As you look at the group's current beliefs, important questions might include:

What is their current level of knowledge about the topic? This might include education, basic skills, and specialized training from the past.

How important is the issue to the target group? We know from adult learning theory that adult learners are practical—they seek out and resonate with information that they perceive as beneficial for their lives.

How do they talk about it? Analyzing a variety of editorial formats—such as blogs and editorials—can give you valuable insights into consumer views on a variety of current topics. Attitude surveys can also provide a helpful window into the attitudes of consumers and some of the emotional aspects of the topic.

Another important area is identifying and describing any consumers' misperceptions about the issue. A good example goes back to the country's early experience with promoting the use of seat belts. Surveys found that in those early years, many drivers erroneously believed that being restrained by a seat belt was deadly and that it was better to be thrown out of a car than to be trapped inside and injured by an explosion. In response, the early seat belt campaigns focused on correcting the misperception by teaching consumers about the dangers of driving without any seat belt restraint.

Finally, you need to identify what the consumer needs to know. In the case of seat belts, consumers needed to learn that the danger of driving without seat belts was far greater than driving with the seat belt. This and all other need-to-know information then becomes the core content of your marketing program. Because this information may be based on assumptions about the needs and beliefs of your target group, it may be helpful at this point to clarify the assumptions about the target group with a group of advisers before proceeding to the development phase.

At this point, ask yourself: *Is there any thing else I need to know about my audience?*

Worksheet 6: An Appeal That Resonates
(*Resonate*)

This step of the process involves the crafting of messages that will have real appeal for your target audience. At this stage you have already spent time reviewing the objectives of your agency and the program you're developing, researching, and identifying the demographics of your target audience, and understanding their knowledge, attitudes and beliefs, and any misperceptions they may have about the issue. Now, you roll up your sleeves and begin the artful crafting of the campaign messages that will resonate with your audience.

We say that this stage involves "artful crafting" because message development is really an art and not a science. Although we follow general design principles, there are still plenty of decisions to be made that require judgment and an intuitive sense of what is right for the audience. These decisions can be organized into three categories:

Style: Here is where you decide on your campaign's mark of distinction that sets your campaign apart from others. Are you portraying a slice of good ole' American life or a fantasy to a new enchanted land? Is the mood somber and alarming (like some AIDS campaigns or those for global warming) or cheerful and hopeful like some campaigns for recycling and clean water? Are you portraying a lifestyle choice that you wish your target audience to select, or is your focus on the science and technology? Will your message be anonymous or will it be carried by a famous celebrity who endorses the program?

Tone: The tone of your messages carries a distinctive sound that sets the stage for your messages. Like style, this characteristic must be appropriately matched to the content of your messages and the overall purpose of the campaign. Depending on the issues at hand, you can use a rational tone that clearly and authoritatively explains the "why" of the campaign or the issue. You can use humor to give an issue instant appeal and the ability to draw the target audience into the issue. Or you can strike a serious tone by crafting a more judgmental, critical, or moral tone.

Positioning: In this dimension you decide on the final element—the spin. Given the complexity involved in most issues that involve the public, you have choices about the direction of the message's spin. Will it be funny and easy to consume? Will you go for shock value instead by including shocking, graphic pictures, and testimonials? Will you appeal to the compassionate side of simply being human— the generous side—or perhaps the patriotic side?

Remember...the key message about crafting your appeal is—know your audience, know your mission. *From there, you can craft messages that are in sync.*

WORKSHEET 7: ACTION TO TAKE
(ACTION)

In this third phase of the TRACK method, you move from analysis and planning to incite your audience to take action. Think of it this way—you've laid a solid foundation for change, made a convincing appeal that resonates with members of the target group, and clarified why this issue is important to THEM. And you have done a smart job of crafting the campaign messages in ways that match the intent and the intended outcomes. But at this point, all marketing programs require that the consumer take some action.

Depending on the nature of the marketing campaign, these actions can be quite varied. Examples include calling a hotline, visiting a website, requesting more information by sending an e-mail, completing a baseline survey, learning about an issues and then taking a test, registering for either a class or a special event related to the campaign, providing feedback on the content and presentation of information presented on a campaign, volunteering to serve as a participant in a focus group or interview session, or completing an online dietary analysis.

One of the key points to remember about this "action-packed" phase is that successful change in behavior is typically achieved in small steps rather than large leaps. For example, a new campaign designed to increase exercise levels in sedentary individuals doesn't start by having them run a marathon! Instead, a smart campaign will build a solid case for the benefits of exercise and then encourage the target group to start walking—first for a short period of time and then for gradually longer periods.

Another key point of this action phase is the importance of designing campaign materials and instructions that are customer friendly and easy to understand and use. The US-DA's food pyramid is a good example of a public health campaign that needed some redesign work after initial feedback from consumers showed that the first version was far too complex for average citizens to understand.

Whatever the campaign, those who market public programs must be experts at leading others. *They do this through a series of small action steps that lead to positive consequences.*

Worksheet 8: Barriers - Competing Actions
(Action)

After you have identified the actions you wish members of your audience to take, you need to pause and consider the "competition." Why? Because behaviors do not exist in a vacuum in everyday life—there are typically a number of choices that compete directly with the desired action you are recommending. Identifying these competitors can help you design marketing programs that acknowledge the complexity of human behavior, the number of available choices, and the benefits and distinguishing characteristics of the recommended action.

This worksheet provides an outline that can help you frame your thinking about the competition. You will analyze, compare, and contrast the desired action and other competing actions through three different lenses or views.

For each action, it is important to begin by writing a clear, concise statement of the action and the actions that compete directly with it. Then for each action, discuss the following:

> **The "messenger(s)":** Who is the messenger? For anti-smoking programs, the messengers typically include advocates such as federal agencies like the National Heart Lung and Blood Institute, and non-profit organizations like the American Lung Association. These traditional sources of health messages have stiff competition, however, from the advertising and music world where characters that have appeal for young adults can be shown smoking cigarettes and being "cool."

Perceived benefits: In this section, you will explain all the direct and indirect benefits that the individual might realize from taking the specific action or from engaging in the competing action. This includes monetary and non-monetary benefits as well.

For example, stopping smoking has great immediate and long-term health benefits. In contrast, continuing to smoke has benefits as well, such as those associated with the pleasurable aspects of tobacco and nicotine, the potential social benefits from smoking, and for some, the weight control benefits.

Perceived costs: Since smoking is addictive, there are potential short-term costs to stopping in terms of irritability, agitation, weight gain, and the possible need for and cost of nicotine substitutes. These are also monetary benefits from the dollars saved from not buying cigarettes and other tobacco products and societal benefits gained from less air pollution. The costs of continuing to smoke include the high costs of tobacco products, advanced wrinkling of the skin, the eventual loss of productivity due to lung disease, lung cancer, and other complications that result from smoking.

So, in this section ask yourself: Who is my program's main competitor? *How can I address what my competitor is offering?*

WORKSHEET 9: ADDITIONAL BARRIERS
(ACTION)

Now that you have analyzed competing behaviors and messages, you need to do some more thinking. This involves putting yourself squarely in the shoes of your audience, and identifying any other potential barriers that might get in the way of their taking the steps you are recommending, and then figuring out how to overcome the barrier. This can include a variety of factors—big and small, perceived or real, physical, social or emotional—that might get in the way of new behaviors, such as:

Lack of information: Information is key to understanding and to behavior change. And in this fast-moving cyber age, it's difficult to keep up with all the information that's available to us. To address this barrier, you need to access relevant baseline data, which can show you the target group's starting point about a particular issue. From there, you can develop a plan to providing the right kind of information that can fill the gap between what the audience knows and what they need to know.

Lack of efficacy: This means simply believing that the required task is beyond one's control or ability. To address this, you can use testimonials from others who have mastered something new, and other success stories, such as someone who recovered from a heart attack and is now leading a full, active life.

Lack of tools to respond: This barrier might include not having access to a computer, speaking a language different from what is being offered, or not having the educational background to understand very complex material. As the program designer, your task is to identify these and to identify alternatives that can make accessing your program easier for more individuals. This involves assessing the language level of all your program materials, and assuring that they meet federal standards.

Lack of convenience: This is important because today, people lead very busy lives with many challenging demands on their time—both personally and professionally. Overcoming the inconvenience factor means making program information and activities available at times when average citizens can access them. This can mean making information available online and in other formats, offering exhibit hours that include evenings and weekends, and also building partnership with community groups that can facilitate outreach activities into neighborhoods and communities.

So, in this section—ask yourself: What might get in the way? *What can I do to make it easier for citizens to take advantage of public programs?*

WORKSHEET 10: PLANNING FOR EVALUATION
(TARGET, RESONATE, ACTION)

At this point, it is critical that you begin planning for how you will evaluate the success of your public program. There are two very important points to remember about evaluation. First, the most effective evaluations are those designed in the early stages of program planning, rather than the later stages. Why? Because evaluation requires establishing all the different types of data you will need to collect, and then having those systems in place before the program is implemented. Second, evaluation is especially important in designing public programs because you must demonstrate that you have used public funds wisely to achieve the goals of your agency. That requires ongoing, rigorous evaluation, which can show the impact of your work. Remember that e-valu-a-tion means to show the value of a program, product or activity, and to do what you will need to collect data in a precise way.

There are important questions that you need to answer as you design an evaluation plan:

What types of data are available as "baseline" data? Baseline data—or data that exist at the start of a program—are important because they represent the starting point of any change. Thus, baseline data are essential because you will measure progress from this starting point. Depending on the program, there will be many different types of data available for your use. These could include data related to consumer action such as hits to a website, requests for brochures, or calls to a toll-free hotline—or survey data that is related to knowledge and attitudes, which can be used as pre- and post-test measures.

How can you best evaluate how you are doing during a campaign? To design an effective evaluation, you will need to consider the baseline data that are available and any other data that could be collected. One way is to think about members of the target audience and what they experience after their first contact with the campaign. "Walking through" the steps of the campaign will give you ideas that can be captured as measures of success. Second, it is critical for you to identify the best type of data to collect—the data that can actually show the value of your work. Third, at this point, it is helpful to remind yourself of the purpose of the campaign or program. For example, in the campaign designed to increase the number of citizens who are receiving treatment for high cholesterol levels, evaluation measures should include not only cholesterol testing but also data on follow-up care with a physician. In this case, screening is important but it is the actual care of the individual that is the most important goal.

In this section, ask yourself: *How will I demonstrate the value of my program?*

WORKSHEET 11: RESEARCH PLAN
(*TARGET, RESONATE, ACTION*)

In this section you will assemble all your questions into a research plan that will give you direction and critical answers that pave the way for your program's success. In your research plan, there are three areas of focus: resources, partners, and research methods.

Resources: This is an important area because you certainly want to be able to utilize existing resources rather than "re-inventing the wheel." One of the logical places to look for information is past campaigns. To do this, you need to take a look at archives of previous public campaigns. Look at the successful campaigns that are similar to the one you are designing. Or, read published articles about that campaign. What worked? What didn't? What was unique about the campaign messages or the communication vehicles? Were there any surprises? What were the lessons learned? After becoming familiar with the campaigns, don't forget to access one of your most important resources—your colleagues. Tapping the expertise of government colleagues makes good sense because you can share information—and it saves time and effort.

External Partners: Studying the archives and networking with colleagues who develop public programs are invaluable steps in developing your research plan. But it's also important not to forget your program partners. In these days where collaboration and partnerships are so common, your partners who are not part of the federal government are great resources as well. Why? Because, like your agency, your partners have years of experience, records, and data that they may be willing to share with you. By tapping into these resources, you may find a goldmine of data that you may need.

Research methods: As you search for information, you will be able to use a number of research methods that can help you obtain the critical data you need. The Internet can be a good starting point, although you need to be careful to check on the authenticity of all sources. You may need to search professional databases that contain all the relevant literature published on your subject. There may be existing surveys which might be helpful, or you may need to conduct your own, although this can be costly and time consuming. Focus groups and interviews are other possibilities that you can use if you need to explore a subject in a different direction or depth. The most important thing to remember about research methods is that the reliability of your findings will be enhanced if you use multiple sources of data.

Questions to ask yourself about your research plan: *Have I explored all internal and external resources? Have I chosen the right research methods? Have I checked the accuracy of my information with multiple sources?*

WORKSHEET 12: CONNECT WITH YOUR AUDIENCE
(CONNECT)

You have clarified your objectives, identified your target audience, accessed the archives of past campaigns, networked with colleagues, and developed a rigorous evaluation plan. Now it's time to think about connecting with your target audience. Connecting involves reaching out through multiple channels that you have strategically identified as the best routes to your target group and using the appropriate tactics and methods to leverage these for maximum impact.

Think about the following:

Advertising: Depending on your budget, you can place ads in magazines that are matched to your audience's profile. Or, you can place public service announcements on television channels and radio stations. Research may be required to study audience profiles or subscriber data. The two keys to using advertising successfully are proper placement; making sure that the vehicle you use, be it TV or radio, has the potential to reach large numbers of your target group; and crafting your advertisement creatively and smartly so that your message resonates with the target group.

Public relations: Even in this age of the Internet, newspapers and press releases are traditional routes that are used to spread the news about new public programs. As with advertising, the timing of notices in the newspaper, the content, and the exact location of the placement, for example, can make a real difference. Press releases are increasingly being distributed through online, mass distribution systems.

Print media: The Internet has not done away with the print media as a popular communication vehicle. This might include colorful, informative brochures placed in high traffic areas, or posters that can appear in transportation vehicles or community buildings.

Promotional items: These are popular with groups because they are practical or fun and are typically provided free of charge. The choices available today are endless, such as key rings, t-shirts, hats, mascots, carrying cases, water bottles, pens, bottle openers, bumper stickers, and coffee mugs.

Signage/displays: Large roadside signs and exhibit signs can also reach out to many people at high traffic locations either indoors or outdoors.

Personal selling: Since high touch is desirable in our high-tech world, don't forget the power of personally connecting with your target audience. By attending relevant meetings and seminars, you can share your knowledge and your passion for your subject and inspire others to take action.

Pop media: Since public programs serve the entire public, it's important not to forget accessing the public through pop culture. This could involve popular songs, comedians, celebrities, or even the comics.

World Wide Web: For public campaigns to survive and be successful, they must be cyber savvy. This means using the web and weblogs to full advantage through search engine optimization. This will help spread your campaign's message to greater numbers of people.

At the end of this section ask yourself: *Have I reached out to my target group in the most strategic way? Have I activated every possible channel that can carry our campaign message?*

Worksheet 13: Prepare for Connections (Connect)

Identifying the channels through which you will connect with your target audience is the first step in this connect phase. After you have made the crucial decisions about the channels, you need to get busy preparing for the interactions that will occur after you begin your campaign.

Generally, there are four major areas you need to consider:

Funding: Conducting a campaign with extensive public outreach is expensive. There are design and printing costs, as well as a host of costs related to the required staffing. All of the costs must be detailed in your project budget so that additional funding can be requested and received prior to the beginning of the campaign.

Staffing: This is an important category because all campaigns require hands-on staff who keep the operations of the campaign running. The nature of campaign and the varied staffing requirements often dictate that some of the staffing be hired from temporary agencies or from the pool of part-time contract workers or volunteers. Prior to recruiting these staffers, you will need to define the core skills and knowledge required to handle the tasks. It is also important to write a staffing plan so that all tasks are delegated to specific employees or groups of employees. This might include responding to telephone inquiries, opening mail requests for more information, or staffing an exhibit at a community meeting.

Training: A critical aspect of this stage is providing training for all staff. This is important for several reasons. First, all staff need to understand the rationale and details of the campaign so they can answer consumer questions in a consistent manner. Second, the staff must be trained in performing skills that are unique to the campaign. This might include knowing how to complete a particular data collection form or using an online scheduling system. The staff also needs to be cross-trained in a number of different functions so that the campaign operation can continue smoothly through staff rotations.

Technology: Given the important role that technology plays in communications, it is wise to enlist the assistance of a technology expert in assessing your technology capability. Special equipment and telephone lines may be required, and this takes time and funding. For example, if you are planning to run public service announcements with a toll-free number, you need to be sure that your system can handle a high call volume. In the campaign about women and heart disease with the "Golden Girls," this was critical because there were times when more than six thousand calls came into the system in one day.

As you prepare for making connections with consumers, ask yourself: Have I thought of all the details that must be ready when the audience responds to our calls for action?

WORKSHEET 14: PARTNERSHIPS
(KEEP)

In this final stage of the TRACK process, you will focus your attention of developing and nurturing a variety of partnerships that can help you extend the reach and impact of a public program. For each potential partner, you will need to consider reciprocity—or what each partner brings to the relationship and what they can expect to gain. These benefits may be quite different depending on the nature of the organization. Consider these possibilities:

Other federal agencies: It's always wise to start with your federal colleagues who may have similar interests and experiences. The advantage here is that everyone involved will more likely be familiar with federal regulations, guidelines, and procedures.

Non-profit organizations: These organizations may share a common bond with your program or campaign because they are usually driven by a cause-related mission vs. one that is focused exclusively on profits, such as those in the private sector. These organizations are also interested in cost-sharing arrangements that can help them do more with less.

Health clinics: These types of health facilities are interested in partnerships because they are constantly seeking new ways to motivate healthy behavior.

Foundations: Like non-profits, foundations make good partners because they too are motivated by work devoted to important public causes.

Manufacturers/vendors: Both of these depend on partnerships with other groups that can offer them access to a population in exchange for reduced or no-cost supplies or devices.

Unions: Unions have a special interest in partnering with good causes because maintaining the health of their members is important to their survival and their budgets.

Schools: Like health centers, schools seek partnerships because they are in constant need of new materials. They can offer access to large groups of students and parents.

Religious organizations: In today's society, religious organizations have become increasingly interested in programs that minister to their members' health, as well as their faith.

Community groups: The vast number of community-based organizations provides a wealth of partnership opportunities of all kinds. Sharing costs and resources for the benefit of everyone is appealing to these groups because they may be operating under strict budgets.

Media: One of the ways in which the local media are viewed is their commitment to partnering with worthy organizations. Thus, partnerships can help to position the media as concerned about community causes and not simply profit.

When building partnerships ask yourself: *Have I considered every possible group that might have an interest in joining forces with us?*

WORKSHEET 15: KEEPING MOMENTUM
(KEEP)

Yes it's exciting when a new campaign begins—there's plenty to learn, people to meet, ideas to make a reality. But what will you do to keep the momentum of your campaign? How can you keep the excitement and the interest in your campaign? In this section, there are three areas for you to consider as you identify strategies for each:

Moving the momentum forward: One of the most powerful strategies for sustaining momentum is to be sure that you are publicizing real results at periodic intervals. Whether by using evaluation data or personal stories and testimonials, results can serve as part inspiration and part motivation for individuals and for groups. While pre-campaign publicity is important, real results sell the story of the campaign. They encourage others to take a chance on trying new behaviors. Another helpful strategy is the use of contracts or commitments that specify in writing, an individual's willingness to state their goal in terms of behaviors and to meet it within a prescribed time period.

Keeping the audience's attention: Keeping the campaign on your audience's radar screen requires ongoing communication and an extra burst of creativity. To avoid the "out of sight, out of mind" phenomenon, you may need to create a system of reminders that are sent out periodically. You may create activities that highlight those who have realized a goal or who have given extra effort to the campaign. Retention efforts keep the campaign in your audience's awareness, and they give you the freedom to create some new and different ways of communicating.

Sustaining behavior: After the anticipated behavioral change has occurred, it is important to provide reinforcement, which can be a periodic boost to morale, motivation, and maintenance of the change. This is critical because behavioral change requires reinforcement to continue. Without this, behavior can slowly slip back to the original state. Specific strategies related to sustaining behaviors include creating reminder gifts, recognition awards, and other types of motivational items.

At this stage stop and ask yourself: *Have I paid enough attention to designing strategies that can keep the momentum of the campaign moving forward?*

WORKSHEET 16: MEASUREMENT
(KEEP)

When all is said and done, the designers of public programs or campaigns come to a critical point at which they are held accountable for the "success" of a campaign or program. At this point, there are important questions to be answered about how the campaign was implemented and the impact of the campaign on the identified action or change. This evaluation approach looks at the sum total of all the program activities and assesses both change indicators and process measures:

Change indicators: As discussed briefly in an earlier section, all public programs begin with needs, objectives and clearly identified indicators that can demonstrate change. These indicators can include a variety of different types of campaign responses (telephone calls, requests for information, participation in events); changes in the intent of individuals to make a specified change, such as exercising more or eating healthier foods; changes in knowledge, attitudes, beliefs, or habits; and changes in the actual behaviors. Sometimes these indicators are referred to as outcomes or outcome measures.

Process measures: Sometimes referred to as process evaluation, this involves analyzing and evaluating the effectiveness of the program or campaign's implementation. In contrast to the change indicators, this involves assessing the internal effectiveness of the program in moving from design concept to implementation. The actual measures vary by the type of program, but in general, these may include: adherence to the implementation timetable, changes in policy, exposure in the media, amount of materials distributed, and the extent of external contributions.

The questions to ask yourself at this final step are: *Have we done an efficient job in implementing the program and have we made a difference that will benefit society?*

TIME TO BEGIN YOUR CAMPAIGN: NEXT STEPS

We hope that we've provided an inspirational review of the history of marketing public programs and given you some new insights that you can apply to your specific campaigns. We truly believe that the government does many things right every day and often does not receive credit for many of these accomplishments. You believe passionately about the work of your agency and by applying many of the principles covered in this book, it is our hope that the public will have a better understanding of what your agency does every day, as well as a better understanding of their role as an active citizen who can create change in society.

As a resource, we'd like to offer our website (www.marketingpublicprograms.org) where you can do the following:

Sign up for courses where you can meet your peers and learn more about marketing public programs.

Search 100's of campaigns to get ideas.

Watch videos of your peers who share their experiences. Some of the people interviewed for this book appear in the videos and this can provide you with more inspiration for tackling your campaign.

Download copies of the worksheets to assist you in planning your campaign.

Please contact us at anytime to speak about your specific challenges and how we might be able to provide some assistance.

We offer a free no-obligation consultation to any federal employee involved in outreach, communication, or public affairs. We'd love to hear from you and we wish you much success in marketing your public program.

David Ehrlich
Alan Minton,
Co-founders, The Track Group and
The Track Center for Marketing Public Programs

www.trackg.com
www.marketingpublicprograms.org

END NOTES

PART ONE: *THE ROOTS OF MARKETING PUBLIC PROGRAMS*

Roots

4. Cutlip, S.M. & Center, A.H. (1978). Effective public relations. Englewood Cliffs, NJ: Prentice-Hall, Inc.

5. Quail, R. Theodore Roosevelt, the conservationist. Accessed June 15, 2006 at: http://www.esf.edu/resorg/rooseveltwildlife/Roosevelt.htm

6. Jones, V. C. (1971). Roosevelt's Rough Riders. Garden City, NY: Doubleday & Company.

7. The White House Historical Association. The President and the Power to Conserve the American Frontier. Accessed on June 14, 2006 at: http://www.whitehousehistory.org/04/subs/images_subs/primary_1906.pdf

8. Theodore Roosevelt – conservationist. Accesses on June 14, 2006 at: http://en.wikipedia.org/wiki/Conference_of_Governors

9. US Fish & Wildlife Service. America's national wildlife refuge system: A century of conservation. Accessed on June 20, 2006 at: http://fws.gov-midwest-Refuges-documents0chronology,pdf.url

10. Fuller, D. Theodore Roosevelt - Conservation as the guardian of democracy. Accessed on June 14, 2006 at: http://pantheon.cis.yale.edu/~thomast/essays/filler/filler.html

11. Roosevelt, Teddy - quotes. Accessed on June 19, 2006 at: http://kenfran.tripod.com/teddy.htm

Creel Committee

12. Baltimore's two hundredth anniversary – Theodore Roosevelt during Liberty Loan Drive – 19818. Accessed on June 23, 2006 at: http://www.hellobaltimore.com/History.Cfm

13. President Woodrow Wilson's War Message. Accessed on June 30, 2006 at: http://www.lib.byu.edu/~rdh/wwi/1917/wilswarm.html

14. Source watch. The committee on public information. Accessed on June 23, 2006 at: http://www.sourcewatch.org/index.php?title=Committee_on_Public_Information

15. Creel G. (1920). How We Advertised America. New York: Harper & Brothers.

16. Hanc. G. (2001, December 5) Rallying the public: A look back at government efforts to 'spin' a war. Newsday, p.B-03

17. Library of Congress. American treasures of the Library of Congress – The most famous poster. Accessed on June 30, 2006 at: http://www.loc.gov/exhibits/treasures/trm015.html

18. New York Times, February 1, 1920, p. 9

19. Creel G (1922, September) The battle in the air lanes. Popular Radio, pp. 3-10.

20. Mock, J.O. & Larson, C. (1939). Words that won the war. Princeton, NJ: Princeton University Press.

21. Cutlip, S.M. & Center, A.H. (1978). Effective public relations. Englewood Cliffs, NJ: Prentice-Hall, Inc.

22. DeCorte, T. The Red Scare In Nevada, 1919-1920. Accessed on June 24, 2006 at http://www.geocities.com/gvwrite/redscare.htm

Medicine versus morality

23. Weisberger, B.A. (2006, June/July). The persistence of the serpent – The emergence of AIDS has added new urgency to the work of an organization that turns eighty this year. American Heritage Magazine, 57 (3).

24. Commissioned Officers Association of the U.S. Public Health Service. The history of public health. Accessed on June 24, 2006 at: http://www.coausphs.org/phhistory2.cfm

25. Family Health International. Reproductive health. Accessed on June 29, 2006 at: http://www.fhi.org/en/RH/Pubs/Network/v16_3/nt1638.htm

26. Brandt, A. (1985). No Magic Bullet: A Social History of Venereal Disease in the United States since 1880. Oxford, England: Oxford University Press.

27. National Library of Medicine. Visual culture and public health posters. Accessed on June 24, 2006 at: http://www.nlm.nih.gov/exhibition/visualculture/venereal.html

28. National Library of Medicine. To your health. Accessed on June 24, 2006 at: http://www.nlm.nih.gov/hmd/pdf/health.pdf

Intermezzo

29. History of the Anti-Saloon League. Accessed on July 5, 2006 at: http://www.publichistory.org/reviews/View_Review.asp?DBID=84

30. The temperance movement. Accessed on July 5, 2006 at: http://www.u-s-history.com/pages/h1054.html

31. The Anti-Saloon League. Accessed on July 5, 2006 at: http://www.ohiohistorycentral.org/entry.php?rec=845

32. Jarmul, D. 'Roaring Twenties' a Time of Economic and Social Change. Accessed on July 5, 2006 at: http://www.voanews.com/specialenglish/2006-06-07-voa1.cfm

33. Al Capone. Accessed on July 6, 2006 at: http://www.chicagohs.org/history/capone.html

34. U.S. Constitution - Amendment XIX: Women's Suffrage - Right to Vote. Accessed on July 5, 2006 at: http://www.u-s-history.com/pages/h1097.html

35. Winslow, B. Sisters of Suffrage: British and American Women Fight for the Vote. Accessed on July 5, 2006 at: http://www.historynow.org/03_2006/historian5.html

36. Women's suffrage. Accessed on July 3, 2006 at: http://www.spartacus.schoolnet.co.uk/USAsuffrage.htm

37. National Museum of Women's History. Woman suffrage: A sophisticated political movement. Accessed on July 5, 2006 at: http://www.nmwh.org/exhibits/exhibit_frames.html

38. Freeman, J. (1995).From suffrage to women's liberation: Feminism in twentieth century America. In Women: A Feminist Perspective, Jo Freeman (ed.) Mountain View, CA: Mayfield 5th edition, pp. 509-28.

New Deal, New War

39. Franklin D. Roosevelt. Accessed on July 10, 2006 at: http://www.whitehouse.gov/history/presidents/fr32.html

40. The new deal. Accessed on July 9, 2006 at: http://en.wikipedia.org/wiki/New_Deal

41. The new deal and World War II. Accessed on July 12, 2006 at: http://usinfo.state.gov/products/pubs/histryotln/newdeal.htm

42. The new dealers. Accessed on July 11, 2006 at: http://www.digitalhistory.uh.edu/database/article_display.cfm?HHID=470

43. The National Recovery Administration. Accessed On July 9, 2006 at: http://www.digitalhistory.uh.edu/database/article_display.cfm?HHID=472

44. New Deal-era promo for the NRA (National Recovery Administration)... Accessed on July 14, 2006 at: http://www.archive.org/details/National1933

45. FDR's fireside chat on the purposes and foundations of the recovery program. Accessed on July 10, 2006 at: http://www.archives.gov/education/lessons/fdr-fireside

46. Mankowski, D. & Jose, R. Flashback: The 70th anniversary of FDR's fireside chats. The Museum of Broadcast Communications Accessed on July 12, 2006 at: http://www.museum.tv/exhibitionssection.php?page=79

47. Franklin Delano Roosevelt fireside chats & speeches. Accessed July 9, 2006 at: http://www.otrcat.com/fdr.htm

48. Teaching Political Cartoons: FDR's Court-Packing Plan, 1937. Accessed on July 11, 2006 at: http://www.authentichistory.com/images/1930s/political_cartoons/FDRcourtpacking.htm

49. The FDR portfolio project. Accessed on July 14, 2005 at: http://www.nisk.k12.ny.us/fdr

50. By the people, for the people: Posters of the WPA. Accessed July 14, 2006 at: http://memory.loc.gov/ammem/wpaposters/wpahome.html

51. Franklin D. Roosevelt Executive Order 9182 Establishing the Office of War Information. Accessed on July 15, 2006 at: http://www.presidency.ucsb.edu/ws/print.php?pid=16273

52. OWI Pacific psyop six decades ago. Accessed on July 15, 2006 at: http://www.psywarrior.com/OWI60YrsLater.html

53. Office of War Information. Retrieved on July 12, 2006 at: http://history.acusd.edu/gen/st/~ksoroka/hollywood3.html

54. Cutlip, S.M. & Center, A.H. (1978). Effective public relations. Englewood Cliffs, NJ: Prentice-Hall, Inc., p. 90.

55. Powers of Persuasion: World War II Posters from AIHA's Collections. Accessed on July 9, 2006 at: http://www.albany-institute.org/exhibits/wwII.posters.htm

56. War aims through art: The U.S. Office of War Information. Accessed on July 9, 2006 at: http://americanhistory.si.edu/victory/victory5.htm

Women working for the war

57. Harvey, S. Rosie the Riveter: Real Women Workers in World War II. Accessed on July 11, 2006 at: http://www.loc.gov/rr/program/journey/rosie-transcript.html

58. Campbell, D. (1984).Women at War with America: Private Lives in a Patriotic Era. Cambridge, MA: Harvard University Press.

59. Gluck, S. (1987).Rosie the Riveter Revisited: Women, the War and Social Change. Boston: Twayne.

Rising from the ashes

60. Smokey's artist. Accessed on July 12, 2006 at: http:// www.goodbyemag.com/aug00/wendelin.html

61. Smokey Bear. Accessed on July 11, 2006 at: http:// www.pbs.org/weekendexplorer/newmexico/ruidoso/ruidoso_ smokey.htm

62. Phillips, B. Image: 1944 vs. 2004 Makeover for Smokey. Accessed on July 11, 2006 at: http://www.wsutoday.wsu.edu/ Print_completestory.asp?StoryID=1071

63. Harry S. Truman quotes. Accessed on July 24, 2006 at: http://home.att.net/~howingtons/dem/truman.html

64. History of Education: Selected Moments of the 20th Century. Accessed on July 24, 2006 at: http://fcis.oise.utoronto. ca/~daniel_sch/assignment1/1944gibill.html

65. Blackwell, J. (1951). American dream houses, all in a row. Trentonian. Accessed on July 24, 2006 at: http://www. capitalcentury.com/1951.html

66. The fifties. Accessed on July 24, 2006 at: http://www.historychannel.com/exhibits/fifties

67. John F. Kennedy. Accessed on July 24, 2006 at: http:// www.quotesandsayings.com/sjfk.htm

68. Assassination and funeral of President John F. Kennedy. Accessed on July 27, 2006 at: http://www.museum.tv/archives/etv/K/htmlK/kennedyjf/kennedyjf.htm

69. Vaill, P. (1996). Learning as a way of being. San Francisco: Jossey-Bass Publishers.

PART TWO: *THE TRENDS OF TODAY AND TOMORROW*

Welcome to the wild wired world

1. Naisbitt, J. (1982). Megatrends: Ten new directions transforming our lives. New York: Warner Books, Inc.

2. Kappelman. T. Marshall McLuhan "The Medium is the Message." Accessed July 16, 2006 at: http://www.leaderu.com/orgs/probe/docs/mcluhan.html

3. Friedman, T. (1999). The lexus and the olive tree. New York: Farrar, Straus& Giroux.

4. U.S. Census Bureau. Computer and Internet Use in the United States: 2003 Accessed on July 26, 2006 at: www.census.gov/prod/2005pubs/p23-208.pdf

5. A brief history of the Internet. Accessed on July 26, 2006 at: http://www.isoc.org/internet/history/brief.shtml

6. Barabasi, Albert-Laszlo. (2002). Linked: The new science of networks. Cambridge, MA: Perseus Publishing.

7. Prensky, M. (2001). Digital game-based learning. New York: McGraw-Hill.

8. Business 2.0 50 people who matter Now Accessed on August 30, 2006 at: http://money.cnn.com/magazines/business2/peoplewhomatter

9. Reiss, S. (2006, July 14). "His space". Wired Magazine. Accessed on August 31, 2006 at: http://www.wired.com/wired/archive/14.07/murdoch.html

10. Arnold, T. K. (2006, August 1). "The MySpace invaders." USA Today.

11. Snider, M. (2006, August 16). "Microsoft to let players design own games." USA Today.

12. University of Oregon Libraries. Blogs, wikis and other animals. Accessed on July 27, 2006 at: http://libweb.uoregon.edu/guides/blogs

13. Puente. M/ (2006, August 23). "Artists take paintings to the masses." USA Today.

14. Sullivan, A. (2002, May). The Blogging Revolution - Weblogs Are To Words What Napster Was To Music. Wired Magagzine. Accessed on July 27, 2006 at: http://weblogs. about.com

15. Robel, S. (2003, March 3). Harvard Business Review calls blogs a breakthrough idea for 2005. Accessed on July 27, 2006 at: http://www.webpronews.com/news/ebusinessnews/ wpn-45-20050303HarvardBusinessReviewCallsBlogsa-BreakthroughIdeafor2005.html

16. Hart, K. (2006, August 5). "Barging into the blogger's circle". The Washington Post.

17. Jones, D. (2006, August 1). "Authorship gets lost on Web." USA

Public relations in the digital age

18. PR Blog. "The way forward according to Edelman – 1/3/06" Accessed on September 1, 2006 at: http://reuven.pr-blogs.org/2006/01/03/the-way-forward-according-to-edelman

19. McClure, J. "Jen's top ten – my predictions of new communications trends for 2006. Accessed on September 1, 2006 at: http://www.newcommblogzine.com/?p=344

20. Larry Bodine's Professional Service Marketing Blog. "4 top PR trends" – April 16, 2005. Accessed on September 1, 2006 at: http://pm.typepad.com/professional_marketing_bl/2005/04/4_top_pr_trends.html

21. Dawson, R. "Six facets of the future of PR"- May 5, 2006. Accessed on September 1, 2006 at: http://www.rossdawson-blog.com/weblog/archives/2006/05/six_facets_of_t.html

22. Blogs establishing journalistic legitimacy, say Sargent. Accessed September 1, 2006 at: http://www.cbsnews.com/ blogs/2006/06/09/publiceye/entry1696964.shtml

23. Pilgrim, M. "What Is RSS". Accessed on September 1, 2006 at: http://www.xml.com/pub/a/2002/12/18/dive-into-xml. html

24. King. A. "Introduction to RSS." Accessed on September 1, 2006 at: http://www.webreference.com/authoring/languages/xml/rss/intro/

25. Lawrence, E. "The rise of marketing PR" – August 21, 2006. Accessed on September 1, 2006 at: http://www.b2bmarketingtrends.com/abstract.asp?id=239&groupid=7

26. Principles of Marketing – Part 16 – Public Relations. Accessed on September 1, 2006 at: http://www.knowthis.com/tutorials/principles-of-marketing/public-relations/14.htm

27. Crowther, D. "Where PR is going and how to make sure you get there first." July 16, 2004. Accessed on September 1, 2006 at: http://www.globalprblogweek.com/archives/tomorrows_pr_today.php

28. Paluszek, J. PR Tactics. Accessed on September 1, 2006 at: www.prsa.org

29. Bowman, S. & Willis. "We media; How audiences are shaping the future of news and information." Accessed on September 1, 2006 at: http://www.futureofpr.com

Multiculturalism

30. de Tocqueville, A. (1959) Democracy in America. (ed.) RD Heffner. New York: New American Library.

31. El Nasser, H. (2006, July 5, 2006) A nation of 300 million. USA Today.

32. Takaki, R. (1993). A different mirror: A history of multicultural America. Boston, MA: Little, Brown and Co.

33. Schlesinger, A.M. Jr. (1992). The disuniting of America: Reflections on a multicultural society. New York: W.W. Norton & Company.

34. Anderson, B. (1991). Imagined communities. New York: Verso.

35. Purdy, J. (2003). Being America. New York: Alfred A. Knopf.

36. U.S. Small Business Agency. "Ethnic marketing - turning obstacles into opportunities." Accessed September 3, 2006 at: http://www.sba.gov/gopher/Business-Development/Success-Series/Vol8/obstacle.txt

37. Hall, E.T. (1959). The silent language. New York: Anchor Books.

38. Tharp, M.C. (2001). Marketing and consumer identity in multicultural America. Sage Publications. CA: Thousand Oaks.

39. Guion, L. Ethnic Marketing: A Method to Market Programs to Ethnically Diverse Audiences in Extension. Accessed on September 3, 2006 at: http://www.ediversitycenter.net/audiences/ethnic_marketing.php

40. Stoy, D.B. (2000) "Developing intercultural competence: An action plan for health educator." Journal of Health Education, 31: 16-20.

Skepticism: Who do YOU trust?

41. Lobe, J. "Skepticism grows among US voters". Accessed on September 4, 2006 at: http://www.atimes.com/atimes/Front_Page/EK15Aa02.html

42. Allen, M. "Bush faces new skepticism from Republicans on Hill: - January 28, 2005. Accessed on September 4, 2006 at: http://www.washingtonpost.com/wp-dyn/articles/A42895-2005Jan27.html

43. "Lack of skepticism leads to poor reporting on Iraq weapons claims" March 25, 2003. Accessed on September 4, 2006 at: http://www.commondreams.org/news2003/0325-12.htm

44. Reuters News Agency. Skepticism of U.S. model rising in EU since Enron, May 23, 2002 Toronto Globe & Mail. Accessed September 4, 2006 at: http://www.commondreams.org/headlines02/0522-03.htm

45. Balko, R. "When the catastrophe is government," September 07, 2005. Accessed on September 4, 2006 at: http://www.foxnews.com/story/0,2933,168732,00.html

46. The Washington DC Examiner. Big government failure is Katrina's lesson - Aug 30, 2006 Accessed on September 4, 2006 at: http://www.examiner.com/a-51807~Editorial__Big_Government_failure_is_Katrina_s_lesson.html

47. CBS News. "Low ratings for Congress." May 24, 2005 Accessed September 5, 2006 at: http://www.cbsnews.com/stories/2005/05/24/opinion/polls/main697548.shtml

48. Powell, A. SPH works to restore public's trust in health care system: Conference examines problems, solutions for erosion in medical trust. Harvard Gazette. Accessed on September 5, 2006 at: http://www.news.harvard.edu/gazette/2002/11.21/09-trust.html

49. Massachusetts Study predicts high failure rate under "No Child Left Behind" Accessed on September 5, 2006 at: http://www.massteacher.org/news/headlines/news_2005-06-23.cfm

50. Edelman. 2006 Edelman Trust Barometer. Accessed on September 3, 2006 at: http://www.edelman.com/image/insights/content/FullSupplement_final.pdf

51. Edelman. "A person like me" now most credible spokesperson for companies; trust in employees significantly higher than in CEOs, Edelman Trust Barometer finds. January 23, 2006. Accessed on September 3, 2006 at: http://www.edelman.com/news/ShowOne.asp?ID=102.

52. The benefits of skepticism: A look at the positive aspects of the skeptical approach. Accessed on September 4, 2006 at: http://www.skeptics.org.uk/article.php?dir=articles&article=the_benefits_of_skepticism.php

53. Discover skepticism. Accessed on September 5, 2006 at: http://www.skeptic.com/about_us/discover_skepticism.html

54. Sagan, C. "The burden of skepticism." Accessed on September 3, 2006 at http://www.is.wayne.edu/mnissani/2030/burden.htm

55. Berresford, S. V. (1997-1998, Winter). At work in an age of skepticism. Advancing Philanthropy. Vol 5, No. 4. Accessed on September 5, 2006 at: http://www.fordfound.org/news/view_speeches_detail.cfm?news_index=103

Bi-polar nation

56. Patton, P. (2004, September 24) "One Fate, Two Fates, Red States, Blue States," Accessed on September 8, 2006 at: http://designforum.aiga.org/content.cfm?ContentAlias=%5Fg etfullarticle&aid=%23%2FN%23%28%0A

57. Burke, T. "Red and Blue Bunny." November 24, 2004. Accessed on September 6, 2006 at: http://hnn.us/blogs/entries/8572.html

58. White, J. K. (2002). The Values Divide: American Politics and Culture in Transition. Hanover, NH: University Press of New England.

59. Wikipedia. "Red state vs. blue state divide," Accessed on September 8, 2006 at: http://en.wikipedia.org/wiki/Red_state_vs._blue_state_divide

60. Barone, M. (2001, June 9) "The 49 Percent Nation," National Journal.

61. Brooks, D. (2001, December 1). "One nation, slightly divisible." Atlantic Monthly.

62. Langlieb, D. (2004, November 14). Ask the Cleaning Lady: Are all "blue state voters" latte drinking yuppies? Not even close. The Bi-College On-line. Accessed on September 7, 2006 at: http://www.biconews.com/article/view/1423

63. Issenberg, S. (2004, April). "Boo-Boos in Paradise." Philadelphia Magazine. Accessed on September 8, 2006 at: http://www.phillymag.com/articles/booboos_in_paradise/

64. Wilentz, S. (2004, November 7) The Red State, Blue State Myth. Los Angeles Times.

65. Muro, M. & Berube, A. (2004, August 15). Red and Blue States Not Black-and-White: Sharp Demarcations on Electoral Map Don't Match Reality. San Francisco Chronicle. Accessed on September 7, 2006 at: http://www.brook.edu/views/op-ed/berube/20040815.htm

66. Pearson Longman. "New Book Debunks Commonly Accepted Picture of a Polarized Electorate." Accessed on September 8, 2006 at: http://www.pearsoned.com/pr_2004/071504A.htm

67. Glaeser, E.L. & Ward, B.A. "Myths and Realities of American Political Geography" (2006, January). Harvard Institute of Economic Research Discussion Paper No. 2100 Accessed on September 8, 2006 at: http://ssrn.com/abstract=874977

68. Potorti, D. (2004, November 6). "One State, Two State, Red State, Blue State". Accessed on September 7, 2006 at: http://www.commondreams.org/views04/1106-21.htm

69. Cool Blue Reason. (2005, November 27). Mental Gerrymandering: The "red state / blue state" dichotomy. Accessed September 8, 2006 at: http://www.dailykos.com/story/2005/11/27/215455/23

70. Malek, C. (2005, July). Red / Blue Polarization. Accessed on September 6, 2006 at: http://www.beyondintractability.org/case_studies/Red_Blue.jsp

71. Rosen, J. (2004, November 15). "House Divided," The New Republic. Accessed on September 6, 2006 at: http://www.beyondintractability.org/case_studies/Red_Blue.jsp

72. Yankelovich, D. (2004, October 15). Toning down our opinions will ratchet up our understanding - and the welfare of the nation. The Christian Science Monitor. Accessed on September 6, 2006 at: http://www.csmonitor.com/2004/1015/p10s02-coop.html

Terror, terror, terror

73. Tanielian. T. & Stein, B.D. Understanding and preparing for the psychological consequences of terrorism. Accessed on September 11, 2006 at: www.rand.org/pubs/reprints/2006/RAND_RP1217.pdf

74. Pangi. R. (2002, August). "After the attack: The psychological consequences of terrorism," Accessed on September 11, 2006 at: www.mipt.org/pdf/ksg_popno7.pdf

75. Beaton, R. & Murphy, S. (2002). "Psychosocial Responses to Biological and Chemical Terrorist Threats and Events: Implications for the Workplace," Journal of the American Association of Occupational Health Nurses 50(4): 182–9.

76. Schuster, M.A., Stein, B.D., Jaycox, L. et al., (2001) "A National Survey of Stress Reactions after the September 11, 2001, Terrorist Attacks," New England Journal of Medicine 345: (20): 1507–12.

77. Galea,S., Ahern, J., Resnick, H. et al., (2002). "Psychological Sequelae of the September 11 Terrorist Attacks in New York City," New England Journal of Medicine 346(13): 982–7.

78. Cohen Silver, R., Holman, E.A., McIntosh, D.N., Poulin, M., Gil-Rivas, V. (2002). Nationwide Longitudinal Study of Psychological Responses to September 11. JAMA. 288:1235-1244.

79. National Mental Health Association. Coping with Tragedy: The Fifth Anniversary of 9/11 Accessed on September 12, 2006 at: http://www.nmha.org/reassurance/9-11anniversary/index.cfm

80. Transportation Security Administration. Our history – how we began. Accessed on September 12, 2006 at: http://www.tsa.gov/research/tribute/history.shtm

81. McCullagh, D. (2006, September 7). Post-9/11 anti-terror technology: A report card. Zdnet News. Accessed on September 11, 2006 at: http://news.zdnet.com/2100-1009_22-6113064-3.html?tag=st.num

82. Davidson, K. (2006, September 6). Anti-terror fish guard S.F.'s water - Bluegills monitored to detect an attack on city's drinking supply. Accessed on September 11, 2006 at: http://sfgate.com/cgi-bin/article.cgi?f=/c/a/2006/09/06/FISH.TMP

83. Sandhana, L. (2003, April 5). Plants: New Anti-Terror Weapon? Accessed on September 11, 2006 at: http://www.wired.com/news/technology/0,1282,58118,00.html

84. The New Anti-Terror Protection Industry. (2006, August 30). Accessed on September 11, 2006 at: http://www.pbs.org/nbr/site/onair/transcripts/060830c/

85. Van, J. (2006, September 11) Advertising angle part of the package for anti-terror technology. Accessed on September 11, 2006 at: www.chicagotribune.com/technology/chi-060 9110146sep11,1,7824998.story?coll=chi-technology-hed

86. 9/11's 'astonishing unity' has given way to bitter partisanship. (2006, September 12). Accessed on September 12, 2006 at: http://www.cnn.com/2006/POLITICS/09/11/terror-warpolitics.ap/index.html

87. Regan. K. (2006, June 27). "Bush Condemns Media Outlets for Leaking Anti-Terror Program," Accessed on September 12, 2006 at: http://www.technewsworld.com/story/51378. html

88. Slone, M. (2000). Responses to media coverage of terrorism. Journal of Conflict Resolution. 44(4): 508-522. Accessed on September 11, 2006 at: www.jcr.sagepub.com/cgi/reprint/44/4/508.pdf

89. Anderson, L. (2006, August 11). Numb to unnerved, but few surprised. The Chicago Tribune. Accessed on September 12, 2006 at: www.chicagotribune.com/news/nationworld/chi-0608110168aug11,1,6049952.story?coll=chi-newsnation-world-utl

90. Tanielian. T., Pincus, H., Stein, B.D. & Burnam, A. (2002, Summer). The path of greatest resilience. Rand Review. Accessed on September 11, 2006 at: www.rand.org/publications/randreview/issues/rr.08.02/resilience.html

91. Hampson, R. (2006, September 11). Does 2001's shadow of fear still linger? USA Today.

92. Eversley, M. (2006, September 12). Lower Manhattan: A neighborhood coming back. USA Today.

93. Saltonstall, D. (2996, September 5). 'A horrible thing' New York Daily News. Accessed on September 11, 2006 at: http://www.nydailynews.com

94. Redlener, I., Markenson, D., Grant, R., Berman, D. & McKenzie, R. (2004, November). How Americans feel about terrorism and security: three years after September 11 Accessed on September 11, 2006 at: www.ncdp.mailmancolumbia.edu/files/Annual_Survey_2004.pdf

95. National Science and Technology Council. Combating Terrorism - Research priorities in the social, behavioral and economic sciences. Accessed on September 11, 2006 at: www. ostp.gov/nstc/html/terror.pdf

Nervous energy

96. Energy Information Administration. Annual Energy Outlook, 2004. Accessed on October 11, 2006 at: http://www. nrdc.org/air/transportation/gasprices.asp

97. Samuelson, R. (2006, October 18). An oil habit America cannot break. The Washington Post.

98. Natural Resources Defense Council. (2001, October 3). Reducing U.S. Oil Dependence: A Real Energy Security Policy. Accessed on September 21, 2006 at: http://www.nrdc. org/air/energy/fensec.asp

99. Natural Resources Defense Council. (2004, July). Reducing America's Energy Dependence Breaking our addiction to oil is the real solution to high gas prices. Accessed on September 21, 2006 at: http://www.nrdc.org/air/transportation/gasprices.asp

100. Saxton, J. & Enge, E. (2005, October 3). Energy security and oil dependence Accessed on September 21, 2006 at: http://www.washingtontimes.com/commentary/20051002-093822-1999r.htm

101. Mufson, S. (2006, June 8). Greenspan testifies on oil dependence, and few pay attention. Accessed on September 21, 2006 at: www.washingtonpost.com/wp-dyn/content/article/2006/06/07/AR2006060700625.html

102. Hunt, K. (2006, September 26). Proposition 87 fires up California energy debate: Measure would impose tax on oil production to fund alternative programs. Accessed on October 17, 2006 at: www.marketwatch.com/News/Story/Story.aspx?dist=newsfinder&siteid=google&guid=%7BE6D8B96D-903F-4EC

103. EPA proposes strategy to reduce foreign oil dependency. (2006, September 7). Accessed on October 17, 2006 at: http://yosemite.epa.gov/opa/admpress.nsf

104. Bush Administration proposes fuel economy changes - New weight-based proposal to increase pollution and oil dependence. (2003, September 22). Accessed on September 21, 2006 at: http://www.sierraclub.org/pressroom/releases/pr2003-12-22a.asp

105. An inconvenient truth. Accessed on October 17, 2006 at: http://www.climatecrisis.net/aboutthefilm/

106. Booth, W. (2006, January 26). Al Gore, Sundance's leading man: 'An Inconvenient Truth' documents his efforts to raise alarm on effects of global warming. The Washington Post. Accessed on October 17, 2006 at: http://www.washingtonpost. com/wp-dyn/content/article/2006/01/25/AR2006012502230. html

107. Brazil reaches out to Al Gore for help with rain forest proposal (2006, October 17). Accessed on October 17 , 2006 at: http://www.foxnews.com/story/0,2933,221857,00.html

108. Fetterman, M. (2006, September 26). Wal-Mart grows 'green' strategies. USA Today.

109. Hajela, D. (2006, September 21). Branson to pledge billions at Clinton Global Initiative. Accessed on October 17, 2006 at: http://www.clintonglobalinitiative.org/NETCOM-MUNITY/Page.aspx?&pid=725&srcid=457

110. Branson bets billions to curb global warming. (2006, September 21). Accessed on October 17, 2006 at: http://www.ms-nbc.msn.com/id/14936341/

111. ICF, Inc. Strategic Communications and Marketing for the Energy Industry. Accessed on October 17, 2006 at: http:// www.icfi.com/Markets/Energy/efficiency-communications. asp

A helping hand

112. Gunderson, S. (2006, May). FOUNDATIONS: Architects of Social Change. eJournal USA: Society & Values. Accessed on October 23, 2006 at: http://usinfo.state.gov/journals/itsv/0506/ijse/ijse0506.htm

113. Points of Light Foundation. (2006, July 11). Volunteer Centers: A History In America. Accessed on November 4, 2006 at: www.pointsoflight.org/downloads/doc/center/resources/HistoryRevised22206.doc

114. Ellis, S. (1987). We the People: The History of Volunteerism in America. Accessed on November 4, 2006 at: http://www.warwickri.gov/humanserv/volunteens/resources/volunteerism.html

115. Bellah, R.N., Madsen, R., Sullivan, W.M., Swider, A., & Tipton, S.M. (1985). Habits of the Heart: Individualism and Commitment in American Life. NY: Harper & Row, Publishers.

116. Friedman, M. J. Lifting Someone Else: Government Encouragement of Volunteer Efforts Accessed on October 19, 2006 at: http://usinfo.state.gov/journals/itsv/0506/ijse/friedman.htm

117. About the Peace Corps. Accessed on October 31, 2006 at: http://www.peacecorps.gov/index.cfm?shell=learn.whatispc

118. Corporation for National and Community Service. What is AmeriCorps? Accessed on November 3, 2006 at: http://www.americorps.org/about/ac/index.asp

119. US Department of Labor. (2003, December 17). Volunteering in the US: 2003. Accessed on October 23, 2006 at: http://www.pointsoflight.org/downloads/pdf/networks/business/membersonly/3_Bureau_of_Labor_Statistics_Volunteer_Service_Indicator-2003.pdf

120. Business Strengthening America. 2003 Report to the Nation. Accessed on October 24, 2006 at: http://www.pointsoflight.org/downloads/pdf/networks/business/membersonly/2_BSA_2003_Report_to_the_Nation.pdf

121. Yeager, R.L. Approaches To Giving. (2006, May). FOUNDATIONS: Architects of Social Change. eJournal USA: Society & Values. Accessed on October 23, 2006 at: http://usinfo.state.gov/journals/itsv/0506/ijse/ijse0506.htm

122. Allstate Foundation. The corporate volunteer program as a strategic resource: The link grows stronger. Accessed on October 23, 2006 at: http://www.pointsoflight.org/downloads/pdf/networks/business/membersonly/7_Link_Grows_Stronger_Executive_Summary-2000.pdf

123. About the virtual volunteering project. Accessed on October 24, 2006 at: http://www.serviceleader.org/old/vv/vvabout.html#funding

124. VolunteerMatch. 21st Century Volunteering. Accessed on November 3, 2006 at: http://www.volunteermatch.org

125. 1-800-Volunteer.org Tops Century Mark: More than 100 Volunteer Centers Use System to Recruit Volunteers. Accessed on November 2, 2006 at: http://www.pointsoflight.org/about/mediacenter/releases/2006/10-12.cfm

126. Corporation For National And Community Service. Marketing volunteer opportunities to baby boomers. Accessed on November 3, 2006 at: http://nationalserviceresources.org/epicenter/practices/index.php?ep_action=view&web_id=33141

127. Strigas, A.E. (2006, April). Making the Most of Volunteers. Accessed on November 3, 2006 at: http://www.nrpa.org/content/default.aspx?documentId=3972

128. Nonprofits failing to maximize impact of corporate volunteers. (2006, April 24). Accessed on November 3, 2006 at: http://www.causemarketingforum.com/page.asp?ID=437

129. Alaska Division of Parks and Recreation. Ten year strategic plan 2006-2006. Accessed on November 3, 2006 at: www.dnr.state.ak.us/parks/plans/strategicplan/partnershp.pdf

130. Points of Light Foundation & Volunteer Center National Network. Accessed on October 24, 2006 at: http://www.pointsoflight.org

Self-help nation

131. Center for Disease Control and Prevention. Health United States, 2005. Accessed on November 22, 2006 at: http://www.cdc.gov/nchs/data/hus/hus05.pdf

132. The self-help marketplace. Accessed on November 20, 2006 at: http://en.wikipedia.org/wiki/Self-help

133. American Obesity Association. (2005). Consumer Protection - Weight Management Products & Service. Accessed on November 20, 2006 at: http://www.obesity.org/subs/fastfacts/Obesity_Consumer_Protect.shtml

134. National Institute on Aging. (2005, March 16). Obesity Threatens to Cut U.S. Life Expectancy, New Analysis Suggests. Accessed on November 5, 2006 at: http://www.nih.gov/news/pr/mar2005/nia-16.htm

135. Centers for Disease Control and Prevention. Weight and obesity. Accessed on November 6, 2006 at: http://www.cdc.gov/nccdphp/dnpa/obesity

136. Harvard University. (2006, May 1), Obesity Levels in U.S. States Are Grossly Underestimated. Accessed on November 6, 2006 at: http://www.hsph.harvard.edu/press/releases/press05012006.html

137. CBS News. (2004, January 4). Fast Food Linked To Child Obesity. Accessed on November 7, 2006 at: http://www.cbsnews.com/stories/2004/01/05/health/main591325.shtml

138. Schlosser, E. Fast Food Nation: The Dark Side of the All-American Meal. Accessed on November 6, 2006 at: http://www.mcspotlight.org/media/books/schlosser.html

139. Nestle. M. (1998, July/August). Supersize Food, Supersize People. Nutrition Action Newsletter. Accessed on November 6, 2006 at: http://www.cspinet.org/nah/7_98eat.htm

140. U.S. Food and Drug Administration. (2004, March 12). Report of the Working Group on Obesity. Accessed on November 6, 2006 at: http://www.fda.gov/oc/initiatives/obesity/backgrounder.html

141. The News. The cost of obesity. (2006, November 8). Accessed on November 10, 2006 at: http://www.thenews.com.pk/daily_detail.asp?id=2936

142. Bariatric Surgery Statistics. Accessed on November 6, 2006 at: http://www.bariatric-surgery.info/statistics.htm

143. Mann, D. (2003, October 3). Life after weight loss surgery. Accessed on November 6, 2006 at: http://www.webmd.com/content/Article/74/89372.htm

144.American Society of Plastic Surgeons. Plastic Surgery Today, (2004, May).

145.Harper, J. (2006, October 26). Obesity drives up U.S. fuel appetite. The Washington Times. Accessed on November 7, 2006 at: http://www.washtimes.com/national/20061026-120133-4620r.htm http://www.plasticsurgery.org/news_room/PST-04-05.cfm

146.National Health Council (1997). Americans Talk About Science and Medical News. Washington, DC: National Health Council. Accessed on November 20, 2006 at: http://www.nationaldairycouncil.org/NationalDairyCouncil/Health/Digest/dcd72-Page4.htm

147.The Salt Institute. Salt & Health. Accessed on November 20, 2006 at: http://www.saltinstitute.org/28.html

148.Fletcher, A. (2006, September 12) 'Oversimplifying obesity' creating consumer confusion. Accessed on November 20, 2006 at: http://www.nutraingredients.com/news/ng.asp?n=70500-obesity-calories-fat

149.Pallarito, K. Consumer Confusion Persists on Painkillers' Safety. Lifespan Health News. Accessed on November 20, 2006 at: http://www.lifespan.org/healthnews/2005/03/21/article524610.html

150.Huntingford C.A. (2004). Confusion over benefits of hormone replacement therapy. Lancet, 363(9414):1078-9.

151.Campbell, D. (2006, September 29). Poor math skills feed food label confusion: study. The Reporter. Accessed on November 20, 2006 at: https://www.mc.vanderbilt.edu/reporter/index.html?ID=5045

152.Flaherty, C. (2004, November 22). From nutrition confusion to individual nutrition prescriptions. Montana State University News. Accessed on November 25, 2006 at: http://www.montana.edu/cpa/news/nwview.php?article=2043

153.Institute of Medicine. (2004). Health Literacy: A Prescription to End Confusion. Accessed on November 20, 2006 at: http://fermat.nap.edu/books/0309091179/html/19.html

154. National Network of Libraries of Medicine. Health Literacy. Accessed on November 20, 2006 at: http://nnlm.gov/outreach/consumer/hlthlit.html

155. National Dairy Council. (2001). Good Science: Its Role In Setting the Record Straight - How Media Contribute to Consumer Confusion. Accessed on November 20, 2006 at: http://www.nationaldairycouncil.org/NationalDairyCouncil/Health/Digest/dcd72-5Page4.htm

156. Food Marketing Institute and PREVENTION Magazine. (2000). Shopping for Health. Self-Care Needs and Whole Health Solutions. Washington, DC: Food Marketing Institute and Emmaus, PA: PREVENTION Magazine. Accessed on November 20, 2006 at: http://www.nationaldairycouncil.org/NationalDairyCouncil/Health/Digest/dcd72-5Page4.htm

157. Trust for America's Health. (2006, August 26). America's Obesity Epidemic Getting Worse; New Report Finds Adult Obesity Rates Up In 31 States; The South Is The "Biggest Belt." Accessed on November 25, 2006 at: http://healthyamericans.org/reports/obesity2006/

158. Saletan, W. (2006, November 26). All about girth control. The Washington Post.

Mine, yours and ours

159. The Quotations Page. Quotations about family. Accessed on November 30, 2006 at: http://www.quotationspage.com/quote/37853.html

160. Frey, W.H. (2003, March 1). Married With Children - Decline in traditional-family households. Accessed on November 20, 2006 at: http://findarticles.com/p/articles/mi_m4021/is_2_25/ai_97818968

161. National Stepfamily Resource Center. Families built through divorce, remarriage, adoption, birth. Accessed on November 26, 2006 at: http://www.stepfamilies.info/faqs/faqs.php

162. The Stepfamily Foundation. (2005). The statistics are staggering. Accessed on November 26, 2006 at: http://www.stepfamily.org

163. Successful stepfamilies. (2006). Build a Local Stepfamily Ministry. Accessed on November 27, 2006 at: http://www.successfulstepfamilies.com/view/30

164. TheStepFamilyLife Newsletter (2004). Accessed on November 26, 2006 at: http://www.thestepfamilylife.com/NewsletterSpring04.htm

165. Business Wire. Your Stepfamily Magazine Partners With Stepfamily Association of America (2002, Feb. 19). Accessed on November 26, 2006 at: http://www.findarticles.com/p/articles/mi_m0EIN/is_2002_Feb_19/ai_83021784

166. Welcome to the National Stepfamily Resource Center. (2005). Accessed on November 26, 2006 at: http://www.stepfamilies.info/

167. The Positive Way. (2006). Resources for stepparents. Accessed on November 26, 2006 at: http://www.positive-way.com/stepfamily_resources_and_reading.htm

168. Crosby, J. (2004, May 16). 'People now recognize we are out there'. Cape Cod Times. Accessed on November 26, 2006 at: http://www.capecodonline.com/special/gaymarriage/gayfamilies16.htm

169. Bowe, J. (2006, November 16). Gay donor of gay dad? The New York Times Magazine.

170. Wilke, M. (2003, May 15). Volvo Bids for Gay Families: "Some families are carefully planned. Others, you just meet along the way." Accessed on November 26, 2006 at: http://www.thegully.com/essays/gay_mundo2/wilke/030515_gay_les_family_ads.html

171. Broadway World News. HBO Documentary on Rosie O'Donnell's Gay Family Cruise Premieres April 6. (2006, April 3). Accessed on November 27, 2006 at: http://broadwayworld.com/viewcolumn.cfm?colid=8702

172. Donaldson-Evans, C. (2004, May 26). Fortune 500 Companies See Money In Gay Families. Fox News. Accessed on November 26, 2006 at: http://www.foxnews.com/story/0,2933,120902,00.html

173. Jayson. S. (2005, October 31). Feds: 1.5 million babies born to unwed moms in '04. Accessed on November 29, 2006 at: http://www.usatoday.com/news/nation/2005-10-31-unwed-families_x.htm

174. Fox News. (2005, October 28). Births to Unwed Mothers at Record High. Accessed on November 26, 2006 at: www.foxnews.com/story/0,2933,173850,00.html

175. Price, J. H. (2005, October 14). Half of new unwed mothers in poverty. The Washington Times.

176. New Medical.Net. (2005, October 4) It's more difficult for unwed mothers to get married, and if they do, they tend to not marry well. Women's Health News. Accessed on November 26, 2006 at: http://www.news-medical.net/?id=13557

177. U.S. Bureau of Census. (2004, November). America's Families and Living Arrangements: 2003. Accessed on November 26, 2006 at: www.census.gov/population/www/socdemo/hh-fam.html

178. Alternative to Marriage Project. (2004). Living Alone. Accessed on November 29, 2006 at: http://www.unmarried.org/statistics.html

179. Putnam, R. D. (1995). Bowling Alone: America's Declining Social Capital. Accessed on November 26, 2006 at: http://128.220.50.88/demo/journal_of_democracy/v006/putnam.html

180. O'Brien, K. (2006, June 4). Single Minded. The Boston Globe. Accessed on November 29, 2006 at: http://www.boston.com/news/globe/magazine/articles/2006/06/04/single_minded

181. Learned, A. (2006). Single and Loving It: A New Perspective on Marketing to Solo Women. Accessed on November 26, 2006 at: http://www.mpdailyfix.com/2006/06/single_and_loving_it_a_new_per_1.html

PART THREE: *LEARN FROM SUCCESS*

Energy Star

1. Dijksterhuis, E.J. (1987). Archimedes. Princeton, NJ: Princeton University Press.

2. U.S. Environmental Protection Agency. "Energy Star - The power to protect the environment through energy efficiency". Accessed on 5/16/06 at: www.energystar.gov/ia/partners/downloads/energy_star_report_aug_2003.pdf

3. U.S. Environmental Protection Agency. "Energy Star – Overview of 2005 achievements". Accessed on 5/17/06 at: (Available at www.energystar.gov/is/news/downloads/2005_acheivements.pdf)

4. Lewin, K. (1951). Field theory in social science. NY: Harper & Row.

5. Collins, J. & Porras, J.I. (1994). Built to last: Successful habits of visionary companies. New York: HarperBusiness.

Seat belts

6. National Highway Traffic Safety Administration. Accessed on 5-3-06 at http://www.buckleupamerica.org/

7. Bellis, M. The History of Seat Belts. Accessed on 5-4-06 at: http://inventors.about.com/library/inventors/bl_seat_belts.htm

8. Royal Society for the Prevention of Accidents. (2005, April). Seat Belts: History. Birmingham, England.

9. Gantz T. & Henkle, G. (2002, October). "Seatbelt: Current Issues," Prevention.

10. Yellow Cab Company. (1965, March). "Yellow Cab Celebrates 50 Years of 'Service to the Public.'" Chicago, IL: Trips 'n' Tips.

11. Jonah, B.A, (1982, May 9-12). Driver Behaviour, Legislation and Enforcement. Proceedings of the Canadian Multidisciplinary Road Safety Conference I, Halifax, Nova Scotia Technical University of Nova Scotia.

12. Cohen, A. & Einav, L. (2001). "The Effect of Mandatory Seat Belt Laws on Driving Behavior and Traffic Fatalities." Harvard Law School Olin Paper No. 341. Boston, University.

Military recruiting

13. John Paul Jones. Accessed on 6/04/06 at: http://www.geocities.com/CapitolHill/Lobby/3020/jones.html

14. Robinson, J.D. (1998). Finding a crew for the Ranger. Accessed on 6/4/06 at: http://seacoastnh.com/Maritime_History/John_Paul_Jones

15. Jones, J. P. (1777, July 26). "Encouragement for seamen". The Freeman's Journal (NH Gazette). Accessed on June 4, 2006 at: http://seacoastnh.com/Maritime_History/John_Paul_Jones/First_US_Navy_Recruiting_Poster

16. National Research Council. (2003). Attitudes, aptitudes, and aspirations of   American youth: Implications for military recruitment. Committee on the Youth Population and Military Recruitment. P. Sackett & A. Mavor, Eds., Washington, D.C.: National Academy of Sciences.

17. Department of Defense. (2006, April 10). DoD announces recruiting and retention numbers in March. Accessed on June 3, 1006 at: http://www.defenselink.mil/releases/2006/nr20060410-12786.html

18. Department of Defense. (2006, February). Department of Defense Budget, Fiscal Year 2007. Accessed on 6/6/06 at: http://www.dod.mil/comptroler/defbudget/fy2007/fy2007_o1.pdf

19. Quigley, S.L. (2005, October 17). "New, joint DoD ads urge parent-to-kid talks about military". American Forces Press Service. Accessed on June 1, 2006 at: http://www.defenselink.mil/cgi-bin/dlprint.cgi?http://www.defenselink.mil/news/Oct2005/20051017_3075.html

20. Sample, D. (2005, June 17). "General Cites Influencers as Part of Recruiting Challenge. American Forces Press Service. Accessed on 6/1/06 at: http://www.defenselink.mil/news/Jun2005/20050617_1759.html

21. Cave, D, (2005, June 3). "Growing Problem for Military Recruiters: Parents." New York Times.

22. Ephron, D. (2006, May 29). The pizza offensive. Newsweek, 30.

23. Kennedy, H. (2002, November). Computer games liven up military recruiting, training. Accessed on 6/1/06 at: http://www.nationaldefensemagazine.org/issues/2002/Nov/Computer_Games.htm

24. Hall, K. (2006, March 20). First $1,000 referral bonus earned in new SMART program. Army News Service. Accessed on 6/1/06 at: http://www4army.mil/ocpa/print.php?story_id_ket=8708

25. Miles, D. (2005, July 6). "Army values concept sells in tough recruiting environment." American Forces Information Service. Accessed on 6/1/06 at: http://www.defenselink.mil/news/Jul2005/20050706_1984.html

26. US Army Recruiting Command. (2006, January 18). Army raises enlistment age, doubles cash enlistment bonuses. Accessed on 6/1/06 at: http://www.usarec.army.mil/hq/apa/download/40-20Kbonus-age%20limit%201-06.pdf

27. Leipold, J.D. (2006, March 15). Army changes tattoo policy. Accessed on 6/1/06 at: http://www4army.mil/ocpa/print.php?story_id_key=8692

28. Stafford, R. (2006, April 5). Why parents must mind MySpace - Posting too much information on social networking sites may be dangerous. Accessed on August 8, 2006 at: http://www.msnbc.msn.com/id/11064451

29. The Associated Press. Marines looking for a few good MySpace pals - Corps sets up profile on social networking Web site in bid for recruits. Accessed on July 24, 2006 at: http://www.msnbc.msn.com/id/14007210/from/ET/

Printed in the United States
221908BV00002B/1/A

9 781934 248331